Eternal Treblinka

Eternal Treblinka

*Our Treatment of Animals
and the Holocaust*

———◆———

Charles Patterson

Lantern Books • New York
A Division of Booklight Inc.

2002

Lantern Books

One Union Square West, Suite 201

New York, NY 10003

The cover photo showing a World War II German soldier carrying off live geese is in the State Museum of the History of the Great Patriotic War in Minsk, Belarus.

Printed in the United States of America

Library of Congress Cataloging-in-Publication Data

Patterson, Charles
Eternal Treblinka : our treatment of animals and the Holocaust / Charles
Patterson.
p. cm.
Includes bibliographical references and index.
ISBN 1-930051-99-9 (alk. paper)
1. Animal welfare. 2. Holocaust, Jewish (1939–1945) I. Title

HV4708 .P384 2002
179'.3—dc21

2001050536

In memory of

Isaac Bashevis Singer (1904–1991)

In his thoughts, Herman spoke a eulogy for the mouse who had shared a portion of her life with him and who, because of him, had left this earth. "What do they know—all these scholars, all these philosophers, all the leaders of the world—about such as you? They have convinced themselves that man, the worst transgressor of all the species, is the crown of creation. All other creatures were created merely to provide him with food, pelts, to be tormented, exterminated. In relation to them, all people are Nazis; for the animals it is an eternal Treblinka."

—Isaac Bashevis Singer, "The Letter Writer"

TABLE OF CONTENTS

FOREWORD

In *Eternal Treblinka*, not only are we shown the common roots of Nazi genocide and modern society's enslavement and slaughter of non-human animals in unprecedented detail, but for the first time we are presented with extensive evidence of the profoundly troubling connections between animal exploitation in the United States and Hitler's Final Solution. Dr. Patterson does not let us forget, moreover, that the practices of the quintessentially American institution of the slaughterhouse that served as a model for the slaughter of human beings during the Nazi Holocaust flourish to this day.

However, *Eternal Treblinka* does not stop there. By exploring the entrenched racism in mainstream American culture that Hitler often cited as exemplary, the book details American support for human eugenics and forced sterilization and the role that their advocates played in contributing to the the Final Solution. This examination is long overdue, for without it, American culture is unlikely ever to reconsider the values that still make it the most animal-exploiting civilization in history.

As disturbing as *Eternal Treblinka*'s revelations are to read, the book's message is one of hope. The last part of the book takes pains to tell the stories of individuals whose links to the Holocaust, both as victims and perpetrators, helped steer them into animal liberation advocacy. If the experience of suffering can generate some good, then the work of those whose memory of suffering moves them to alleviate the suffering of others is that good.

My own parents are an example of individuals whose experiences of suffering did not stifle their impulse to alleviate the suffering of others. They both adored animals and empathized deeply with their plight. For my father, the passion was for horses. At one point in his unusual military career, he could no longer bear to subject horses to the weight of a human passenger, so he ended his equestrian days forever. My mother, who, to this day, makes the lengthy acquaintance of each dog she encounters on busy Manhattan streets, has more diverse interests. When small, furry fauna and large insect colonies could still be found everywhere in the borough of Queens, she regularly called my sisters and me away from other tasks to show us some amazing new accomplishment of a local squirrel or earthworm. And yet our requests to keep companion animals were steadfastly rejected, even as families around us, headed by parents less interested in animal life, went through generations of dogs and cats.

The reason always given was the inadvisability of becoming attached to a creature who would eventually die or be killed. My parents were adamant that we not be placed needlessly in situations in which we would have to experience loss and grieving. Only over time did I come to understand that it was the indescribable scale of their own losses during the Nazi era that imbued them with this excessive protectiveness. I eventually came to learn that my father had once had two young daughters and a wife, who were murdered as he watched, shortly before he himself was deported to a series of seven concentration camps, including Auschwitz-Birkenau. My mother, only an adolescent, and newly married, was torn from family in Budapest in 1944 for transport to forced labor, where she survived by employing her artistic gifts as a mender of SS uniforms and regalia. These two uprooted and nearly spent souls ultimately met in a Displaced Persons camp in Salzburg and married quickly, as did so many survivors who somehow formed the resolve to start life anew.

Though my parents wished for me and my two sisters lives of light-heartedness, it was inevitable that we would be drawn by our empathy for their suffering to causes that attempt to uplift the downtrodden.

Eventually, when I came to understand that the oppression of non-humans on this Earth eclipses even the ordeal survived by my parents, my fate as an advocate for animals was sealed. At a time when few attorneys could find paid employment in the animal rights movement, I was blessed to spend years of practice working as investigations counsel for People for the Ethical Treatment of Animals. Today, as I enter the field of public administration, the animals' plight will continue to direct my choices.

During my work on behalf of animal liberation, I have been renewed countless times by the literary masterpieces of Nobel Laureate Isaac Bashevis Singer. *Eternal Treblinka* is the first work of its kind to describe, in splendid detail, the enormous contribution of this literary genius, who stands, for me and many, as the animals' most compassionate champion in modern literature.

All who are not afraid to understand that the suffering that humans have so relentlessly inflicted on animals over the course of our species' history is one and the same with the suffering that humans often inflict on each other, must read and re-read this book.

Lucy Rosen Kaplan, Esq.
Baltimore, Maryland

PREFACE

While in New York doing graduate work at Columbia University, I became close friends with a German Jewish refugee, traumatized by her experience of living under the Nazis for six years. Her story moved me deeply, so I took courses and read extensively to learn more. Yuri Suhl, author of *They Fought Back: The Story of the Jewish Resistance in Nazi Europe*, and Lucjan Dobroszycki of the YIVO Institute of Jewish Research, editor of *The Chronicle of the Lodz Ghetto, 1941–1944*, were especially helpful.

Later when I became a history teacher and looked for, but could not find, a book on the background of the Holocaust suitable for my students, I wrote *Anti-Semitism: The Road to the Holocaust and Beyond* to fill the gap. The summer after its publication I attended the Yad Vashem Institute for Holocaust Education in Jerusalem, where I learned more from Yehuda Bauer, David Bankier, Robert Wistrich, and other Holocaust scholars. Back in the United States, I began reviewing books for *Martyrdom and Resistance*, a bimonthly now published by the International Society for Yad Vashem.

My awareness of the scope of our society's exploitation and slaughter of animals has been a more recent development. I grew up and spent most of my adult life oblivious to the extent to which our society is built on institutionalized violence against animals. For a long time it never occurred to me to challenge or even question the practice or the attitude behind it. The late AIDS and animal activist Steven Simmons described the attitude: "Animals are innocent casualties of the world view that asserts that some lives are more valuable than others, that the powerful are entitled to exploit the powerless, and that the weak must be sacrificed for the greater good." Once I realized this was the same attitude behind the Holocaust, I began to see the connections that are the subject of this book.

I am dedicating the book to the great Yiddish writer Isaac Bashevis Singer (1904–91), who was the first major writer to focus on the "Nazi" way we treat animals. The first two parts of the book (Chapters 1–5) put the issue in historical perspective, while the last part (Chapters 6–8) profiles people—Jewish and German—whose animal advocacy has been, at least to some extent, shaped by the Holocaust.

The conviction of Albert Camus that "it is a writer's responsibility to speak for those who cannot speak for themselves" helped me persevere through the writing of this book. And when it looked as if I might never find a publisher brave enough to publish it (some said the book was "too strong"), I took comfort from Franz Kafka's view: "I think we ought to read only books that bite and sting us. If the book we are reading doesn't shake us awake like a blow to the skull, why bother reading it in the first place? So it can make us happy? Good God, we'd be just as happy if we had no books at all....A book must be the ax for the frozen sea within us."

If the issue of the exploitation and slaughter of animals moves to center stage in the twenty-first century the way the issue of human slavery did in America in the nineteenth century—and I think it will—my hope is that this book will be in the thick of the debate.

I

A FUNDAMENTAL DEBACLE

True human goodness, in all its purity and freedom, can come to the fore only when its recipient has no power. Mankind's true moral test, its fundamental test (which lies deeply from view), consists of its attitude towards those who are at its mercy: animals. And in this respect mankind has suffered a fundamental debacle, a debacle so fundamental that all others stem from it.

— Milan Kundera, The Unbearable Lightness of Being

We have been at war with the other creatures of this earth ever since the first human hunter set forth with spear into the primeval forest. Human imperialism has everywhere enslaved, oppressed, murdered, and mutilated the animal peoples. All around us lie the slave camps we have built for our fellow creatures, factory farms and vivisection laboratories, Dachaus and Buchenwalds for the conquered species. We slaughter animals for our food, force them to perform silly tricks for our delectation, gun them down and stick hooks in them in the name of sport. We have torn up the wild places where once they made their homes. Speciesism is more deeply entrenched within us even than sexism, and that is deep enough.

— Ron Lee, founder of the Animal Liberation Front

CHAPTER ONE

THE GREAT DIVIDE

Human Supremacy and the Exploitation of Animals

Sigmund Freud put the issue of human supremacy in perspective in 1917 when he wrote: "In the course of his development towards culture man acquired a dominating position over his fellow-creatures in the animal kingdom. Not content with this supremacy, however, he began to place a gulf between his nature and theirs. He denied the possession of reason to them, and to himself he attributed an immortal soul, and made claims to a divine descent which permitted him to annihilate the bond of community between him and the animal kingdom."[1] Freud called man's self-appointed lordship over the other inhabitants of the earth "human megalomania."[2]

Several centuries earlier the French writer Michel Montaigne (1533–92) had expressed similar thoughts about "these excessive prerogatives which [man] supposes himself to have over other existences." He believed that man's "natural and original disease" was presumption. "The most calamitous and fragile of all creatures is man, and yet the most arrogant....Is it possible to imagine anything so ridiculous as that this pitiful, miserable creature, who is not even master of himself, should call itself master and lord of the universe?"[3] His conclusion was: "It is apparent that it is not by a true judgment, but by foolish pride and stubbornness, that we set ourselves before other animals and sequester ourselves from their condition and society."[4]

This chapter discusses the emergence of the great divide between man and other animals and man's might-makes-right attitude toward others—what Montaigne called human arrogance and Freud called human megalomania.

The Great Leap Forward

Man's emergence as the dominant species is a very recent development. Carl Sagan writes that if the fifteen-billion-year lifetime of the universe were compressed into a single year, it would not be until September that the solar system forms (September 9), the earth condenses out of interstellar matter (September 14), and life begins on earth (September 25). Dinosaurs emerge on Christmas Eve and become extinct four days later. The first mammals appear on December 26, the first primates on December 29, and the first hominids (our bipedal primate ancestors) on December 30. Modern humans (*homo sapiens*) do not appear until 10:30 P.M. on New Year's Eve, with all recorded human history not taking place until the last ten seconds of the year.[5]

The paleontologist Richard Leakey and Roger Lewin provide another way of understanding time when they ask the readers of *Origins* to think about the history of the earth as a 1000-page book. If each page covers four and a half million years, it would take 750 pages just to reach the beginnings of life in the sea. Hominids would not appear until three pages from the end of the book, and the first use of stone tools would show up halfway down the final page. The story of *homo sapiens* would be told in the very last line of the book, with everything from cave paintings and the pyramids to the Holocaust and computer age jammed into the final word.[6]

According to Carl Sagan and Ann Druyan, several features characterize our status as the dominant species: "our ubiquity, our subjugation (politely called domestication) of many animals, our expropriation of much of the primary photosynthetic productivity of the the planet, our alteration of the environment at the Earth's surface."[7] They ask, how did "one primate species, naked, puny, and vulnerable, manage to subordinate all the rest and to make this world, and others, its domain?"[8] Harvard professor Edward O. Wilson writes that our emergence as the dominant species has hardly been a felicitous development for the planet. "It was a misfortune for the living world in particular, many scientists believe, that a carnivorous primate and not some more benign form of animal made the breakthrough."[9]

The dramatic technological advance for the human species—what came to be called the "Great Leap Forward"—occurred about 40,000 years ago, writes Jared Diamond, when our *homo sapiens* ancestors developed tools, musical instruments, lamps, a talent for art, and the beginnings of trade and culture. "Insofar as there was any single point in time when we could be said to have become human, it was at the time of that leap."[10] Since the genetic make-up of humans is so close to that of chimpanzees, whatever caused the breakthrough involved just a tiny fraction of human genes. Many scientists, Diamond included, think the key factor was the ability to use verbal language.[11]

Others contend that what makes us "human" goes back more than two million years to the long period when our foraging ancestors spread throughout the world and lived as hunters and gatherers. Allen Johnson and Timothy Earle write, "The very long growth and dispersion of human hunters and gatherers served as the context for our biological evolution and as the foundation for all later cultural development."[12] Similarly, Sherwood Washburn and C. S. Lancaster write that while the agricultural revolution, followed by the industrial and scientific revolutions, is now freeing us from the conditions and restraints of ninety-nine percent of our history, "the biology of our species was created in that long gathering and hunting period."[13]

Barbara Ehrenreich also believes that our "human nature" was forged during those more than two million years when we mostly lived in small bands and ate plants and the slain prey of other animals. However, she argues that we have managed to repress almost entirely the traumatic memory of our long history, not of hunting, but of being hunted and eaten by animals far more skilled at hunting. She maintains that our later rituals of blood sacrifice and our penchant for war and violence "celebrate and terrifyingly reenact the human transition from prey to predator."[14]

Diamond writes that what prevented other primates from developing our ablity to use complex verbal language "seems to involve the structure of the larynx, tongue, and assorted muscles that give fine control over spoken sounds." Because the human vocal track is an intricate mechanism that depends on the precise operation of many tissues and muscles, "it's plausible that the missing ingredient may have been some modifications of the protohuman vocal tract to give us finer control and permit formation of a much greater variety of sounds."[15] Since the mouth and throat of the chimpanzee are not configued for speech the way ours are to produce several of the most basic human vowels, their capacity for language is limited to just a few vowels and consonants.[16] Thus, the absence of "mutations for altered tongue and larynx anatomy" that made human vocalization possible has consigned captured chimpanzees to "primate centers" and exploitation in zoos, nightclub acts, space flights, and medical experiments. Carl Sagan has asked the pertinent question: "How smart does a chimpanzee have to be before killing him constitutes murder?"[17]

This so-called "Great Leap Forward" that allowed language-using humans to develop agriculture, use metals, invent writing, and spread themselves over the earth, also allowed them to exploit the earth's "voiceless" inhabitants. "It was then but a short further step to those monuments of civilization that distinquish humans from animals," writes Diamond, "monuments such as the 'Mona Lisa' and *Eroica Symphony*, the Eiffel Tower and Sputnik, Dachau's ovens and the bombing of Dresden."[18] He might well have added animal laboratories, factory farms, and slaughterhouses.

The Domestication of Animals
The exploitation of goats, sheep, pigs, cattle, and other animals for their meat, milk, hides, and labor—euphemistically called their "domestication"—began about 11,000 years ago in the ancient Near East when a number of communities began to shift from a diet sustained by gathering and hunting to one supported by domesticated plants and animals.[19] For hundreds of thousands of years our ancestors had been food gather-

ers who relied on hunting, fishing, and foraging for fruit, vegetables, nuts, shell-fish, grubs, and other wild foods.[20]

The transition to herding and farming happened gradually. Those who hunted wild sheep and goats attached themselves to a particular herd, which then became "their" herd to follow and exploit. Since it is easier to capture and domesticate young animals, the first herders killed protective adults so they could capture and keep the young animals away from their natural living area and breeding community. In the process of killing animals for their meat and exploiting them for their milk, hides, or labor, herders learned how to control the animals' mobility, diet, growth, and reproductive lives through the use of castration, hobbling, branding, ear cropping, and such devices as leather aprons, whips, prods, and eventually chains and collars.[21] "The price [domesticated animals] have paid is their evolutionary freedom," writes Desmond Morris. "They have lost their genetic independence and are now subject to our breeding whims and fancies."[22]

To produce the kinds of animals most useful for their needs, herders killed or castrated most of the males to ensure that the "selected" breeding males impregnated the females.[23] Male animals were also castrated to make them more manageable, as Carl Sagan explains:

> Bulls, stallions, and roosters are made into steers, geldings, and capons because humans find their machismo inconvenient—the very same male spirit that the castrators likely admire in themselves. One or two skilled motions of the blade—or a deft bite by a reindeer-herding Lapp woman—and the testosterone levels are down to manageable proportions for the rest of the animal's life. Humans want their domestic animals to be submissive, easily controlled. Intact males are an awkward necessity; we want just enough of them to father a new generation of captives.[24]

The way present-day herders manage their flocks provides us with a look at the likely methods early herders used to control their flocks. Castration continues to be the centerpiece of animal husbandry. The

Nuer in Africa select the bull calves of their best milking cows for breeding and castrate all the rest. That leaves one breeding calf intact for about every thirty or forty castrated calves. In northern Scandinavia the Lapps castrate most of the reindeer bucks in their herds and then use them as draft or pack animals. The Tuang castrate camels because they find they grow larger humps, last longer as riding animals, and are easier to control than bull camels in rut.

In the case of most animals, such as cattle, horses, camels, and pigs, herders cut open their scrotum and cut out their testicles. African herdsmen use either a knife or the blade of a spear, while people in New Guinea castrate their pigs with a bamboo knife. Some herders destroy or damage the testicles of their animals without removing them. One common practice is to tie the scrotum tightly with a cord until the testicles atrophy. The Lapps restrain the reindeer, wrap his scrotum in a cloth, and then bite and chew it with their teeth until the testicles are crushed. The Sonjo of Tanzania castrate their he-goats when they are about six months old by strangulating their scrotum with a bow-string and then crushing their testicles with a long stone implement. The Masai pound the testicles of their rams with two stones. Herders rarely control reproduction by tampering with female animals. However, the Tuareg—Berbers of the Sahara—sometimes insert a small stone into the uterus of the she-camels they use for riding in the belief that it makes for a smoother gait.

Present-day herders manipulate the timing of the reproduction of their herds to ensure that milk and meat become available when they are most wanted. Kazak herders in Asia control the reproduction of their rams by wrapping them in leather aprons, while the Tuareg bind the prepuce of their he-goats with a cord that they then tie to their scrotum.[25]

To exploit female animals for milk, herders have devised various ways to keep the milk from getting to their children. Since the calf usually needs to be present to get the mother's milk to start flowing, the Nuer, Basuto, and Tuareg have the calf begin sucking, but once the mother's milk starts flowing, they take the calf away and milk the mother for themselves.

If a calf dies or the herders decide to eat the calf, getting the mother to give up her milk becomes more difficult. Some herdsmen will skin the dead calf, stuff the skin with straw or grass, and then bring it to the mother. The Nuer smear the dummy with the mother's urine to give it a more familiar scent. The Rwala sometimes kill a camel calf at birth so they can eat him and then smear another calf with the dead calf's blood and bring him to the she-camel. Herders in northern England used to mount the skin of a dead calf on a rocker and then have the rocker butt against the female's udder. In East Africa herders activate the female animal's "milk-ejection reflex" by manually stimulating her genital tract or inflating her vagina with air.

Making suckling and sucking painful and difficult, if not impossible, is another way herders keep milk away from the offspring for whom it is intended. The Nuer tie a ring with thorns around the calf's muzzle, which pricks the mother's udder. Some herders tie pointed sticks to a muzzle behind the calf's head, which keeps the calf from getting close to his mother. To keep a camel calf from sucking his mother, the Rwala insert a sharp peg under the nostrils of the camel calf, which pricks her udder. They also tie a pouch or net, often made of goat's hair, over the she-camel's udder, so that the calf can't reach his mother's milk. The Lapps smear excrement on the udders of reindeer does in order to keep their fawns from sucking them.

The Tuareg put a stick in the back of a calf's mouth, like a bit, and then tie it to the calf's horns so he cannot suck his mother. They also pierce a kid's cheek with a stick to achieve the same result. Another method the Tuareg use on their cattle is to pierce the nasal septum of the calves with a forked stick that makes sucking painful. To keep camel calves from their mothers the Tuareg pierce their upper lip and insert a root which they tie in a knot at both ends. This makes suckling uncomfortable for the mother and sucking extremely difficult and painful for the calf. The Tuareg also cut the noses of camel and cattle calves to keep them from sucking their mothers.[26]

Herders restrict the movement of their animals, either to keep them from mating or to prevent them from wandering too far away while grazing or during a halt when they are used as transport or pack animals. The Tuareg "hobble" their rams by tying their front and back legs tightly together on one side. They also hobble camel calves to keep them from reaching their mothers. The Gonds of Madhya Pradesh attach a heavy wooden hobble to the feet of their cattle to keep them from wandering away from the herd.

In New Guinea people have devised several different ways to keep pigs from foraging freely or rooting where they're not supposed to. In northern New Guinea they cut off a slice of the pig's snout to keep it raw so that it will be painful for the pig to root. People at the headwaters of the Sepik restrict the mobility of their pigs by scooping out their eyes, piercing them with a stick "to let the water out," and then returning the damaged eyes to their sockets. Then when the time comes, they kill and eat the blinded pigs.[27]

Today, in the United States, a common method of castration is to pin the animal down, take a knife, and slit the scrotum, exposing the testicles. Each testicle is then grabbed and pulled on, breaking the cord that attaches it.[28] Another method is to use a ring. American rancher Herb Silverman describes what happens: "I hate castrating them. It's really horrible. After you put the ring on its scrotum, the calf will lie down and kick and wring its tail for half an hour or more, before the scrotum finally goes numb. It's obviously in agony. Then it takes about a month before its balls fall off."[29]

The story of the "domestication" of animals is traditionally paired with the cultivation/domestication of plants as part of the "Agricultural Revolution," trumpeted as the key element in the triumphant march of our species from the Stone Age to civilization. However, the story rarely describes the cruelty involved.

Ruthlessness and Detachment

The enslavement/domestication of animals affected the way humans related to their captive animals and in turn to each other. In hunter-gatherer societies there had often been a sense of kinship between humans and animals, reflected in totemism and myths which portrayed animals, or part-animal part-human creatures, as creators and progenitors of the human race. Hunted animals lived free of human control until they were tracked and killed.[30] However, once animals were "domesticated," herdsmen and farmers adopted mechanisms of detachment, rationalization, denial, and euphemism to distance themselves emotionally from their captives.[31]

The main coping mechanism humans employed was the adoption of the view that they were separate from and morally superior to the other animals, the attitude Freud described at the beginning of the chapter. The relationship of humans to other beings became what it is today—one of domination, control, and manipulation—with humans making life-or-death decisions concerning what were now "their" animals. "Like dependents in the household of a patriarch," writes Tim Ingold, "their status is that of jural minors, subject to the authority of their human master."[32]

Since violence begets violence, the enslavement of animals injected a higher level of domination and coercion into human history by creating oppressive hierarchical societies and unleashing large-scale warfare never seen before. Some anthropologists believe that the advent of herding and farming gave rise to an interventionist approach to political life. They point out that in societies, like Polynesia, where people live by growing vegetables and crops that require little intervention, people believe that nature should be left to take its course and they in turn should be trusted to fend for themselves with a minimum of control from above.

The historian Keith Thomas likewise believes that the domestication of animals created a more authoritarian attitude since "human rule over the lower creatures provided the mental analogue on which many political and social arrangements were based."[33] Jim Mason maintains that making intensive animal agriculture the foundation of our society has built ruthlessness, detachment, and socially acceptable violence and cruelty into the very bone marrow of our culture, thus cutting us off from a greater sense of kinship with the other inhabitants of the natural world.[34]

Once animal exploitation was institutionalized and accepted as part of the natural order of things, it opened the door to similar ways of treating other human beings, thus paving the way for such atrocities as human slavery and the Holocaust.[35] As Aviva Cantor writes, "Nowhere is patriarchy's iron fist as naked as in the oppression of animals, which serves as the model and training ground for all other forms of oppression."[36]

The English philosopher Jeremy Bentham (1748–1832), who recognized the domestication of animals as tyrannical, looked forward to the day when things might be different: "The day may come when the rest of the animal creation may acquire those rights which never could have been withheld from them but by the hand of tyranny."[37]

Human Slavery

Karl Jacoby writes that it seems "more than coincidental that the region that yields the first evidence of agriculture, the Middle East, is the same one that yields the first evidence of slavery."[38] Indeed, in the ancient Near East, he writes, slavery was "little more than the extension of domestication to humans."[39] Most studies of human slavery have failed to emphasize how the enslavement of animals served as the model and inspiration for the enslavement of humans, but there have been notable exceptions.[40]

Elizabeth Fisher believes that the sexual subjugation of women, as practiced in all the known civilizations of the world, was modeled after the domestication of animals. "The domestication of women followed the initiation of animal keeping," she writes, "and it was then that men began to control women's reproductive capacity, enforcing chastity and sexual repression."[41] Fisher maintains that it was the vertical, hierarchical positioning of human master over animal slave that intensified human cruelty and laid the foundation for human slavery. The violation of animals expedited the violation of human beings.

In taking them in and feeding them, humans first made friends with animals and then killed them. To do so, they had to kill some sensitivity in themselves. When they began manipulating the reproduction of animals, they were even more personally involved in practices which led to cruelty, guilt, and subsequent numbness. The keeping of animals would seem to have set a model for the enslavement of humans, in particular the large-scale exploitation of women captives for breeding and labor.[42]

Fisher believes that the violence involved in the subjugation and exploitation of animals that paved the way for men's sexual domination of women, created the high level of oppressive control inherent in patriarchal societies.[43] She also believes that men learned about their role in procreation from domesticated animals and that the forced mating of animals planted in their minds the idea of raping women. Mary O'Brien also believes the enslavement of animals was the training ground for male violence.[44]

In Mesopotamia, warfare between rival city-states typically ended with the mass slaughter of male captives and the enslavement of women and children. Not only were female slaves useful as workers, but they were valuable because they could produce more slaves. Young girls stayed with their mothers in female work gangs, while boys were castrated like oxen and assigned to slave labor camps. The victorious city-states which did not automatically kill all their male captives castrated them instead and often blinded them as well, before they put them to work as slaves.

Sumer, one of the earliest and most powerful of the ancient Mesopotamian city-states, managed its slaves the same way it managed its livestock. The Sumerians castrated the males and put them to work like domesticated animals, and they put the females in work and breeding camps. The Sumerian word for castrated slave boys—*amar-kud*—is the same word the Sumerians used for young castrated donkeys, horses, and oxen.[45]

Slaves as Domestic Animals

In slave societies, the same practices used to control animals were used to control slaves—castration, branding, whipping, chaining, ear cropping. The ethic of human domination that removed animals from the sphere of human concern and obligation, writes Keith Thomas, "also legitimized the ill-treatment of those humans who were in a supposedly animal condition."[46] And certainly no humans were in more of an "animal condition" than slaves. In European colonies, he points out, "slavery, with its markets, its brandings and its constant labour, was one way of dealing with men thought to be beastlike."[47]

An English traveller reported that the Portuguese branded slaves "as we do sheep, with a hot iron," while another traveller who visited the slave market in Constantinople saw buyers take slaves indoors to inspect them naked and handle them "as we handle beasts, to know their fatness and strength." One eighteenth century goldsmith advertised "silver padlocks for blacks and dogs." English advertisements for runaways often showed them with collars around their necks.[48]

In American colonies such as the Carolinas, Virginia, Pennsylvania, and New Jersey, castration of slaves was punishment for such things as striking a white person or running away. In some colonies, the castration laws were worded so that they applied to all blacks, whether free or slave. Having no basis in English law, castration was a uniquely American experiment that many Americans defended as necessary to subdue and restrain a lecherous and barbarian people.[49] "Castration of blacks clearly indicated a need in white men to persuade themselves that they were really masters and in all ways masterful," writes Winthrop Jordan, "and it illustrated dramatically the ease with which white men slipped over into treating their Negroes like their bulls and stallions whose 'spirit' could be subdued by emasculation."[50]

Branding was used as a way to mark and identify slaves throughout the Americas until the late 1700s.[51] The Spanish branded Indian slaves on the face, using a new set of letters each time the slave was sold to a new owner, so that some slaves had so many marks, in addition to the royal brand, that their faces were covered with letters.[52] In the 1800s in the American South, branding was used to punish runaways and insubordinate slaves, but it was still sometimes used as a means of identification. South Carolina allowed branding and permitted slave owners to crop the ears of slaves accused of a crime until 1833.[53] One Georgian slave owner punished his runaways by pulling out one of their toenails with a pair of pincers.[54]

In Latin America when runaway slaves were returned, their masters branded them on their shoulders. However, when the slave masters discovered that slaves considered the brand a badge of honor, they "hobbled" their returned runaways by severing the Achilles tendon on one of their feet.[55] In 1838 a North Carolina slave owner advertised that his runaway had recently been "burnt with a hot iron on the left side of her face; I tried to make the letter M." Ten years later a Kentucky slave owner identified his runaway by a brand mark "on the breast something like L blotched."[56]

While branding and mutilating slaves was on the decline by the mid-1800s, the practice remained legal in some places. Mississippi and Alabama continued to punish slaves with a "burning in the hand" for penalties other than the death penalty. In 1831 a Louisiana jailer reported that he had in his custody a runaway who "has been lately gelded, and he is not yet well." Another Louisianian reported that his neighbor "castrated three of his men."[57] A man caught helping slaves trying to escape was branded on the hand with SS (slave stealer).[58]

Slave owners fettered their slaves for the same reason herders fettered animals—to limit their mobility. A Mississippi slave owner had his runaway Maria "ironed with a shackle on each leg connected with a chain." When his runaway Albert was returned, the owner "had an iron collar put on his neck." He also "put the ball and chain" on Woodson, a habitual runaway. A Kentuckian remembered seeing slaves in his state wearing iron collars, some of them with bells attached. However, these fetters apparently did not accomplish what they were supposed to, since many advertisements for runaways in Southern newspapers described the missing slaves as wearing fetters when they escaped. Three entries in a 1844 diary read: "Alonzo runaway with his irons on" (July 17); "Alonzo came in with his irons off" (July 30); "...re-ironed Alonzo" (July 31). A Louisiana runaway named Peter "had on each foot when leaving, an iron ring, with a small chain attached to it."[59] American blacks—free as well as slave—were legally in the same category as domestic animals.[60]

Man's Dominion Over Animals

By the time civilizations emerged in the river valleys of ancient Egypt, Mesopotamia, India, and China, the exploitation of captive animals for food, milk, hides, and labor was so firmly entrenched that the religions that emerged in these civilizations, including the Judeo-Christian tradition, sanctified the notion that the world had been created for the sake of the human species.[61]

According to Genesis, God created "the beasts of the earth according to their kinds and the cattle according to their kinds, and everything that creeps upon the ground according to its kind." God then made man in his image and gave him "dominion over the fish of the sea, and over the birds of the air, and over the cattle, and over all the earth, and over every creeping thing that creeps upon the earth."[62] Philip Kapleau writes that some environmentalists and historians think "those fateful words of the Bible have determined the destructive course of Western civilization for 2,000 years."[63] In a lecture which the environmentalist and social critic Ian McHarg gave on the question of Western man's attitude toward the natural world, he said, "If you wanted to find one text which, if believed and employed literally, or simply accepted implicitly, without the theological origins being known, will explain all the destruction and all the despoliation accomplished by Western man for at least these 2,000 years, then you do not have to look any further than this ghastly, calamitous text."[64]

If, as the Genesis story relates, man first sinned when Adam ate the forbidden fruit in the Garden of Eden, writes Kapleau, then "surely his second great sin was succumbing to the temptation to kill and eat his fellow creatures." He believes the transition to meat eating may have first taken place during one of the glacial periods in prehistoric times when plant life, man's original diet, disappeared under sheets of ice, or it may have happened because of the prestige associated with the killing of the large mammals that dominated large portions of the earth. "In any case, terror, violence, bloodshed, the slaughter of men, and ultimately war, it can be argued, all grew out of that fateful encounter."[65]

The Genesis passage which grants man dominion over other creatures reflected the political and social reality that existed at the time it was written.[66] As Milan Kundera observes, Genesis was written from man's point of view:

> The very beginning of Genesis tells us that God created man in order to give him dominion over fish and fowl and all creatures. Of course, Genesis was written by a man, not a horse. There is no certainty that God actually did grant man dominion over other creatures. What seems more likely, in fact, is that man invented God to sanctify the dominion that he had usurped for himself over the cow and the horse. Yes, the right to kill a deer or a cow is the only thing all of mankind can agree upon, even during the bloodiest of wars.[67]

While the Hebrew Bible upholds the principle of divinely sanctioned human supremacy, its laws against causing animals physical and psychological pain and suffering (*tsa'ar ba'alei chayim*) and its disapproval of cruelty to animals moderate this principle to some degree. "Judaism is radical in accepting that in practice animals have certain basic rights," write Dan Cohn-Sherbok and Andrew Linzey. "These are revealed in a variety of prescriptions found in Hebrew law, which while allowing human use of animals teach that humans are to refrain from causing distress to any of God's creatures."[68]

This Jewish tradition of compassion for animals is rooted in the Torah, which requires animals to rest on the Sabbath, prohibits the yoking of strong and weak animals together, requires that threshing animals be allowed to graze, and so forth. Isaiah put the matter bluntly, as prophets are wont to do: "He who slaughters an ox is like him who kills a man."[69]

The later Talmud and responsa expanded on this tradition by banning blood sports, including hunting for "pleasure," and by requiring Jews to feed their animals before feeding themselves. So important was the duty to take care of one's animals that a Jew was legally authorized to interrupt the performance of a rabbinic commandment to feed them.[70] The *Code of Jewish Law* (*Sefer Hasidim*) expressed the requirement succinctly: "It is forbidden, according to the law of the Torah, to inflict pain upon any living creature. On the contrary, it is our duty to relieve the pain of any creature."[71]

The Bible remembers less violent earlier times and hopes for less violent times to come in the future. According to Genesis, at the beginning of human history there was an Eden where Adam and Eve and the animals lived in peace and harmony and where God's intention for all living creatures was that they should eat plants, not each other.[72] "Whether or not we find it practical and desirable," writes the Protestant theologian Karl Barth, "the diet assigned to men and beasts by God the Creator is vegetarian."[73] Moreover, Jewish tradition envisions that in the messianic age to come the nonviolent atmosphere that prevailed at creation will be restored. In the meantime, in Judaism, which for the most part has yet to evolve beyond meat eating, the tradition of compassion for animals remains a promising potential waiting to be fully realized.

No such humane sentiments infuse the extant texts of Greco-Roman civilization. Aristotle and the other writers of classical antiquity constructed a high, thick wall between humans and other animals, maintaining that since animals lacked reason, they were in the same category as inanimate objects. In his *Politics*, Aristotle wrote that "animals existed for the sake of man" and nature made all animals for his sake.[74] The Stoics taught similarly that nature existed solely to serve man's interests.[75]

Aristotle maintained that man's dominion over animals extended to slaves and women as well, another view that mirrored the political reality of the day, since human slavery and the subordination of women were the norm in ancient Greece. In his *Politics*, Aristotle wrote that such "uncivilized" people as the neighboring Achaeans and Thracians "are slaves by nature, as much inferior to their fellows as the body is to the soul, or as beasts are to men."[76] Aristotle believed it was as permissible to enslave people who did not possess "reason" as it was to enslave animals. "Slaves and animals do little for the common good, and for the most part live at random."[77] Anthony Pagden writes that since the slave is condemned to a life of perpetual servitude, "his obligations are indistinquishable from those of the beast of service, and his acquisition may be likened to hunting."[78]

In the first century B.C.E., Cicero, the Roman philosopher and statesman, maintained that everything in the world was created for the sake of something else: "Thus the corn and fruits produced by the earth were created for the sake of animals, and animals for the sake of man."[79] A character in one of his writings declares that "men can make use of the beasts for their own purposes without injustice."[80] Cicero expressed the Greco-Roman view of human lordship over nature when he proclaimed:

> We are absolute master of what the earth produces. We enjoy the mountains and the plains. The rivers are ours. We sow the seeds and plant the trees. We fertilize the earth. We stop, direct, and turn the rivers; in short, by our hands and various operations in this world we endeavor to make it as it were another nature.[81]

Roman law—like our law today—classified animals as property and hence things without any inherent rights. The right of humans to deprive animals of their lives and natural liberties was so ingrained in Roman thought and law that it was always assumed and never had to be justified.[82] Matt Cartmill writes that in the Greco-Roman world "animals were routinely treated with a mixture of brutal indifference and sadism."[83] In fact, only two instances of anything resembling disapproval of cruelty to animals can be found in Greco-Roman literature. In one instance, Plutarch wrote that the Athenians expelled a man from the city because he skinned a ram while he was still alive.

The second instance took place in 55 B.C.E. at a staged hunt sponsored by Pompey in a large Roman amphitheater. Different kinds of captured animals, from lions to deer, were forced into the arena where heavily armed men chased and killed them to entertain the spectators. According to Dio Cassius, on one of the final days of Pompey's games, the Romans drove eighteen elephants into the arena. When the armed men attacked them, however, instead of fighting back, the wounded elephants "went round holding up their trunks to heaven and lamenting bitterly," and "the crowd took pity on them, contrary to [Pompey's] intentions."[84] Cicero, who was present, wrote to a friend that "the whole affair was attended by a sort of pity, and a feeling that these huge animals have something in common with humankind."[85]

Christianity absorbed the human supremacy views of both the Greeks and the Hebrew Bible (minus its teachings about compassion to animals). Augustine (354–430) wrote that the sixth commandment ("Thou shalt not kill") applied only to humans, not to "irrational living things, whether flying, swimming, walking, or crawling, because they are not associated in a community with us by *reason*....Hence it is by a very just ordinance of the Creator that their life and death is subordinated to our use."[86]

The medieval theologian Thomas Aquinas (1225–74) declared that it is all right to kill animals because "the life of animals...is preserved not for themselves, but for man."[87] Not only did he deny rationality to animals, but he denied them an afterlife as well. Like Aristotle, whose work he incorporated into his theology, Aquinas believed that only the reasoning part of the soul survived after death. Since animals lacked the capacity to reason, he claimed that their souls, unlike human souls, did not survive their death.

By denying animals an afterlife, Aquinas protected Christians from the disturbing prospect of encountering in the hereafter the vengeful spirits of the animals they victimized on earth. His view helped reassure Christian Europe that it had no reason to feel morally concerned about other species or guilty about exploiting or killing them. He even went so far as to reinterpret the Old Testament passages that advocated kindness toward animals to help buttress his contention that people had no moral obligation to animals whatsoever.[88]

This tradition of church support for the human/animal divide notwithstanding, there has long been a pro-animal undercurrent in Christianity from the early apocryphal literature on. It includes the fourth-century church fathers Basil and Ambrose, the Celtic saints, St. Francis of Assisi, St. Anthony of Padua, St. Bonaventure, C. S. Lewis, and many contemporary theologians and scholars like Andrew Linzey, John Cobb, and others.[89] In an article—"For a More Just Relationship with Animals"—printed in the December 7, 2000 issue of the Vatican newspaper, *L'Osservatore Romano*, papal official Marie Hendrickx wrote that human "dominion" over the natural world does not mean indiscriminate killing and the infliction of needless suffering on animals. She questioned the morality of the way animals are currently treated, especially the cruelty involved in food production, animal experimentation, the wearing of fur, and bull fighting.[90]

The Great Chain of Being
The idea of the Great Chain of Being, created by Aristotle's teacher, Plato, formalized the belief of the Greeks that they ranked higher than non-Greeks, women, slaves, and, of course, animals. To the question of why a perfect creator would make a world with imperfect beings, Plato's answer was that the completeness of the world demanded a full range of different beings ranked hierarchically on a chain that descended from the immortal gods on high, down through humans to animals, plants, stones, and dust at the very bottom. The human part of the chain was likewise ranked hierarchically from the civilized Greeks at the top to slaves at the bottom.[91]

Medieval Christendom translated Plato's image into a ladder which had God at the top and European Christians on the highest rung, a position that granted them a divine mandate as God's overseers and stewards to rule over the rest of the ladder below. The idea that (European) man, flawed and sinful though he might be, occupied a position on earth comparable to God's position in the universe became a central idea in the religious and philosophical thought of Western civilization regarding man's place in nature.[92] Thus, (European) man had virtually unlimited authority to rule the natural world as "the Viceregent and Deputy of Almighty God."[93]

The fifteenth-century jurist Sir John Fortescue viewed the hierarchical arrangement of all things as a reflection of God's perfect ordering of the universe, in which "angel is set over angel, rank upon rank in the kingdom of heaven; man is set over man, beast over beast, bird over bird, and fish over fish, on the earth in the air and in the sea." He maintained that "there is no worm that crawls upon the ground, no bird that flies on high, no fish that swims in the depths, which the chain of this order does not bind in most harmonious concord." His conclusion was that in our perfectly hierarchical universe "from the highest angel down to the lowest of his kind there is absolutely not found an angel that has not a superior and inferior" and "not from man down to the meanest worm is there any creature which is not in some respect superior to one creature and inferior to another."[94]

The Great Chain of Being explained why certain social classes were by nature subordinate to others in a society in which each class had its divinely determined place. In medieval Christian art, writes John Weiss, "princes and priests were depicted at the apex of society followed by nobles; behind them trailed merchants, craftsmen, and peasants, the beggars, actors, and prostitutes, with Jews bringing up the rear."[95]

This hierarchy, including the social rankings within human society, was thought to be continuous since the perfect fabric of God's creation could have no gaps. The theologian Nicolaus Cusanus wrote that "the highest species of one genus coincides with the lowest of the next higher genus, in order that the universe may be one, perfect, continuous."[96]

This view of a continuously graded hierarchy of nature led to the creation of a category of "subhuman" being, writes Anthony Pagden, "a 'man' so close to the border with the beast, that he is no longer fully recognisable by other men as a member of the same species."[97] Most members of this subhuman category were destined to be what Aquinas called "animated instruments of service" (slaves). However, the lowest members of this borderline category were thought to possess a human lineage so corrupt that, as Hayden White writes, they "are men who have fallen below the condition of animality itself; every man's face is turned against them, and in general they can be slain with impunity."[98] This was the belief of Europeans having their first encounters with the native peoples of Africa, Asia, and the Americas.

As late as the Renaissance and Enlightenment, Europe's leading thinkers continued to believe in the interconnectedness of overlapping species as envisioned in the Great Chain of Being. Philosophers as distinguished as Gottfried Leibniz and John Locke believed in the existence of creatures who were part-man and part-animal. Carolus Linnaeus, who created the modern scientific classification of plants and animals, found room in his system for *homo ferus*, a wild man who was "four-footed, mute and hairy."[99] The reports of newly encountered peoples in Africa, Asia, and the Americas which made their way back to Europe fueled the popular imagination with fanciful accounts of creatures who were half-man and half-animal.[100]

The Human/Animal Divide

By the early modern period the notion that man was the apex of creation was the prevailing point of view. "Man, if we look to final causes, may be regarded as the centre of the world," wrote Francis Bacon (1561–1629), "insomuch that if man were taken away from the world, the rest would seem to be all astray, without aim or purpose."[101] According to this humanocentric view, animals were made for man, each one created specifically to serve a human purpose. Apes and parrots were made "for man's mirth," while singing birds were created "on purpose to entertain and delight mankind."[102]

The most far-reaching attempt to widen the gulf between humans and animals was a doctrine originally put forward in 1554 by a Spanish physician, but independently formulated and made famous from the 1630s onward by the French philosopher and scientist, René Descartes. This doctrine, as it was developed and elaborated further by his followers, declared that "animals were mere machines or automata, like clocks, capable of complex behaviour, but wholly incapable of speech, reasoning, or, on some interpretations, even sensation."[103]

Descartes's followers maintained that animals did not feel pain and claimed that the cries, howls, and writhings of animals were only external reflexes, unconnected to inner sensation. Widening the gulf between man and animal to such an extent provided by far the best rationalization yet for the human exploitation of animals. Cartesianism not only absolved God of the charge of unjustly causing pain to innocent animals by permitting humans to mistreat them, but it also justified the ascendancy of men and freed them, as Descartes put it, from "any suspicion of crime, however often they may eat or kill animals."

Keith Thomas writes that denying the immortality of animals "removed any lingering doubts about the human right to exploit the brute creation."[104] For, as the Cartesians observed, if animals really had the potential for immortality, then "the liberties men took with them would be impossible to justify; and to concede that animals had sensation was to make human behaviour seem intolerably cruel."[105]

By designating men as the lords of nature, Descartes created an absolute break between man and the rest of nature that cleared the way for the unimpeded exercise of human domination. James Serpell writes that the early Christian (and Aristotelian) belief that animals were created solely for the benefit of mankind, combined with the Cartesian view that animals were incapable of suffering, gave us "a licence to kill; a permit to use or abuse other life-forms with total impunity."[106]

In England and elsewhere in the western world, this doctrine of human supremacy became the established, uncontested truth. "In the ascent from brutes to man," wrote Oliver Goldsmith (1730–74), "the line is strongly drawn, well marked, and unpassable." The naturalist William Bingley (1774–1823) wrote that "the barrier which separates men from brutes is fixed and immutable." For a civilization that routinely exploited, killed, and ate animals, to think otherwise would have raised too many troubling ethical questions.[107]

Negative views of animals allowed people to project onto them qualities they did not like about themselves and helped them define themselves by contrasting animal behavior with what was alleged to be distinctive and admirable about human behavior. "Men attributed to the animals natural impulses they most feared in themselves—ferocity, gluttony, sexuality," writes Thomas, "even though it was men, not beasts, who made war on their own species, ate more than was good for them, and were sexually active all the year round."[108]

This great divide between human and non-human animals justified and continues to justify hunting, meat eating, animal experiments, and all manner of crueltics inflicted on animals. As Carl Sagan and Ann Druyan write, "A sharp distinction between humans and 'animals' is essential if we are to bend them to our will, make them work for us, wear them, eat them—without any disquieting tinges of guilt or regret." Their loss is of no consequence to us because animals are not like us. "Animals whom we have made our slaves," wrote Charles Darwin, "we do not like to consider our equals."[109]

Less Than Human

The great divide between humans and animals provided a standard by which to judge other people, both at home and elsewhere. If the cssence of humanity was defined as consisting of a specific quality or set of qualities, such as reason, intelligible language, religion, culture, or manners, it followed that anyone who did not fully possess those qualities was "subhuman." Those judged less than human were seen either as useful beasts to be curbed, domesticated, and kept docile, or as predators or vermin to be eliminated.[110]

This hierarchical thinking, built on the enslavement/domestication of animals that began 11,000 years ago, condoned and encouraged the oppression of people regarded as animals or animal-like. The ethic of human domination which promotes and justifies the exploitation of animals legitimized the oppression of humans alleged to be in an animal condition. The German biologist and philosopher Ernst Haeckel (1834–1919), whose ideas had a strong influence on Nazi ideology, maintained that since non-European races are "psychologically nearer to the mammals (apes and dogs) than to civilized Europeans, we must, therefore, *assign a totally different value to their lives.*"[111]

Europeans considered colonialism the natural extension of human supremacy over the animal kingdom since "it seemed clear to many Europeans that the white race had proved itself superior to the lower races of man by bringing them under its sway, just as the human species as a whole had proved itself superior to the other animals by dominating and subduing them."[112] In Africa, India, and other European colonies big-game hunting expeditions became perfect symbols of the dominion of European whites over the land, its animals, and its people.

In British East Africa, for example, a white hunter on safari usually used 40–100 black natives as equipment carriers and servants. They were called *boy* and slept in the open, while the hunter, clad in a distinctive formal hunting outfit, was addressed as *master* and slept in an elaborate tent. The natives trekked day after day balancing 60-pound packs on their heads, while the hunter carried nothing, not even his gun, which a gunboy carried for him. The hunting ritual left no doubt in anyone's mind who was in charge. As the renowned tiger hunter Ralph Stanley-Robinson reminded his companions before one safari, "The object of this hunt is imperial. We are the rulers here."[113]

Thus, with animals already defined as "lower life" fated for exploitation and slaughter, the designation of "lesser" humans as animals paved the way for their subjugation and destruction. In *Genocide: Its Political Use in the Twentieth Century*, Leo Kuper writes, "The animal world has been a particularly fertile source of metaphors of dehumanization," so that people designated as animals "have often been hunted down like animals."[114]

The next chapter looks at the practice of vilifying people by designating them as animals and how it serves as a prelude to their persecution, exploitation, and murder.

CHAPTER TWO

WOLVES, APES, PIGS, RATS, VERMIN

Vilifying Others as Animals

In the same essay in which Freud wrote about the wide gulf man placed between himself and his fellow creatures, he went on to point out that "this piece of arrogance" is the result of "a later, more pretentious stage of development" and that this stage is foreign to children because a child can see no difference between his own nature and that of animals ("he is not astonished at animals thinking and talking in fairy-tales"). It is not until the child is grown up, writes Freud, that "he becomes so far estranged from animals as to use their names in vilification of others."[1]

Not only did the domestication of animals provide the model and inspiration for human slavery and tyrannical government, but it laid the groundwork for western hierarchical thinking and European and American racial theories that called for the conquest and exploitation of "lower races," while at the same time vilifying them as animals so as to encourage and justify their subjugation.

European explorers and colonists, who at home abused, slaughtered, and ate animals to a degree unmatched in human history up to that time, sailed forth to other parts of the world, in the words of David Stannard, as "representatives of a religious culture that was as theologically arrogant and violence-justifying as any the world had ever seen."[2] The European designation of the people of Africa, Asia, and the Americas as "beasts," "brutes," and "savages" raised the level of murderousness with which they encountered them.

Calling people animals is always an ominous sign because it sets them up for humiliation, exploitation, and murder. It is significant, for example, that in the years leading up to the Armenian genocide, the Ottoman Turks referred to Armenians as *rajah* (cattle).[3] "The use of animal imagery is particularly foreboding," writes Neil Kressel, "as in Nazi depictions of the Jews as rats and Hutu references to Tutsis as insects. Such allusions to the subhumanity of enemies can be an early sign of the potential for mass bloodshed."[4]

Africans

The Europeans who sailed to Africa in the sixteenth century described the people they encountered there as "rude and beastlie" and "like to bruite beasts." One English voyager complained that he could not make out what the people of Mozambique were saying because they spoke "so confoundedly and chatteringly lyke apes."[5]

The English saved their harshest criticism for the "ugly and loathsome" Hottentots whom they described as an "ill-look'd stinking, nasty People" who went about in "heardes" like their animals and seemed "rather to cackle like hens or turkeis, then speak like men." In 1626 Sir Thomas Herbert wrote, "Their words are sounded rather like that of Apes, then Men.... And comparing their imitations, speech, and visages, I doubt many of them have no better Predecessors then Monkeys." In 1714 Daniel Beeckman declared of the Hottentots, "These filthy animals hardly deserve the name of rational creatures."[6] The Reverend John Ovington, who sailed to Africa in 1696 as chaplain of the *Benjamin*, a ship owned by the East India Company, described the Hottentots as "the very Reverse of Human Kind," comparing them to the Helachors (East Indian outcasts), "only meaner and more filthy." His conclusion was that "if there is any medium between a Rational animal and a Beast, the Hotantot lays fairest claim to the Species."[7]

In the 1600s and 1700s there were many discourses on the animal nature of negroes, both slave and free, and their beastlike sexuality and brutish nature, which placed them low down on the hierarchical ladder next to the animals.[8] In his *History of Jamaica* (1774) Edward Long wrote that the orangutan was closer to the negro than the negro was to the white man. In 1799 the English surgeon Charles White analyzed the "regular gradation from the white European down through the human species to the brute creation, from which it appears that in those particulars wherein mankind excel brutes, the European excels the African."[9]

By the 1800s European scientists were constructing various theories of human inequality based on race, gender, and class that set white European males above non-Europeans, women, Jews, and, at the bottom of the ladder, Africans. Western scientific thought accepted as self-evident the superiority of the white race and the possession of greater intelligence by the educated and wealthy. Employing the widely held belief that intelligence was directly related to brain size, scientists established a hierarchical ranking of races and classes that put whites on top, Indians below whites, and blacks below everybody else, close to the animals.

"The brain of the Bushman leads towards the brain of the Simiadae (monkeys)," wrote Sir Charles Lyell (1797–1875), the founder of modern geology. "Each race of Man has its place, like the inferior animals."[10] Georges Cuvier (1769–1832), a pioneer in the science of comparative anatomy who was hailed in France as the Aristotle of his age, described Africans as "the most degraded of human races, whose form approaches that of the beast."[11] After the death in Paris of an African woman known as the "Hottentot Venus," Cuvier wrote that she had a way of pouting her monstrously large lips "exactly like what we have observed in the orang-utan" and that she moved in a manner "reminding one of the ape." He concluded that she had the characteristics of an animal. "I have never seen a human head more like an ape than that of this woman."[12]

Paul Broca (1824–80), a French pathologist, anthropologist, and pioneer in neurosurgery, measured human skulls to support the thesis that brain size was related to intelligence. He argued that the brains and hence the intelligence of well-established white men were greater than those of women, poor people, and the non-European "lower races." His conclusion was that "in general, the brain is larger in mature adults than in the elderly, in men than in women, in eminent men than in men of mediocre talent, in superior races than in inferior races."[13]

Broca's research on the relative location of the hole in the base of the skull called the *foramen magnum*, which found it farther forward in humans than in the great apes and even more so than in other mammals, led him to study the skulls of whites and blacks. Finding the *foramen magnum* of whites in a more anterior position, he concluded that "the conformation of the Negro, in this respect as in many others, tends to approach that of the monkey."[14] In a similar vein, the German anthropologist, E. Huschke, wrote in 1854 that the Negro brain has a spinal cord which "approaches the type of brain found in higher apes."[15]

American scientists did their part to uphold white prejudices that ranked blacks and other "inferior" people at the bottom of the racial ladder. The American paleontologist and evolutionary biologist Edward D. Cope (1840–97) declared that lower forms of human beings belonged to four groups—women, nonwhites, Jews, and the lower classes within superior races.[16]

In the nineteenth century American scientists, who used skulls to measure brain size (called craniometry) and to rank people hierarchically, declared that foreigners and people at the bottom of the social ladder at home were made of intrinsically inferior material (flawed brains, poor genes, or whatever). Samuel George Morton (1799–1851), a distinquished Philadelphia physician and researcher in natural history, amassed a huge collection of human skulls, mostly of American Indians, which he used to measure brain size and rank human races. In his three major published works on human skulls, Morton ranked the races hierarchically, with whites on top, Indians in the middle, and blacks at the bottom. He called Hottentots "the nearest approximation to the lower animals" and described their women as "even more repulsive in appearance than the men."[17] He further sub-divided whites and ranked them hierarchically—Teutons and Anglo-Saxons on top, Jews in the middle, and Hindus on the bottom.[18]

Jim Mason writes that White America's conception and treatment of Africans as domesticated animals both during and after slavery was part of "white society's urge to confine and control 'bestial' black Africans. That control required even more emotional intensity than did the control of their domestic animals, for the threat and the stakes were so much higher."[19] In *The Paradox of Cruelty*, Philip Hallie writes that after the Civil War white prejudice "kept the Negro a passive victim of white power, a domesticated animal."[20]

In 1893 the *Southwestern Christian Advocate*, published in New Orleans, printed an article by the Hon. B. O. Flower—"Burning of Negroes in the South"—in which he criticized a recent lynching, while at the same time saying he felt little sympathy for the victim. "If we weighed this crime from the standpoint of that higher justice, it would be seen that this poor brute was at best only a few degrees removed from the gorilla or the lion of his native Africa. Some of his ancestors probably belonged to the most brutal and degraded tribes of the dark continent."[21]

In an article published in the *American Journal of Anatomy* in 1906, Robert Bennett Bean, a Virginia doctor, wrote that on the basis of his measurements of the brains of American whites and blacks, which found that the posterior part of the black brain was larger than the anterior, he was able to conclude that blacks were intermediate between man and the orangutan.[22] An editorial in the April 1907 issue of *American Medicine* praised Bean's views, stating that he provided "the anatomical basis for the complete failure of the negro schools to impart the higher studies— the brain cannot comprehend them any more than a horse can understand the rule of three."[23]

Native Americans

Native Americans were vilified in a similar way as a prelude to their destruction. Like the Nazis in Europe who came after them, writes Stannard, the European explorers and colonists who came to America "produced many volumes of grandiloguently racist apologia for the genocidal holocaust they carried out." Not only did they consider the "lower races" they encountered in the Americas dark, sinful, carnal, inhuman, and un-Christian—hence dangerously close to animals—but they regarded contact with them as moral contamination.

Stannard writes that Christian Europe believed "God was always on the Christians' side. And God's desire, which became the Christians' marching orders, was that such dangerous beasts and brutes must be annihilated."[24] He also points out that Christian Europe's "long-entrenched and pathological hatred of Jews and all things Jewish"[25] served as the background to its encounter with the peoples of America. He thinks it is significant that Columbus set sail for the New World in 1492—the same year the Spanish drove the Jews out of Spain.

Given the way Europeans treated animals, their designation of Native Americans as "wild beasts" was a deadly presentiment of what lay ahead.[26] The most educated and cultured members of Columbus's second voyage—which Stannard calls "the true beginning of the invasion of the Americas"—were contemptuous of the native people they encountered. The Italian nobleman Cuneo, a boyhood friend of Columbus, called them "beasts" because they slept on mats instead of beds and because "they eat when they are hungry." The physician on board, Dr. Diego Chanca, described the natives as barbarous and unintelligent creatures whose "degradation is greater than that of any beast in the world."[27]

In his account of the early years of the Spanish Conquest, Bartolomé de Las Casas (1474–1566) described the Spanish atrocities against Native Americans as similar to the way the Spanish treated animals back home. "Christians, with their horses and swords and pikes began to carry out massacres and strange cruelties against them," he wrote. "They attacked the towns and spared neither the children nor the aged nor pregnant women nor women in childbed, not only stabbing them and dismembering but cutting them to pieces as if dealing with sheep in the slaughterhouse."[28] At one massacre he witnessed in Cuba, Spanish soldiers attacked a group of men, women, children, and old folk "to cut and kill those lambs." When they entered a large house nearby, they killed so many people inside "that a stream of blood was running, as if a great number of cows had perished."[29] They forced the Indian survivors of their massacres to carry cargo like "beasts of burden" and to squat down on their haunches "like tame sheep."[30]

The Spanish worked their Indian slaves to death, killing outright those who were reluctant, because, as Juan de Matienzo expressed it, Indians were "animals who do not even feel reason, but are ruled by their passions."[31] According to Tzvetan Todorov, targeted Indians were "identified with animals for the slaughterhouse, all their extremities are cut off, nose, hands, breasts, tongue, sexual organs, thereby transforming them into shapeless trunks, as one might trim a tree."[32]

The Europeans who settled North America were equally contemptuous of the native peoples they encountered. From the beginning the English constantly referred to them as "beasts," with all the pent up violence ready to be unleashed that the term implied. The English mariner Martin Frobisher (1535?-94) found Native Americans in Canada living in caves and hunting their prey "even as the bear or other wild beasts do." Robert Johnson, author of *Nova Britannia* (1609), observed Indians wandering "up and down in troops, like herds of deer in a forest."[33]

Samuel Purchas (1577?-1626), an English clergyman and compiler of travel literature, reported in the 1620s that the Indians in America had "little of humanitie but shape" and were "ignorant of Civilitie, of Arts, of Religion; more brutish than the beasts they hunt, more wild and unmanly then that unmanned wild countrey, which they range rather then inhabite."[34] When the Indians in Virginia began to resist the growing numbers of English settlers, John Smith (c.1580–1611) declared that the Indians were "cruel beasts" with "a more unnatural brutishness than beasts."[35] The English philosopher Thomas Hobbes (1588–1679) wrote that the "savage people" in America live in a "brutish manner," keeping the company of "hound-dogs, apes, asses, lions, barbarians, and hogs."[36] In 1689 an English clergyman, who had returned from the West Indies, spoke of the Indians as "just one degree (if they be so much) remov'd from a monkey."[37] According to Richard Drinnon, until the conquest and destruction of Native Americans was complete, the message was always the same: "In times of trouble natives were always wild animals that had to be rooted out of their dens, swamps, jungles."[38]

Hugh Brackenridge (1748–1816), a jurist and novelist, wrote that extermination would be most fitting for "the animals vulgarly called Indians."[39] In 1823 U.S. Supreme Court Chief Justice John Marshall (1755–1835) wrote, "The tribes of Indians inhabiting this country were fierce savages, whose occupation was war, and whose subsistence was drawn chiefly from the forest....That law which regulates, and ought to regulate in general, the relations between the conqueror and conquered was incapable of application to a people under such circumstances."[40] Such language placed Indians, like animals, beyond the reach of moral obligation and legal protection. "To call a man a savage," writes Francis Jennings in *The Invasion of America*, "is to warrant his death and to leave him unknown and unmourned."[41]

Josiah Clark Nott, a craniologist and co-author of the popular *Types of Mankind* (1856), concluded from his study of human skulls that whereas Caucasians had those parts of the skull developed which indicated intellect, Indian skulls indicated a strong "animal propensity." His conclusion was that Indians were "scarcely a degree advanced above brutes of the field." Although Francis Parkman (1823–93), the most honored historian of his time, viewed with regret the approaching extermination of the Indians—whom he described as "man, wolf, and devil all in one"—he believed that the Indian was responsible for his own destruction. Since he "will not learn the arts of civilization, he and his forest must perish together."[42]

Stannard writes that in California, as elsewhere, whites described Indians "as ugly, filthy, and inhuman 'beasts,' 'swine,' 'dogs,' 'wolves,' 'snakes,' 'pigs,' 'baboons,' 'gorillas,' and 'oran-gutans,' to cite only a few of the press's more commonly published characterizations." Some whites gave the Indians the benefit of the doubt and declared them not quite animals, but merely the people in North America closest to quadrupeds. However, others were less charitable, maintaining that simply touching an Indian created "a feeling of repulsion just as if I had put my hand on a toad, tortoise, or huge lizard." Needless to say, writes Stannard, the eradication of such loathsome creatures "could cause little trouble to most consciences."[43]

Oliver Wendell Holmes (1809–94), the famous Harvard professor of anatomy and physiology and father of the later Supreme Court justice of the same name, declared that Indians were nothing more than a "half-filled outline of humanity" whose extermination was a logical and necessary final solution to the problem. He believed they were meant to be in America only until the white man ("the true lord of creation") should come and claim it. He thought it was only natural for the white man to hate the Indian and "hunt him down like the wild beasts of the forest," so that "the red-crayon sketch is rubbed out, and the canvas is ready for a picture of manhood a little more like God's own image."[44]

Charles Francis Adams, Jr. (1835–1915) believed that although America's treatment of Indians had been "harsh," its conquest of them had "saved the Anglo-Saxon stock from being a nation of half-breeds." Stannard finds Adams' words "both a terrible echo of past warrants for genocidal race war and a chilling anticipation of eugenic justifications for genocide yet to come, for to this famous scion of America's proudest family, the would-be extermination of an entire race of people was preferable to the 'pollution' of racial intermixture."[45] On the occasion of the nation's centennial celebration in 1876, the country's leading literary intellectual, William Dean Howells (1837–1920), advocated "the extermination of the red savages of the plains," whom he called hideous demons "whose malign traits can hardly inspire any emotion softer than abhorrence."[46]

Shortly before the massacre of almost 200 Indian men, women, and children at Wounded Knee in South Dakota in 1890, L. Frank Baum, the editor of the state's *Aberdeen Saturday Pioneer*, who later achieved fame as the author of *The Wizard of Oz*, advocated the extermination of the Indians.

The nobility of the Redskin is extinquished, and what few are left are a pack of whining curs who lick the hand that smites them. The Whites, by law of conquest, by justice of civilization, are masters of the American continent, and the best safety of the frontier settlements will be secured by the total annihilation of the few remaining Indians. Why not annihilation? Their glory has fled, their spirit broken, their manhood effaced; better that they should die than live the miserable wretches that they are.[47]

Following the Wounded Knee massacre, Baum wrote, "we had better, in order to protect our civilization, follow it up and wipe these untamed and untamable creatures from the face of the earth."[48]

Viewing the matter from a global perspective, the country's leading psychologist and educator, Granville Stanley Hall (1844–1924), lauded the rapid extermination of the "hopelessly decadent" lower races around the world, who were "being extirpated as weeds in the human garden." He wrote that concern for those being exterminated was inappropriate since "we are summoned to rise above morals and clear the world's stage for the survival of those who are fittest because strongest."[49]

While White America regarded both Indians and African slaves as animals, it saw them as different kinds of animals: slaves were livestock, while Indians were wildlife (predators and vermin) and were to be treated as such.[50] By the end of the nineteenth century when the extermination of the last of the free Indians was virtually complete, the *California Christian Advocate* wrote that however strongly it sympathized with the Indians "in their sufferings from the white villains who take delight in goading these torpid savages into fury," it cannot release them "from the higher verdict of humanity, that of extermination." The Christian publication reassured its readers that the Indian's "low, beastly, blood-thirsty, tiger nature will inevitably be stamped out by the higher law of civilization."[51]

One of the greatest admirers of the destruction of the native peoples of America was Adolf Hitler. He found the white Anglo-Saxon conquest of the North American continent inspiring, and it convinced him of the practicality of genocidal measures against racially inferior peoples. His biographer John Toland writes that Hitler "often praised to his inner circle the efficiency of America's extermination—by starvation and uneven combat—of red savages who could not be tamed by captivity."[52]

"Injun Warfare" in the Philippines

During wartime the use of animal images and epithets becomes more prevalent and intense since the vilification of enemies as animals encourages killing and makes it easier. "The attachment of stupid, bestial, even pestilential subhuman caricatures on the enemy," writes John Dower, "and the manner in which this blocked seeing the foe as rational or even human facilitated mass killing. It is, at least, for most people, easier to kill animals than fellow humans."[53]

At the end of the nineteenth century when it looked as if America might finally run out of "wild Indians" to hunt down and kill, the conquest of the Philippines in the aftermath of the Spanish-American War (1898) provided the U.S. Army with a whole new set of "Indians." The military campaign, which killed an estimated 20,000 "insurgents" and 200,000 civilians, was reminiscent of the earlier Indian wars in the American West, Indeed, most of the American military officers sent to the Philippines were former Indian fighters with extensive experience hunting "savages."[54]

The first leader of the U.S. Expeditionary Force was Major General Wesley Merritt, a Civil War hero who became a veteran Indian fighter under General George Custer. Merritt's successor, General Ewell Otis, also a Civil War and Indian wars veteran, thought of his job as that of turning Filipinos into "good Indians." Other U.S. generals who went from fighting Indians to fighting Filipinos included Major General Henry Lawton, who captured the great Indian chief Geronimo; Major General Arthur MacArthur, military governor of the Philippines (1900–01); and Major General Adna Chaffee, who worked his way up through the ranks fighting Comanches, Cheyennes, Kiowas, and Apaches.[55]

The Philippines campaign reverberated with much of the same rhetoric and animal imagery of the Indian wars. Filipinos were routinely called "savages," while General Chaffee called them "gorillas" who hid in the bush. In 1901 one of the generals spoke of the problem of not knowing who the enemy was: "the problem is more difficult on account of the inbred treachery of these people, their great number, and the impossibility of recognizing the actively bad from the only passively so"—familiar terminology used during the destruction of Indian communities in America.[56]

In his campaign in Samar, General Jacob ("Hell-Raising") Smith applied the tactics he had successfully used against Geronimo, whom he helped capture, imprison, and send to a reservation. He began by ordering all natives, under pain of death, out of the interior, with those who streamed down to the coast immediately thrown into "concentration camps."[57] American troops described fighting in the Philippines as "Injun warfare" and called Filipinos "niggers," "treacherous savages," and "treacherous gugus" (or "goo-goos")—a derisive term that resurfaced in both World War II and in the Vietnam War as "gook." One soldier told a reporter that "the country won't be pacified until the niggers are killed off like the Indians."

As was often the case with Indian fighting, massacring prisoners, the wounded, and women and children was more often the rule than the exception, and for some it proved to be even more enjoyable than shooting animals.[58] A. A. Barnes of the Third Artillery regiment wrote a letter home in which he described the destruction of Titatia, which involved the slaughter of more than one thousand men, women, and children. "I am probably growing hard-hearted, for I am in my glory when I can sight my gun on some dark-skin and pull the trigger. Tell all my inquiring friends that I am doing everything I can for Old Glory and for America I love so well."[59]

A soldier from the Washington regiment described how shooting Filipinos was more fun than killing rabbits. Although the members of the regiment had to cross a muddy creek with water up to their waists, "we did not mind it a bit, our fighting blood was up, and we all wanted to kill 'niggers.'" Shooting human beings is a "hot game" and "beats rabbit killing all to pieces," he wrote. "We charged them and such a slaughter you never saw. We killed them like rabbits; hundreds, yes thousands of them."[60]

As the campaign turned into a series of massacres, the use of animal epithets intensified. A private in the Utah Battery, who wrote to his folks back home about "the progress of this 'goo goo' hunt," told them that the policy was to "fill the blacks full of lead before finding out whether they are friends or enemies" and that "no cruelty is too severe for these brainless monkeys."[61] A correspondent who visited one of the camps reported that most of the prisoners, who were in rags and dying from disease, "are a miserable-looking lot of little brown rats."[62]

As outright extermination became the order of the day, American officers did not hesitate to defend it. On November 11, 1901, the *Philadelphia Ledger* printed one officer's letter: "Our men have been relentless, have killed to exterminate men, women, and children, prisoners and captives, active insurgents and suspected people, from lads of ten up, an idea prevailing that the Filipino was little better than a dog." Another officer wrote to a reporter, "There's no mincing words. We exterminated the American Indians, and I guess most of us are proud of it, or, at least, the end justified the means; and we must have no scruples about exterminating this other race standing in the way of progress and enlightenment."[63]

Yellow Monkeys

John Dower writes that during World War II the Japanese were vilified as "animals, reptiles, or insects (monkeys, baboons, gorillas, dogs, mice and rats, vipers and rattlesnakes, cockroaches, vermin—or, more indirectly, 'the Japanese herd' and the like)" and that this campaign of vilification paved the way for a "war without mercy" in the Pacific, a war which culminated in the dropping of atomic bombs on Hiroshima and Nagasaki.[64] As the American journalist Ernie Pyle wrote in one of his first reports from the Pacific, "In Europe we felt that our enemies, horrible and deadly as they were, were still people. But out here I soon gathered that the Japanese were looked upon as something subhuman and repulsive; the way some people feel about cockroaches or mice."[65]

When the war started, Japanese-Americans in the United States were treated like animals—literally. Shortly after Pearl Harbor, they were rounded up and forced to live in animal facilities for weeks and even months before their internment in camps. Government officials in Washington State sent two thousand Japanese-Americans to a stockyard where they were crammed into a single building and forced to sleep on gunnysacks filled with straw. In California they had to live in stables at racetracks, such as Santa Anita, from which the horses were removed to make room for 8,500 Japanese-Americans. Other evacuees were assigned to live in horse and cattle stalls in fairgrounds. The Puyallup assembly center in Washington State had Japanese-Americans live in pigpens.[66]

Before the war Churchill told President Roosevelt that he was counting on him "to keep that Japanese dog quiet in the Pacific." Then, after the fighting started, "mad dogs" and "yellow dogs" became common epithets for the Japanese. An American who spent five years in Japan before the war wrote an article about one of his Japanese acquaintances who had been a journalist but was now a "mad dog" military officer. The American's conclusion was that "mad dogs are just insane animals that should be shot."

Bee, ant, sheep, and cattle images were also used to describe the Japanese. An American sociologist called the Japanese "a closely disciplined and conformist people—a veritable human bee-hive or ant-hill." A journalist reported that in battle "the Japs turned into ants, the more you killed the more they kept coming." General Slim, the British commander in Burma, wrote in his memoirs, "We had kicked over the anthill, the ants were running about in confusion. Now was the time to stamp on them." The U.S. Army's weekly magazine *Yank* referred to the "sheep-like subservience" of the Japanese, calling them "stupid animal-slaves." An Australian war correspondent wrote, "Many of the Japanese soldiers I have seen have been primitive oxen-like clods with dulled eyes and foreheads an inch high."[67]

Dower states that the most common animal image employed by western journalists and cartoonists was that of a monkey or ape, since the primate image is "perhaps the most basic of all metaphors traditionally employed by white supremacists to demean nonwhite peoples." Even before the war began, the undersecretary of the British Foreign Office, Sir Alexander Cadogan, regularly referred in his diary to Japanese as "beastly little monkeys." During the early months of the Japanese invasion of Southeast Asia, western journalists called Japanese troops "apes in khaki." In the January 1942 issue of the British magazine *Punch*, a full-page cartoon entitled "The Monkey Folk" showed monkeys swinging through the jungle with helmets on their heads and rifles slung over their shoulders.

American Marines made jokes about tossing a grenade into a tree and blasting out "three monkeys—two bucktooths and the real specimen." In late 1942 the *New Yorker* ran a cartoon, which later reached a much bigger audience when it was reprinted in *Reader's Digest*. It showed white infantrymen lying in a firing position facing a thick jungle where the trees were full of monkeys and several Japanese snipers. "Careful now," one soldier says to another, "only those in uniform." An American radio broadcaster told his audience that the Japanese were monkeys for two reasons: first, a monkey in a zoo imitates his trainer; and second, "under his fur, he's still a savage little beast."

When U. S. Admiral Halsey wasn't calling the Japanese "yellow bastards," he was denouncing them as "yellow monkeys," "monkeymen," and "stupid animals." Before one campaign he declared he was "rarin' to go" to get himself "some more monkey meat." He later told a news conference that he believed a Chinese proverb that "the Japanese were a product of mating between female apes and the worst Chinese criminals who had been banished by China." Simian terminology continued to permeate the American and British media throughout the war: "monkeynips," "Japes" (a combination of "Japs" and "apes"), "jaundiced baboons," "a buck-toothed, near-sighted, pint-sized monkey."[68]

As the tide of battle began to turn, the Japanese were increasingly characterized as vermin to be exterminated. The Marine magazine *Leatherneck* represented the Japanese graphically as a big, grotesque insect with slanted eyes and protruding teeth, which the American Marines were sent to exterminate. Other cartoonists depicted the

Japanese as ants, spiders, "Japanese beetles," and rats to be destroyed. In June 1942, at a huge patriotic parade in New York City, which had half a million participants and three million spectators—the largest parade ever held in New York up until that time—a float called "Tokyo: We Are Coming" was one of the parade's biggest hits. According to the *New York Herald Tribune* (June 14, 1942), the float showed "a big American eagle leading a flight of bombers down on a herd of yellow rats who were trying to escape in all directions." The crowd "loved it."[69]

Chinese Pigs

The Japanese also used animal imagery to demean their enemies, especially the Chinese. Shortly after the fall of Nanking in 1937, a Japanese soldier wrote in his diary that the thousands of Chinese troops they captured "walked in droves, like ants crawling on the ground" and moved "like a herd of ignorant sheep."[70] When a Chinese man tried to prevent Japanese soldiers from raping his wife, the soldiers stuck a wire through his nose and tied the other end of the wire to a tree "just like one would tie up a bull." The soldiers then took turns sticking bayonets into him while they forced his mother to watch.[71]

The Japanese put their new recruits through "desensitization exercises" upon their arrival in China by having them kill Chinese civilians. A Japanese private described his experience: "One day Second Lieutenant Ono said to us, you have never killed anyone yet, so today we shall have some killing practice. You must not consider the Chinese as a human being, but only as something of rather less value than a dog or cat."[72]

In the 1930s Japanese teachers taught their students hatred and contempt for the Chinese people in order to prepare them psychologically for the invasion of the Chinese mainland. In one class the teacher slapped a boy who cried when the teacher told him to dissect a frog. "Why are you crying about one lousy frog?" the teacher shouted. "When you grow up you'll have to kill one hundred, two hundred chinks!"[73]

The Japanese military regarded the Chinese as subhumans whose murder carried no greater moral weight than butchering a hog or squashing a bug. A Japanese general told a correspondent, "I regard the Chinese as pigs," and a soldier wrote in his diary that "a pig is more valuable now than the life of a [Chinese] human being. That's because a pig is edible." An officer in Nanking, who tied Chinese prisoners together in groups of ten, pushed them into pits, and set them on fire, later explained that the feelings he had while he was doing this were identical to those he had when he slaughtered pigs.[74]

The Japanese used to confiscate the beloved and useful buffaloes of Chinese farmers in order to impale and roast them alive.[75] In *Long the Imperial Way*, Hanama Jasaki, a former Japanese soldier, wrote how Japanese soldiers used to seize the Chinese farmer's donkeys and force them to copulate for their entertainment.[76]

Vietnamese Termites and Iraqi Cockroaches

A little more than two decades after the end of the war in the Pacific, similar rhetoric and animal imagery resurfaced in the Vietnam War. American troops referred to Vietnam as "Indian country" and called the Vietnamese "gooks," "slopes," and "dinks" (once they were dead they became "body counts"). According to official government reports, the Vietnamese people "infested" the land. U.S. Public Affairs Officer John Mecklin declared that the minds of the Vietnamese people were the equivalent of "the shriveled leg of a polio victim" and that their power of reason was "only slightly beyond the level of an American six-year old."[77]

In his testimony before Congress General Maxwell Taylor called the Vietnamese "Indians," while U.S. General William C. Westmoreland described them as "termites." Arguing that the United States should not commit too many troops to the conflict, Westmoreland explained that if you try to crowd in too many termite killers, you risk collapsing the floors or the foundation. "We have to get the right balance of termite killers to get rid of the termites without wrecking the house."[78]

During the Gulf War in 1991, American pilots described killing retreating Iraqi soldiers as a "turkey shoot" and called civilians who ran for cover "cockroaches." As always in wartime, animal images dehumanize the enemy and facilitate his destruction. "For among the many things that warfare does," writes Stannard, "is temporarily define the entire enemy population as superfluous, as expendable—a redefinition that must take place before most non-psychopaths can massacre innocent people and remain shielded from self-condemnation."[79] Nothing helps that redefinition take place more than to designate enemies as animals.

Vilification of the Jews
The practice of vilifying Jews as animals goes back to early Christian history. The Patriarch of Constantinople, Saint John Chrysostom (c.347–407), regarded as one of the greatest of the Church Fathers, called the synagogue "a lair for wild beasts" and wrote that "the Jews do not act any better than pigs and goats, in their lewd grossness and extremes of their gluttony." No less a venerable personage than Saint Gregory of Nyssa (c.335–c.394), also a Church Father, called Jewish people "a race of vipers."[80]

In Germany this kind of vilification began long before the Nazis came to power. At first, the leader of the Protestant Reformation, Martin Luther (1483–1546) praised Jews for rejecting the corrupt teachings of the papal "antichrist." But when it soon became clear the Jews weren't all that eager to convert to his brand of Christianity, he denounced them as "pigs" and "mad dogs." He said that if he were ever called on to baptize a Jew, he would drown him like a poisonous serpent. "I cannot convert the Jews...but I can close their mouths so that there will be nothing for them to do but lie upon the ground." According to John Weiss, Luther made it clear that "death was his final solution to the 'Jewish problem.'"[81]

In 1575 a German book of illustrated wonders declared that a Jewish woman near Augsburg gave birth to two small pigs.[82] The German philosopher Georg Wilhelm Friedrich Hegel (1770–1831) maintained that Jews could not be assimilated into German culture because materialism and greed motivated them to follow an "animal existence."[83] In the late 1800s a leading member of the Conservative Party ended his speech attacking Jews in the Reichstag by roaring, "Destroy these beasts of prey!"[84]

Paul de Lagarde (1827–91), a German Orientalist scholar and specialist in Semitic languages, called Jews a "bacillus" and said they were "carriers of decay who pollute every national culture." Destroy these "usurious vermin" before it is too late, he demanded. "You don't talk about what to do with parasites and bacilli. They are exterminated as quickly and as thoroughly as possible."[85] In the early 1900s the German crown prince William II (1859–1941) praised the bloody pogrom against Russian Jews in Kichenev, and when Jewish refugees from Russia entered Germany, he said, "Throw the pigs out!"[86] The German composer Richard Wagner (1813–83) wrote that the Jewish race was the "born enemy of humanity" and that it was polluting German culture like "vermin in a corpse." His wife Cosima constantly reviled Jews as vermin, lice, insects, and bacilli.[87]

Hitler used similar bacteriological language with genocidal overtones. "Don't think you can combat racial tuberculosis without seeing to it that the people is freed from the causative organ of racial tuberculosis," he said in August 1920.[88] Four years later in *Mein Kampf,* he called Jews "germ-carriers" who contaminate art and culture, infiltrate the economy, undermine authority, and poison the racial health of others.[89] In remarks published after the war, Hitler described Jews as "the spider that slowly sucks the people's blood, a band of rats that fight each other until they draw blood, the parasite in the body of other peoples, the eternal leech."[90]

There could be little doubt whom Hitler had in mind when he wrote in *Mein Kampf,* "The nationalization of our masses will succeed only when, aside from all the positive struggle for the soul of our people, their international poisoners are exterminated." However little Hitler had thought through the practical implications of what he was saying in the 1920s, Ian Kershaw writes that "its inherent genocidal thrust is undeniable. However indistinctly, the connection between destruction of the Jews, war, and national salvation had been forged in Hitler's mind."[91] Later, as Hitler was launching the Final Solution, he

once again equated Jews with bacilli and described the struggle to eliminate them as "the same fight Koch and Pasteur had to fight."[92]

John Roth and Michael Berenbaum write that Nazi propaganda
constantly described Jews as "parasites, vermin, beasts of prey—in a
word, subhuman."[93] In 1932, the year before the Nazis came to power,
great enthusiasm greeted a Nazi speech in Charlottenburg, a wealthy
Berlin district, when the speaker called Jews insects who needed to be
exterminated.[94] In the Nazi propaganda film *Der Ewige Jude* ("The
Eternal Jew"), which opens with footage of a mass of swarming rats, the
narrator explains, "Just as the rat is the lowest of animals, the Jew is the
lowest of human beings."[95]

During World War II the German high command on the eastern
front declared that Russian Communists were lower than animals: "We
would insult the animals if we were to describe these men, who are mostly Jewish, as beasts."[96] During a visit to the Lodz ghetto early in the war,
Joseph Goebbels, Nazi propaganda minister, described the Jews he saw
there as "no longer human beings. They are animals."[97] Gendarmerie
chief Fritz Jacob wrote a letter home to Germany in 1942, in which he
told about seeing "frightful Jewish types" in Poland. "These were not
human beings but ape people."[98]

Heinrich Himmler, who regarded the Jew as "spiritually and mentally much lower than any animal,"[99] saw the war as a racial struggle to
the death against the horde of "Asiatic animals" under the control of
Jewish Bolshevism. In 1943, in the German port city of Stettin, he told
an audience of Waffen-SS troops that the war was "an ideological battle
and a struggle of races." On one side was National Socialism, the defend-
er of Germanic Nordic blood ("a whole, a happy, beautiful world full of
culture"), while on the other side was "a population of 180 million, a
mixture of races, whose very names are unpronounceable and whose
physique is such that one can shoot them down without pity and compassion. These animals have been welded by the Jews into one religion,
one ideology, that is called Bolshevism."[100]

Although Germans often called Jews "rats"[101] and insulted them with
other animal names, their favorite epithets were "pig," "Jew-pig,"

"swine," and *Saujuden* ("Jewish swine").[102] Ernst Schumann, a member of one of the *Einsatzgruppen* (mobile killing squads), reported that his superior, Untersturmführer Täubner, laughed at him when he told him he had qualms about shooting women and children because he had a wife and children back home. Täubner "said something to the effect that for him first came pigs, then nothing at all, and only then, a long way down, the Jews."[103] Late in the war in Austria, when the local *Volkssturm* militia received word that the next day a group of Hungarian Jews was to pass through their town, the squad leader told them to get ready to kill them: "These dogs and pigs all deserve to be beaten to death together."[104] When Alois Hafele completed his duties at the Chelmno death camp, he told his former superior that one got used to it. "'Men, women, children, it was all the same, just like stepping on a beetle.' As he talked, Hafele made a scraping motion with his foot on the floor."[105]

The Nazis also used animal names in connection with their biomedical research on humans. At the women's concentration camp at Ravensbrück, the Germans called the inmates given gas gangrene wounds and used in bone-graft experiments "rabbit girls."[106] A prisoner doctor at Auschwitz, Magda V., said that Josef Mengele treated Jews "like laboratory animals" since "we were really biologically inferior in his eyes."[107] Whenever he exploded with anger at prisoner doctors, Mengele called them "dogs and pigs."[108]

This use of animal terms to vilify and dehumanize the victims, combined with the abominably degraded conditions in the camps, made it easier for the SS to do their job, since treating prisoners like animals made them begin to look and smell like animals.[109] "It made mass murder less terrible to the murderers," explains Terrence Des Pres, "because the victims appeared less than human. They *looked* inferior."[110] In *Hitler's Willing Executioners* Daniel Jonah Goldhagen states that the Germans often used Jews as playthings, "compelling them, like circus animals, to perform antics—antics that debased the Jews and amused their tormentors."[111]

For a civilization built on the exploitation and slaughter of animals, the "lower" and more degraded the human victims are, the easier it is to kill them. When Gitta Sereny interviewed Franz Stangl, commandant of Treblinka, in a Düsseldorf prison in 1971, she asked him, "Why, if they were going to kill them anyway, what was the point of all the humiliation, why the cruelty?" He answered, "To condition those who actually had to carry out the policies. To make it possible for them to do what they did."[112]

Designating Jews as animals did not end with the Nazis. In a speech on Iraqi state radio during the Gulf War crisis, Dr. Abd-al Latif Hamin proclaimed that "the Koran has Allah's promise to gather Jews, sons of apes and grandsons of pigs, in one place so that the Moslems can annihilate them."[113] In his weekly Friday prayer sermon broadcast on the Voice of Palestine, the Mufti of the Palestine Authority, Ikrama Sabri, also made reference to the animal ancestry of Jews. "Allah will avenge, in the name of his Prophet, the colonialist settlers who are descendents of monkeys and pigs," he promised. "Forgive us, Oh Muhammad, for the acts of these monkeys and pigs who wished to profane your holiness."[114]

In Russia anti-Semitic rhetoric also refers to Jews as animals. In an article in *Ja-russkij*, in which he praised an anti-Semitic lawmaker, Vladislav Shumsky wrote, "There are no good Jews, like there are no good rats....The Jews are not better than pigs and goats because of their lustfulness and excessive greediness."[115]

Confronting the Holocaust

The artist Judy Chicago writes in *Holocaust Project: From Darkness to Light* about how she came to realize that the designation of Jews as animals was what led to their being treated—and slaughtered—like animals. She admits that it took some time for her to come to that realization, however, because she had always trusted people and believed the world was a relatively fair and just place. She knew terrible things happened, but she saw them as isolated events.

That is why her encounter with the Holocaust shook her to the core and challenged her basic assumptions about people and the world. "Confronting the Holocaust brought me face to face with a level of reality beyond anything I'd experienced before: millions of people murdered, millions more enslaved, millions made to suffer, while the world turned its back on the implementation of the Final Solution."[116] She couldn't take it all in, she says, because it was all too painful and she knew she was a long way from understanding what it all meant about human beings and the world in which she lived.

After she began to see the slaughterhouse-like aspects of the Holocaust, she started to understand the connection between the industrialized slaughter of animals and the industrialized slaughter of people. When she visited Auschwitz and saw a scale model of one of the four crematoria, she realized "they were actually giant processing plants—except that instead of processing pigs they processed people who had been defined as pigs."[117]

As her study of the Holocaust deepened, Chicago learned that since one of the essential steps in being able to slaughter human beings is to dehumanize them, ghettoization, starvation, filth, and brutality all helped to turn Jews into "subhumans." By constantly describing Jews as "vermin" and "pigs," the Nazi regime convinced the German public that it was necessary to destroy them.

At Auschwitz, as Chicago reflected on the model of the crematorium, she "suddenly thought of the 'processing' of other living creatures, to which most of us are accustomed and think little about." She remembered that during the Industrial Revolution pigs were among the first "things" on the assembly line.[118] "I began to wonder about the ethical distinction between processing pigs and doing the same thing to people defined as pigs. Many would argue that moral considerations do not have to be extended to animals, but this is just what the Nazis said about the Jews."[119]

What was so unnerving about being at Auschwitz, she writes, "was how oddly familiar it seemed." Since some of the things the Nazis did in the camps are done all the time in the rest of the world, the "processing" methods used at Auschwitz were "a grotesque form of the same modern technologies upon which we all depend. Many living creatures are crowded together in despicable quarters; transported without food or water; herded into slaughterhouses, their body parts 'efficiently' used to make sausages, shoes, or fertilizer."[120] That is when something inside her suddenly went "click."

> I saw the whole globe symbolized at Auschwitz, and it was covered with blood: people being manipulated and used; animals being tortured in useless experiments; men hunting helpless, vulnerable creatures for the "thrill"; human beings ground down by inadequate housing and medical care and by not having enough to eat; men abusing women and children; people polluting the earth, filling it with poisons that foul the air, the soil, and the water; the imprisonment of dissident voices; the elimination of people of opposing political views; the oppression of those who look, feel, or act differently.[121]

Chicago's holistic vision is a fitting way to conclude the opening part of this book. The next part (Chapters 3–5) examines the interconnectedness of institutionalized violence against animals and people in two modern industrial nations—the United States and Germany.

II

MASTER SPECIES, MASTER RACE

Let me say it openly: we are surrounded by an enterprise of degradation, cruelty, and killing which rivals anything the Third Reich was capable of, indeed dwarfs it, in that ours is an enterprise without end, self-regenerating, bringing rabbits, rats, poultry, livestock ceaselessly into the world for the purpose of killing them.

— *J. M. Coetzee,* The Lives of Animals

Auschwitz begins wherever someone looks at a slaughterhouse and thinks: they're only animals.

— *Theodor Adorno*

CHAPTER THREE

THE INDUSTRIALIZATION OF SLAUGHTER

The Road to Auschwitz Through America

This second part of the book (Chapters 3–5) examines the way in which the industrialized slaughter of animals and people became entwined in modern times and how American eugenics and assembly-line slaughter crossed the Atlantic Ocean and found fertile soil in Nazi Germany.

The historian David Stannard writes in *American Holocaust: The Conquest of the New World* that the road to Auschwitz traveled through America and that the European religious and cultural mentality that produced the genocide against the native peoples of the Americas was the same mentality that produced the Holocaust.[1] He maintains that Elie Wiesel is right when he states that the road to Auschwitz was being paved in the earliest days of Christendom, but he adds that another conclusion is also evident: "on the way to Auschwitz the road's pathway led straight through the heart of the Indies and of North and South America."[2]

The philosopher Theodor Adorno (1903–69), a German Jew who was forced into exile by the Nazis but returned to Germany after the war to a professorship at Frankfurt University, wrote, "Auschwitz begins wherever someone looks at a slaughterhouse and thinks: they're only animals."[3] If Professor Adorno is right, and I think he is, Stannard's conclusion needs to be broadened: the road to Auschwitz begins at the slaughterhouse.

Slaughter in the Colonies

What Jeremy Rifkin calls the "cattlization" of the Americas began with Christopher Columbus's second voyage. Considered the start of the European invasion of America, the voyage brought thirty-four horses and a large number of cattle, which Columbus unloaded on the coast of Haiti in January, 1494. The Spanish galleys which followed brought more cattle and dispersed them throughout the West Indies.

In the early 1500s Gregario de Villalobos took cattle with him when he led a Spanish expedition onto the Mexican mainland. Then, as lieutenant-governor of New Spain, he channeled more settlers, supplies, horses, and cattle into Mexico. After Hernando Cortez defeated the Aztecs, the Spanish populated the rich grazing land between Veracruz and Mexico City with cattle, which they slaughtered for meat and hides.[4]

The European settlers brought with them to the Americas their practice of exploiting animals for labor, food, clothing, and transportion. "It was the Spaniards who introduced horses, cattle, sheep, and pigs to the New World," writes Keith Thomas. "Europeans, moreover, were exceptionally carnivorous by comparison with the vegetable-eating peoples of the East."[5]

Nowhere in Europe was the dependence on animals greater than in England and Holland. The great expansion of the use of horses during the early modern period led to the increased use of oxen for human consumption. Foreign visitors to England were amazed to see so many butcher shops and so much meat eating. "Our shambles [slaughter-houses]," declared the Elizabethan Thomas Muffett, are "the wonder of Europe, yea, verily, of the whole world."[6]

In North America the slaughter of animals began almost immediately with the arrival of the English. When famine faced the first English settlers in Jamestown during the winter of 1607–8, they slaughtered and ate all the pigs, sheep, and cattle they had brought from England. Once the colony's supply of livestock was replenished, the settlers butchered the surplus at the beginning of each winter, so the cold weather could preserve the meat until spring. Soon the settlers were curing, salting, and packing pork into barrels and selling it at bulk rates. By 1635 settlers in the Massachusetts Bay Colony were slaughtering livestock out in the open and selling whole, half, and quarter carcasses to butchers and householders.

The Dutch colony of New Amsterdam became the slaughter capital of North America by the mid-1600s. Jimmy Skaggs, a history professor at Wichita State University, writes that in the colony, which became New York in 1664, slaughterhouses and cattle pens were "almost as conspicuous on the landscape as windmills in Holland."[7] Along the palisade, which later became Wall Street, slaughterhouses straddled the ditch which carried the blood and guts of butchered animals into a small stream called "Bloody Run," which emptied into the East River.

In 1656, when the number of cattle, pigs, and lambs butchered each year in New Amsterdam approached 10,000, the colony began requiring slaughter permits. It also moved its slaughterhouses to the other side of the stockade barrier which ran along Wall Street in deference to the public, wanting to be spared the sights, sounds, and smells of slaughter. As New York expanded, the slaughterhouses kept getting moved north. By the 1830s, they were restricted to the area north of 42nd Street; by the Civil War, they had been moved north of 80th Street.

Since pork preserved better than the flesh of cattle and lambs, colonial butchers preferred pigs. Commercial meatpacking in North America started around 1660 in a warehouse in Springfield, Massachusetts, where William Pynchon slaughtered pigs and transported them to Boston for local and West Indian markets.

Colonial meatpackers clubbed, stabbed, and hung the pigs upside down to drain. Many also plunged the carcasses into vats of scalding water to make it easier to pull out the hair. After they gutted the pigs, they discarded their insides, until the mid-1800s when commercial uses began to be found for them. Workers quartered the carcasses and cut them up into hams, sides, shoulders, and ribs. They rubbed the meat with assorted salt-based compounds, including molasses, and packed it into large barrels called hogsheads.

City of Pork

When Elisha Mills set up a pork factory in Cincinnati in 1818, he became the first commercial meatpacker in the Ohio Valley. Cincinnati quickly became the center of the area's booming pork trade: by 1844 the city had twenty-six slaughterhouses; three years later it had forty. Most of the slaughterhouses were located near stock pens on or close to the Ohio River. Some drovers and farmers killed the pigs at the stockyards and dragged the bodies through the dirt streets to the slaughterhouse (called a packinghouse because it was where they processed and packed the meat); others preferred to drive the pigs to the door of the packinghouse where they beat them into submission with clubs and slit their throats.[8] The rough way Americans treated farm animals made an impression on new European immigrants. One Dutchman wrote back to his friends in the Netherlands that American farmers had no regard for their animals.[9]

The first step toward the division of labor that was soon to transform the American meat industry was already in evidence in Cincinnati by the mid-1800s when some of the city's larger plants started combining their slaughter and meatpacking operations. Skaggs writes that the workers who packed the pigs into a large pen next to the plant "literally walked over their backs, striking each one a killing blow on the head with a two-pointed hammer especially designed for the purpose."[10] Workers then hooked up the dead or stunned animals and hauled them into a "sticking room," where they slashed their throats and hung their carcasses up by the heels to drain, with "the blood running onto the sawdust-covered floors that became coagulated bogs."[11]

After workers plunged the bled carcass into a vat of boiling water, they placed it on a large wooden table where they pulled off the hair and bristles and scraped the skin with sharp knives. Then, they carried the carcass to the next station and hung it up on a hook for the "gutter," who stripped out the pig's intestines, which "dropped onto the sawdust floor and, along with other body fluids, collected until the mess became intolerable."[12]

Once the carcass was cleaned and gutted, it was taken to the "cooling room," which was often simply an area of the warehouse where the winter wind could chill it. There it stayed for twenty-four hours until it was firm enough for cutters to use their cleavers to chop off the pig's head, feet, legs, and knee joints, split the carcass, and cut it up into hams, shoulders, and "middles." The process reduced a 400-pound hog to 200 pounds of pork and forty pounds of lard. At the end of the day, workers swept up the blood-soaked sawdust, collected the entrails and other leftover body parts, and dumped them all into the Ohio River. Since the meat was perishable, and transportation by road and river was slow, Cincinnati's meatpacking business remained seasonal and limited, with few of its plants ever employing more than 100 workers.[13]

Union Stock Yards

While the spread of railroad lines was already shifting the focus of meat production to Chicago by the 1850s and early 1860s, it was the construction of the Union Stock Yards, opened officially on Christmas Day of 1865, that turned meatpacking into a major industry and made Chicago the new slaughter capital of America.

The huge complex, complete with hotels, restaurants, saloons, offices, and an interlocking system of 2,300 connected livestock pens, took up more than a square mile of land in southwestern Chicago. Dwarfing all the other industrial operations of the day, the Union Stock Yards complex was the largest enterprise of its kind in the world. Meatpacking companies like Armour and Swift employed more than 5,000 workers each in their facilities inside the Yards. By 1886 more than 100 miles of railroad track surrounded the Yards, with trains every day unloading hundreds of cars full of western longhorn cattle, sheep, and pigs into the Yards' vast network of pens. In order to handle the growing volume of livestock transported on rail lines strung out across the Great Plains and to satisfy the carnivorous appetites of the expanding population, meatpackers introduced the conveyor belt to increase the speed and efficiency of the nation's first mass-production industry. Rifkin writes that the speed with which this new assembly-line production killed, dismembered, cleaned, and prepared the animals for shipment to the public "was extraordinary."[14]

As its markets and the range of its products increased, the meat industry expanded its networks of branch houses, railroad and storage facilities, and sales organizations. Packers also profited from the growth of by-product industries. Enterprises that made fertilizer, glue, soap, oil, and tallow sprang up in and around slaughterhouses, converting what was once discarded blood, bone, horn, hoof, spoiled meat, and dead animals into commercially valuable commodities. Although many small independent meatpacking firms shared the Yards with Armour, Swift, Morris, National, and Schwartzschild, these Big Five giants slaughtered more than ninety percent of all the animals. From the time the Union Stock Yards opened until 1900, the total number of livestock slaughtered there reached 400,000,000.[15] That number is a drop in the bucket compared to what's going on now. Today, American slaughterhouses kill that number of animals in less than two weeks.

The demand for meat increased with the arrival of new waves of European immigrants from lands where beef and other choice meats had been reserved primarily for the tables of aristocrats and merchants. In Europe, writes Carson I. A. Ritchie, "the sizzling beefsteak, the juicy chop, the cut off the joint were…every bit as much a token of wealth as a starched collar, a broadcloth coat, or a top hat."[16] Meat became a symbol of the newly attained wealth of better-off American workers and a rite of passage into the coveted American middle class. Workers often sacrificed other needs because eating roast beef and steak was a sure sign of success.[17] In some trades American working men flaunted their improved status by eating steak for breakfast every morning.[18] One German immigrant marveled, "Where in the old country do you find a workman who can have meat on his table three times a day?"[19]

The voracious meat eating of Americans could be quite disconcerting to foreign visitors. After a Chinese scholar returned from his first visit to America at the turn of the twentieth century, he was asked if the American people were civilized. "Civilized?" he said. "Far from it. They eat the flesh of bullocks and sheep in enormous quantities. It is carried into the dining room in huge chunks, often half raw. They pluck and slash and tear it apart, and they eat with knives and prongs, which make a civilized being quite nervous. One fancies himself in the presence of sword swallowers."[20]

In 1905, when the meat industry lobby blocked a bill in Congress that would have introduced meat inspection standards, the socialist weekly newspaper, *The Appeal to Reason*, decided to conduct its own investigation. The paper called on Upton Sinclair, a socialist and social critic in the best muckraking tradition of the day, to investigate the Chicago meatpacking industry. Sinclair, a native of Baltimore and a 1897 graduate of City College of New York, had entered Columbia Law School with the intention of practicing law, but he had dropped out to pursue a writing career.

Sinclair spent seven weeks in Chicago learning about the Union Stock Yards and the living conditions of the workers in the surrounding neighborhoods. Each day dressed in ragged clothes and carrying a worker's pail, he entered the Yards and took extensive notes on all he observed. When he returned east, he holed up for nine months in a eight-by-ten-foot cabin in Princeton, New Jersey, and wrote *The Jungle*.

The novel, which is about a family of Chicago slaughterhouse workers, appeared in installments in *The Appeal*, where it quickly attracted attention beyond the paper's working-class audience. Five publishers expressed interest in publishing the installments as a book, but they all backed off because they were intimidated by the power of the meat industry. Sinclair himself wrote a letter to the readers of *The Appeal* asking for prepaid orders so the weekly could publish the installments in book form. When the paper received 1,200 orders, the New York publisher, Doubleday, Page and Company, decided the potential profits from the book outweighed the risks.

To protect itself against possible lawsuits, Doubleday sent one of its own editors, Isaac Marcosson, to Chicago to check out the accuracy of Sinclair's descriptions. "I was able to get a Meat Inspector's badge, which gave me access to the secret confines of the meat empire," Marcosson wrote. "Day and night I prowled over its foul-smelling domain and I was able to see with my own eyes much that Sinclair had never even heard about."[21]

Death on a Monumental Scale

Historian James Barrett writes that in the early 20th century American slaughterhouses were "dominated by the sight, sound, and smell of death on a monumental scale." The machinery of death and the sound of dying animals constantly assaulted the ear. "In the midst of all this squealing," he writes, "gears ground; carcasses slammed into one another; cleavers and axes split flesh and bone."[22]

The Jungle gave its readers their first look inside the world of the slaughterhouse, as seen through the eyes of the novel's protagonist, a young Lithuanian immigrant by the name of Jurgis Rudkus. In the third chapter Rudkus is one of a group of recent Lithuanian immigrants whom a fellow countryman takes to the Union Stock Yards, where Rudkus is to report for work the next day. Inside the Yards, the guide takes the group to a raised gallery where they can look out over the vast expanse of pens filled with "so many cattle no one had ever dreamed existed in the world."[23] The sight leaves Rudkus "breathless with wonder." When one of the group asks what will become of all the cattle, the guide says, "By tonight they will all be killed and cut up; and over there on the other side of the packinghouses are more railroad tracks, where the cars come to take them away."

As the group approaches a nearby building, they see a procession of hogs making their way up a long series of ramps to the top floor. The guide explains that the weight of the hogs will carry them back down through all the processes that will make them into pork. He takes the group up to the visitors' gallery high above the kill floor where they watch a worker grab the rear leg of the first hog who enters and chain her to a great rotating iron wheel that hoists her into the air. The wheel connects her to an overhead trolley that takes her, terrified and shrieking, down the room.

As each new hog is shackled and hung upside down, the cumulative sound of the shrieking becomes so loud that the uproar is overwhelming: There were high squeals and low squeals, grunts and wails of agony; there would come a momentary lull, and then a fresh outburst, louder than ever, surging up to a deafening climax. It was too much for some of the visitors—the men would look at each other, laughing nervously, and the women would stand with hands clenched, and the blood rushing to their faces, and the tears starting in their eyes.

Neither the squeals of the victims nor the tears of the bystanders, however, have any effect on this "pork-making by machinery." Workers slit the hogs' throats "with a swift stroke" that drains their lifeblood.

Seeing the hogs vanish "with a splash into a huge vat of boiling water," Rudkus reflects that even "the most matter-of-fact person could not help thinking of the hogs, they were so innocent, they came so very trustingly; and they were so very human in their protests—and so perfectly within their rights!" From time to time a visitor cries, but "this slaughtering machine ran on, visitors or no visitors." To Rudkus it is "like some horrible crime committed in a dungeon, all unseen and unheeded, buried out of sight and of memory."

Rudkus watches a hog who emerges completely scalded from the vat begin the long process that will take him down through the building floor by floor. Workers scrape his skin, cut off his head ("which fell to the floor and vanished through a hole"), split his carcass, saw his breastbone, and pull out his entrails, which also slide through a hole in the floor. After further scraping, cleaning, trimming, and washing down, workers roll the split carcass into the chilling room where it will stay with the other carcasses overnight.

During the next stage "splitters" and "cleaver men" cut up the chilled carcasses to produce hams, forequarters, and sides of pork. These are then lowered to the pickling, smoke, and salt pork rooms on the floor below, where workers scrape and wash the entrails for use as sausage casings amid "a sickening stench." In another room scraps are boiled to make grease for soap and lard, while in still other rooms packers are "wrapping hams and bacon in oiled paper, sealing and labeling and sewing them." The workers put the processed meat in boxes and barrels, which workers carry to platforms for trucks to transport to waiting freight cars.

The tour continues across the street in a building with a huge room "like a circus amphitheater" where workers slaughter between 400 and 500 steers an hour. When the cattle arrive, the workers drive them into a narrow gallery and then lock them in separate pens where they cannot move or turn around. While the cattle bellow, one of the "knockers," armed with a sledge hammer, leans over the top of the pen, watching for his chance to strike a blow. "The room echoed with the thuds in quick succession, and the stamping and kicking of the steers. The instant the animal had fallen, the 'knocker' passed on to another, while a second man raised a lever, and the side of the pen was raised, and the animal still kicking and struggling, slid out to the 'killing bed.'" As was done with the hogs, a worker puts shackles around the steer's leg and presses a lever that jerks his body up into the air. "There were fifteen or twenty such pens, and it was a matter of only a couple of minutes to knock fifteen or twenty cattle and roll them out. Then once more the gates were opened, and another lot rushed in."

Performing "all highly specialized labor, each man having his task to do," the workers move "with furious intensity." The "butcher" darts from line to line, slitting the throat of each steer with a stroke "so swift that you could not see it—only the flash of the knife." The butcher leaves streams of bright red blood spurting out on the floor behind him. Despite the best efforts of workers to push it through the openings, the sea of blood on the floor is at least half an inch thick.

The bled carcasses are then lowered to a waiting line of workers. A "headsman" saws off the steer's head, and then eight "skinners" cut, strip, and remove the hide, careful not to cut or damage it. As the skinned, decapitated carcass makes its way down the line, workers split it, gut and scrape out the insides, and cut off the feet. After they hose the split carcass down, they move it into the chilling room. The guide explains how each of the leftover parts is put to good use (heads and feet into glue, bones ground into fertilizer). "No tiniest particle of organic matter was wasted."

At the end of the tour the guide tells the group that the Union Stock Yards, which employs 30,000 workers and supports 250,000 people in the surrounding neighborhoods, is "the greatest aggregation of labor and capital ever gathered in one place." Rudkus thinks of the Yards "as tremendous as the universe" and innocently believes that "this whole huge establishment had taken him under its protection."

His naive enthusiasm quickly fades, however, when he starts working. As he moves around the Yards from job to job, he learns the harsh truth about how the system exploits workers as well as animals. Toward the end of the novel, when he remembers his first visit to the Yards when he watched the hog-killing, he thinks "how cruel and savage it was." Although he came away grateful that he was not a hog, he now realizes that "a hog was just what he had been—one of the packers' hogs." What the packers want from a hog is all the profits that can be gotten out of him, Rudkus thinks, and that is exactly what they want from the worker, and also from the public. "What the hog thought of it, and what he suffered, were not considered...there seemed to be something about the work of slaughtering that tended to ruthlessness and ferocity."[24]

The lessons Rudkus learns lead him to embrace socialism and to see diseased, rotten meat as a metaphor for the diseased, rotten capitalist system. He now sees the meat industry as "the incarnation of blind and insensate Greed," "a monster devouring with a thousand mouths," "the Great Butcher," and "the spirit of Capitalism made flesh." Rudkus's revelation ends with a "joyful vision of the people of Packington marching in and taking possession of the Union Stockyards!"[25]

One of the book's most graphic passages describes the making of sausages, the ingredients of which include: spoiled meat returned to the plant; meat dropped on the floor and mixed with dirt, sawdust, and workers' spit; stale water, dirt, rust, and even nails from waste barrels; rat feces deposited on the meat overnight; poisoned bread put out to kill the rats; and every so often...a dead rat![26] It is alleged that when President Theodore Roosevelt read the passage, he threw his breakfast sausages out the White House window.[27]

The Jungle, which contains some of the most harrowing scenes in American literature, created an immediate sensation when it was published in January, 1906. The meat industry issued vehement denials, but to no avail. The public outcry over the diseased and rotten meat it was eating was so strong that within six months of the book's publication, Congress passed two new meat inspection laws—the Pure Food and Drug Act and the Beef Inspection Act. To Sinclair's great disappointment, however, the book's readers were more moved by his exposé of what went into the making of their meat than by his socialist message.

The novel brought its twenty-seven-year-old author immediate fame and quickly established him as a major voice for worker rights. Sinclair went on to write many more books, which were translated into fifty languages. A committee of leading intellectuals, led by Albert Einstein, nominated him for the Nobel Prize for Literature. In 1934—during the Depression—he ran for governor of California on the Socialist ticket and almost won. Sinclair remained a socialist and social reformer until his death in 1968 at the age of ninety. However, his biggest regret remained that his most famous book did so little to establish socialism in the United States. In spite of the phenomenal success of *The Jungle*, Sinclair considered it a failure. "I aimed at the public's heart," he wrote in his autobiography, "and by accident hit it in the stomach."[28]

Not All That Different

The main differences with regard to the slaughter of animals between the early 1900s and today mostly have to do with much faster line speeds and a tremendous increase in volume. Today, what one activist describes as the "cruel, fast, tightly run, profit-driven system of torture and murder in which animals are hardly thought of as living beings and are presumed not to matter in terms of their suffering and deaths"[29] kills more animals in a single day than all the slaughterhouses in Sinclair's day killed in a year.

As for the basics of the operation, however, assembly-line slaughter today is not all that different from what it was 100 years ago. For steers, the process still begins with a "knocker." But instead of using a sledgehammer, the knocker uses a captive bolt pistol called a "stun gun," which fires a five-inch steel bolt into the animal's brain. While the "splitter" continues to be the most skilled worker on the kill floor, he now splits the carcass with a band saw rather than a giant cleaver. "Boners" and "trimmers" still use razor-sharp knives to cut the meat off the carcass, and the knife and the meat hook continue to be the basic tools of the industry.[30]

Even the problem of rats has not changed all that much since Sinclair's day. A recent slaughterhouse inspector's affidavit reads: "A rat came out of the box room and ran across the floor. The inspector shut down the line after the rat ran across her foot. At that point all the boxes should have been inspected for any more rats as well as for droppings that aren't supposed to be mixed in with the beef." But, according to the affidavit, the veterinarian just laughed and had the floor hosed down. Then, after he allowed the line to be turned back on in five to ten minutes, the hunting and killing of rats "turned into something between sport and a bad joke for the inspectors." Company employees told the inspector "rats were all over the coolers at night, running on top of meat and gnawing at it."[31]

Cockroaches, insects, and other rodents also continue to be a problem. One inspector reported: "Insects have had a feast. Rodent infestation and cockroaches up to two inches long have been prevalent." He said pools of urine on the viscera table were in regular contact with the meat products. "The company sprinkled the floor with anti-maggot solution, but the drains are so often stopped up, filthy water splashes on the carcasses even if they don't fall off the rail."[32]

All in the Family

In the 1990s political artist Sue Coe spent six years visiting slaughter houses around the country. In her sketches and descriptions, which appear in her book *Dead Meat,* she provides a first-hand look at a wide range of slaughtering operations—from small, family-owned business-es to giant corporate meatpacking plants using the most up-to-date technology.

Coe describes her visit to a small slaughterhouse in Pennsylvania, located just off a highway "littered with rusting trucks and a couple of farm houses." It is owned by Martha Reed and her brother, Danny, who inherited the business from their father. Coe enters the facility shortly before the lunch break: "We step into a large room, and I look up and see corpses of huge, skinned animals. The fluorescent light gleams off the white fat. I feel like I am in a bizarre cathedral." She follows Martha, deftly ducking to keep from getting hit by the swinging giant corpses of beef, falling stomachs, and power tools. Since the floor is extremely slick, Martha warns her not to slip. "I definitely do not want to fall in all the blood and intestines," writes Coe. "The workers are wearing nonslip boots, yellow aprons, and hard hats. It is a scene of controlled, mechanized chaos."[33]

Like most slaughterhouses, "this place is dirty—filthy in fact—flies swarm everywhere. The walls, floors, everything, everywhere are covered with blood. The chains are caked with dried blood." Steers twelve feet long from hoof to hoof are strung up so high that the workers have to stand on platforms. Since the equipment is fairly up-to-date, Coe figures the plant must be a union shop.

As she walks onto the kill floor to position herself with her sketch-book in the doorway between where the cows are lined up for slaughter and the kill floor, a loud horn suddenly sounds and the workers disperse for lunch. "So I am left alone with six dripping, decapitated corpses. Blood is splashed up walls and is already on my sketchbook. I am get-ting used to being covered with flies, just like the corpses."[34]

Coe sees something move to her right, so she edges closer to the knocking pen to get a better look.

Inside is a cow. She has not been stunned and has slipped and fallen in the blood. The men have gone to lunch and left her. Time passes. Occasionally she struggles, banging the sides of the steel enclosure with her hooves. As this is a metal box, it becomes a loud hammering, then silence, then hammering. Once she raises her head enough to look outside the box, but seeing the hanging corpses, she falls back again. The sounds are blood dripping and FM radio playing over a loudspeaker. It's the Doors, a complete album side.[35]

Coe starts drawing, but when she looks back at the box, she notices that the weight of the cow's body has forced milk from her udders. As the milk flows in a small stream toward the drainage area, it mixes with blood so they go down the drain together. One of the injured cow's legs is sticking out of the bottom of the steel enclosure. "I could weep for this animal, but remove that empathy from my mind, just like the workers do." Later when she tells Martha that the cows seem very young to be going to slaughter, not milked out at all, Martha explains that when the price of milk drops, farmers can't afford to keep their cows, so they dump them on the market.

When the workers return from their lunch break, they tie on their yellow aprons and get back to work. Only two men work on the kill floor itself. "Danny does the throat-cutting, decapitating, washing the head, and taking off the front hooves, then herds a new cow in." The other man, who stands twenty feet off the ground on a platform, does the skinning with a power saw. After he finishes, the conveyor belt takes the cow along to another area.

Coe sees a man she hadn't noticed before come in. He kicks the injured cow hard three or four times to try to get her to stand up, but she can't. Danny leans over into the box to try to shoot her with his compression stunner, which will drive a five-inch bolt into her brain. When he thinks he has a good aim at her head, he fires and "there is a loud crack, exactly like a small handgun."

Danny goes over to a remote control device, presses it, and the side of the pen rises up, revealing the slumped cow. He goes over to her, chains one of her legs, and swings her up. She struggles, and her legs kick as she swings upside down. Coe notices that some animals are totally stunned and some not stunned at all. "They struggle like crazy while Danny is cutting their throats. Danny talks to the unstunned ones as he slits their throats, 'Come on girl, take it easy.'" Coe watches the blood gush out "as though all living beings are soft containers, waiting to be pierced." Danny goes next door and electrically prods the next cow forward. There is a lot of resistance and kicking because the cows are terrified. As he forces them into the knocking pen, Danny says in a singsong voice, "Come on girl."

At small meatpacking plants, workers like Danny do several jobs, unlike at the large plants where the work is divided into repetitive, highly specialized tasks. After Danny shoots a cow with the captive bolt pistol, he cuts her throat. Then when the blood stops gushing and just drips, he cuts off the cow's front hooves, skins her head, and cuts off the skinned head. He takes the head over to the sink, hangs it on a hook, and rinses it with a hose. He then returns to the line of decapitated carcasses and pushes it down to make room for the next one. "The next cow watches everything," writes Coe. "Then her turn comes."[36]

High-Tech Slaughter

Although today's large meatpacking plants employ the same high levels of specialization that Sinclair described in *The Jungle*, their operations are aided by modern technology, including computers.[37] When Coe visited a large, high-tech plant in Utah, she found the atmosphere at the facility very different from the atmosphere at smaller slaughterhouses. Through a contact she made with a rancher who sends his cattle to slaughter at the plant, Coe arranged to take a tour.

The plant, which employs 11,000 workers and slaughters 1,600 cattle a day, looks like "a missile base, with armed guards in security uniforms at many outposts." Coe is sent to a changing room where she puts on "a knee-length white coat, rubber boots, a safety helmet, goggles, earplugs, and hair net." She sees the clothing she has to wear as "an armor, which has already separated us (humans) from the animals, whose terrible vulnerability is no second skin and no skin at all."

The tour leader takes the group to the kill floor, but not to the killing area since it is off limits to visitors, presumably for reasons of safety. However, Coe manages to see that they're using a captive bolt pistol inside a steel box, with a back gate that falls on the back of the animal, forcing him inside. After a worker stuns the steer and hoists him up, another worker cuts his throat and twists his knife deep into the steer's body to puncture his heart.[38]

Conveyor belts extend as far the eye can see. In one room the size of an airport hanger, Coe sees hundreds of skinned heads on a conveyor and hundreds of hearts on another conveyor moving along at the same speed. Workers in another room are working "with inhuman speed" on front and hind quarters as they bob and weave around swinging carcasses. Wearing back harnesses to keep their arms from coming out of their sockets, the workers look "as machine-like as it is possible to imagine."

"This is Dante's Inferno," writes Coe, "steam, noise, blood, smell, and speed. Sprinklers wash off meat, giant vacuum-packing machines use heat to seal twenty-two pieces of flesh a minute." Workers pack ground beef into glycol and water, and long sausage shapes trundle around to be laser scanned and packaged, retail ready. "A computer scans each package to record its destination. Thirty-five thousand boxes a day."[39]

Coe's reference here to "Dante's Inferno" brings to mind the reaction of Franz Stangl to the Treblinka death camp when he arrived to take up his duties as commandant. He described it in his interview with Gitta Sereny:

> "Treblinka that day was the most awful thing I saw during all of the Third Reich"—he buried his face in his hands—"it was Dante's Inferno," he said through his fingers. "It was Dante come to life. When I entered the camp and got out of the car on the square [the Sortierungsplatz] I stepped knee-deep into notes, currency, precious stones, jewelry, clothes. They were every-

where, strewn all over the square. The smell was indescribable; the hundreds, no, the thousands of bodies everywhere, decomposing, putrefying."

Stangl recalled that across the square in the woods just a few hundred yards away on the other side of the barbed-wire fence and all around the perimeter of the camp, "there were tents and open fires with groups of Ukrainian guards and girls—whores, I found out later, from all over the countryside—weaving drunk, dancing, singing, playing music."[40]

On her way out of the Utah plant that reminded her of Dante's Inferno, Coe sees a cow with a broken back lying in the hot sun. She begins to walk towards her, but security guards block her way and escort her off the premises.[41]

"The Holocaust keeps coming into my mind, which annoys the hell of out me," Coe writes at one point in her book. When she sees the Holocaust reference in animal rights magazines, she says she wonders if this is "the comforting measuring rod by which all horrors are evaluated?"

> My annoyance is exacerbated by the fact that the suffering I am witnessing now cannot exist on its own, it has to fall into the hierarchy of a "lesser animal suffering." In the made-for-TV reality of American culture, the only acceptable genocide is historical. It's comforting—it's over. Twenty million murdered humans deserve to be more than a reference point. I am annoyed that I don't have more power in communicating what I've seen apart from stuttering: "It's like the Holocaust."[42]

Recent Developments

The last decades of the twentieth century saw changes in the U.S. meat industry that involved fewer but larger slaughterhouses capable of killing more animals faster. Gail Eisnitz, chief investigator for the Humane Farming Association (HFA) and author of *Slaughterhouse*, writes that during the 1980s and 1990s "more than 2,000 small- to mid-sized slaughterhouses were replaced by a handful of corporate plants capable of killing several million animals per plant per year. There are now fewer plants killing an ever growing number of animals—not only for the domestic market but for the expanding global market."[43]

At the same time, there was a sharp acceleration of line speeds, which doubled and in some cases tripled. The acceleration began during the Reagan Administration when a new USDA policy of "streamlined inspection" resulted in fewer inspectors and greater latitude given to the meat industry to inspect itself. Today, line speeds at slaughterhouses run as fast as 1,100 animals per hour, which means that a single worker has to kill an animal every few seconds. Eisnitz says that one plant she visited slaughters 150,000 hogs a week.[44]

As a result of faster line speeds and the tremendous increase in the number of chickens killed (now over eight billion a year), the number of animals slaughtered in the United States more than doubled in the last quarter of the twentieth century. The number of animals killed rose from four billion to 9.4 billion by the end of the twentieth century (more than twenty-five million a day).[45]

Another trend involves the high wall of legal protection that surrounds what the American meat and dairy industries do to animals. At the very time when many Americans mistakenly assume that humane laws protect farm animals from abuse and neglect, legislatures in state after state are passing laws to exempt "food animals" from state anti-cruelty statutes.[46] Today, in thirty states across the country, writes Gene Bauston, co-founder of Farm Sanctuary, a shelter for rescued farm animals, "horrendous cruelties are considered legal if done to animals used for 'food production' purposes."[47] This development runs counter to what is happening in Europe where the trend is toward *more* protection for farm animals, not less. The American meat and dairy industries have successfully convinced their friends in state legislatures and Congress that what agribusiness does to animals should be "beyond the law."

Henry Ford: From Slaughterhouse to Death Camp

Since this chapter began with the contention that the road to Auschwitz begins at the slaughterhouse, it is fitting that it close with the story of the automobile manufacturer Henry Ford, whose impact on the twentieth century began, metaphorically speaking, at an American slaughterhouse and ended at Auschwitz.

In his autobiography, *My Life and Work* (1922), Ford revealed that his inspiration for assembly-line production came from a visit he made as a young man to a Chicago slaughterhouse. "I believe that this was the first moving line ever installed," he wrote. "The idea [of the assembly line] came in a general way from the overhead trolley that the Chicago packers use in dressing beef."[48]

A Swift and Company publication from that time described the division-of-labor principle that Ford adopted: "The slaughtered animals, suspended head downward from a moving chain, or conveyor, pass from workman to workman, each of whom performs some particular step in the process." Since the authors of the publication wanted to make sure the meatpackers got their due credit for the assembly-line idea, they wrote, "So efficient has this procedure proved to be that it has been adopted by many other industries, as for example in the assembling of automobiles."[49]

This process, which hoists animals onto chains and hurries them along from station to station until they came out at the end of the line as cuts of meat, introduced something new into our modern industrial civilization—the neutralization of killing and a new level of detachment. "For the first time machines were used to speed along the process of mass slaughter," writes Rifkin, "leaving men as mere accomplices, forced to conform to the pace and requirements set by the assembly line itself."[50]

As the twentieth century would demonstrate, it was but one step from the industrialized killing of American slaughterhouses to Nazi Germany's assembly-line mass murder. As noted earlier, it was the German Jew Theodor Adorno who declared that Auschwitz began at the slaughterhouse with people thinking, "They're just animals." In J. M. Coetzee's novel, *The Lives of Animals*, the protagonist Elizabeth Costello tells her audience: "Chicago showed us the way; it was from the Chicago stockyards that the Nazis learned how to process bodies."[51]

Most people are unaware of the central role of the slaughterhouse in the history of American industry. "While most economic historians have been drawn to the steel and automobile industry for clues to America's early industrial genius," writes Rifkin, "it was in the slaughterhouse that many of the most salient innovations in industrial design were first used....It's no wonder historians of a later period were more comfortable extolling the virtues of the assembly line and mass production in the automotive industry."[52] Still, the mental deadening of assembly-line workers, though unsettling, was very far removed from the blood-letting on the "kill floor." Rifkin writes that in the newly mechanized slaughterhouses of Chicago, "the stench of death, the clanking of chains overhead, and the whirr of disemboweled creatures passing by in an endless procession overwhelmed the senses and dampened the enthusiasm of even the most ardent supporters of the new production values."[53]

In his study of Chicago's packinghouse workers in the early 1900s, James Barrett writes, "Historians have deprived the packers of their rightful title of mass-production pioneers, for it was not Henry Ford but Gustavus Swift and Philip Armour who developed the assembly-line technique that continues to symbolize the rationalized organization of work."[54]

Henry Ford, who was so impressed by the efficient way meat packers killed animals in Chicago, made his own special contribution to the slaughter of people in Europe. Not only did he develop the assembly-line method the Germans used to kill Jews, but he launched a vicious anti-Semitic campaign that helped the Holocaust happen.

The campaign began on May 22, 1920, when Ford's weekly newspaper, the *Dearborn Independent*, suddenly changed its format and started attacking Jews. At the time the paper had a circulation of about 300,000[55] and was distributed nationally by Ford automobile dealers.[56] At the time nativism and prejudice were very much part of the national climate, with intense racism and anti-Semitism on the rise and the nation preparing to adopt a national origins quota system to stem the admission of immigrants from eastern and southern Europe. The anti-Semitism evident in 1915 with the lynching of Leo Frank, a Jewish businessman in Atlanta, was increasing with the rapid spread of the anti-black, anti-Catholic, anti-Semitic message of the Ku Klux Klan, which by 1924 had a national membership of more than four million.

During the first phase of Ford's campaign, which lasted until January, 1922, the *Independent* published a series of ninety-one articles based on the text of the *Protocols of the Elders of Zion*, an anti-Semitic forgery written in the 1890s by an agent working for the Russian secret police in Paris. Boris Brasol, a Russian refugee who had worked for the Czarist government and was promoting the *Protocols* in America, gave a copy of the *Protocols* to Ford's right-hand man, Ernest Liebold, who was directing the campaign.[57] The *Protocols* pretended to be a series of twenty-four lectures by the "elders" of Judaism about their secret plan to control the world.

One of the most vicious anti-Semitic tracts ever circulated, it had fueled a series of pogroms against Jewish communities in Russia. The *Protocols* gained worldwide recognition after World War I when the devastation of the war, the Russian Revolution, and the unrest in Germany gave anti-Semites the chance to claim that an international Jewish conspiracy was behind all the turmoil. As Keith Sward wrote, "no manual on Jew-baiting had more to offer."[58]

Ford also published four anti-Semitic brochures, each one based on twenty or more of the ninety-one articles that had appeared in the *Independent*, and a book-length compilation of the articles entitled *The International Jew*. Although the *Independent*'s criticism of Jews was more sporadic from 1922 to 1924, during that time Ford's anti-Semitic publications were spreading throughout the world. *The International Jew* was translated into most of the European languages and widely disseminated by anti-Semites, chief among them the German publisher Theodor Fritsch, an early supporter of Hitler. The brochures and *The International Jew* influenced many readers, writes David Lewis, "all the more because they carried the imprint, not of a crackpot publisher in an alleyway, but of one of the most famous and successful men in the world."[59]

The *Independent's* editor, William J. Cameron, edited and updated the text of the *Protocols* so effectively that the Ford version became the text preferred by anti-Semites around the world. And, thanks to a well-financed publicity campaign and the prestige of the Ford name, *The International Jew* was hugely successful both domestically and internationally. An estimated half million copies circulated in the United States,[60] and the German, Russian, and Spanish translations also reached large numbers of readers.

The International Jew found its most receptive audience in Germany where Ford was enormously popular. When he announced plans to build a plant there, Germans stood in lines all night to buy Ford stock. When Ford's autobiography went on sale in Germany, it immediately became the country's number one bestseller. In Germany *The International Jew* (or *The Eternal Jew* as it came to be known there) became the bible of the postwar anti-Semitic movement, with the Fritsch's publishing house printing six editions between 1920 and 1922.

After Ford's book came to the attention of Hitler and his followers in Munich, the Nazis used a shortened version of it in their propaganda war against the Jews of Germany. In 1923, a *Chicago Tribune* correspondent in Germany reported that Hitler's organization in Munich was "sending out Mr. Ford's books…by the carload."[61] Baldur von Schirach, the leader of the Hitler Youth movement and the son of an aristocratic German father and an American mother (two of whose ancestors signed the Declaration of Independence), said at the postwar Nuremberg war crimes trial that he became a convinced anti-Semite at age seventeen after reading *The Eternal Jew*.[62] "You have no idea what a great influence this book had on the thinking of German youth," he said. "The younger generation looked with envy to symbols of success and prosperity like Henry Ford, and if he said the Jews were to blame, why naturally we believed him."[63]

Hitler regarded Ford as a comrade-in-arms and kept a life-sized portrait of him on the wall next to his desk in his office at the Nazi Party headquarters in Munich. Hitler spoke of Ford in glowing terms to his followers and frequently bragged to them about Ford's financial support.[64] In 1923, when he heard that Ford might run for President of the United States, Hitler told an American reporter that he wanted to help. "I wish that I could send some of my shock troops to Chicago and other big American cities to help in the elections," he said. "We look to Heinrich Ford as the leader of the growing Fascist movement in America. We have just had his anti-Jewish articles translated and published. The book is being circulated in millions throughout Germany."[65]

Hitler praised Ford, the only American to be singled out in *Mein Kampf*. The reference had to do with the struggle in America against Jewish bankers and unionists: "It is Jews who govern the stock exchange forces of the American Union. Every year makes them more and more the controlling masters of the producers in a nation of one hundred and twenty millions; only a single great man, Ford, to their fury, still maintains full independence."[66] In 1931, when a *Detriot News* reporter asked Hitler what Ford's portrait on the wall meant to him, Hitler said, "I regard Henry Ford as my inspiration."[67]

In order to uncover the secret Jewish conspiracy alleged in the *Protocols* and *The International Jew*, Ford ordered Liebold to set up an investigative bureau in New York to spy on prominent American Jews. Ford's detectives shadowed various Jewish leaders, including Supreme Court Justice Louis Brandeis, in hopes of uncovering their plot to take over the world. "When we get through with the Jews," Liebold said, "there won't be one of them who will dare raise his head in public."[68]

When the Anti-Defamation League and other Jewish groups in America objected strongly to the ongoing anti-Semitic campaign of the *Independent* and the publication of *The International Jew*, Ford ignored their objections. Although there was never a formally declared boycott, many Jewish firms and individuals stopped buying Fords.[69] Ford began to have second thoughts about his campaign after a Jewish lawyer, whom the *Independent*'s next series of anti-Semitic articles accused of being part of a Jewish plot to control the wheat market, sued Ford for defamation of character. When the case went to trial in Detroit, Ford settled out of court.[70]

Ford was also put on the defensive by a statement signed by more than 100 prominent Americans, including former president Taft, Jane Addams, Clarence Darrow, and Robert Frost. The statement attacked the authenticity of the *Protocols* and defended the Jewish people. Surprised by the strong reaction, concerned about car sales, and eager to clear his name, Ford signed a letter sent in June, 1927, to Louis Marshall, president of the American Jewish Committee. In it, he claimed he had not been aware of what his paper had been printing and denied responsibility for both the anti-Jewish articles in the *Independent* and *The International Jew*. To demonstrate his sincerity, Ford stopped publishing the *Independent* in late 1927 and agreed to withdraw *The International Jew* from the book market.

In the early 1930s, however, copies of *The International Jew* began turning up again in large numbers throughout Europe and Latin America, and in the United States the German-American Bund distributed widely the German edition of *The International Jew* and English language reprints of the *Independent*'s anti-Semitic articles. In 1933 a congressional committee investigated reports that Ford had contributed heavily to the Nazis in return for Hitler's promise to reprint the *Independent*'s articles.[71]

In spite of the letter Ford wrote to Fritsch, requesting that he stop further publication of the German edition, the influence of *The International Jew* in Nazi Germany continued to be strong and lasting. German anti-Semites continued to advertise and distribute it throughout the 1930s, often putting the names of Henry Ford and Adolf Hitler together on the cover. By late 1933 Fritsch had published twenty-nine editions, each with a preface praising Ford for his "great service" to America and the world for his attacks on the Jews.[72]

Hopes that Ford was really sincere about wanting to distance himself from his anti-Semitic past faded completely in 1938 when, on the occasion of his seventy-fifth birthday in Detroit, Ford accepted the Grand Cross of the Supreme Order of the German Eagle, the highest honor Nazi Germany could bestow on a foreigner. In the ceremony in Ford's office, two German consuls, Karl Kapp of Cleveland and Fritz

Hailer of Detroit, presented him with the Nazi medal (Mussolini was one of the three other foreigners to be so honored).[73] At Ford's birthday dinner that night, Kapp read the citation that accompanied the medal to the 1,500 prominent Detroiters present and extended to Ford Hitler's personal congratulations.[74]

On January 7, 1942—exactly one month after the Japanese attack on Pearl Harbor that brought the United States into the war—Ford wrote a letter to Sigmund Livingston, national chairman of the Anti-Defamation League, in which he sought to "clarify some general misconceptions concerning my attitude toward my fellow citizens of Jewish faith." Ford expressed disapproval of hatred "against the Jew or any other racial or religious group" and strongly urged all his fellow citizens to give no aid to any movement whose purpose it was to promote hatred against any group. "It is my sincere hope," he concluded, "that now in this country and throughout the world, when this war is finished and peace once more established, hatred of the Jews, commonly know as anti-Semitism, and hatred against any other racial or religious group, shall cease for all time."[75]

By the time Ford sent his letter, *Einsatzgruppen* (German mobile killing squads) in the East had already murdered hundreds of thousands of Jewish men, women, and children, and the first German extermination camp at Kulmhof (Chelmno) was already in operation. Several months later the three Operation Reinhard death camps also began functioning—Belzec (March 1942), Sobibor (May 1942), and Treblinka (June 1942). Auschwitz, which Himmler designated as "the centerpiece for 'the final solution of the Jewish question in Europe,'"[76] also began exterminating Jews in the spring of 1942—a few months after Ford sent his letter.

Many years after the war, documents collected by a Washington law firm seeking damages from the Ford Company on behalf of a Russian woman who was forced to work as a slave laborer at Ford's German subsidiary revealed "Ford's energetic cooperation with the Third Reich." After Ford Motor opened its office in Berlin in 1925 and built a large plant in Cologne six years later—two years before Hitler came to

power—Ford's high standing with Hitler and his Nazi followers certainly helped Ford of Germany (later renamed *Ford Werke*) prosper during
the Nazi years.[77] When the Ford subsidiary became a major supplier of
vehicles to the German army, its value more than doubled. Throughout
the war the Ford Motor Co. in Dearborn, Michigan, kept majority control of its German subsidiary that used and profited from slave labor.
After the war the Ford Company helped *Ford Werke* get back on its feet.
In 1948, when the 10,000th Ford truck rolled off the postwar assembly
line in Cologne, Henry Ford's grandson, Henry Ford II, who had
assumed the company's presidency in September 1945, was present to
mark the occasion.[78]

CHAPTER FOUR

IMPROVING THE HERD

From Animal Breeding to Genocide

Henry Ford's propaganda war against the Jews and his slaughter-house-inspired assembly line were not isolated instances of American influence on Germany. They were part of a much broader cultural phenomenon that included efforts to upgrade the populations of both countries. Those efforts, which were inspired and guided by the breeding of domesticated animals—breeding the most desirable and castrating and killing the rest[1]—led to compulsory sterilization in the United States and to compulsory sterilization, euthanasia killings, and genocide in Nazi Germany.

The Emergence of Eugenics
The desire to improve the hereditary qualities of the human population had its beginnings in the 1860s when Francis Galton, an English scientist and cousin of Charles Darwin, turned from meteorology to the study of heredity (he coined the term "eugenics" in 1881).[2] By the end of the nineteenth century genetic theories, founded on the assumption that heredity was based on rigid genetic patterns little influenced by social environment, dominated scientific thought. American and German scientists accepted human inequality as self-evident. They ranked human groups by intelligence and culture, labeling certain human beings as "inferior" because they were allegedly immoral, depraved, criminal, or simply sufficiently different to be threatening.

By the twentieth century the main goal of the eugenics movement was sterilization to control the reproduction of people regarded as a burden to society and a threat to civilization, and in both the United States and Germany eugenicists succeeded in instituting compulsory sterilization.[3] In Germany, where the eugenics movement was to reach its lethal climax, the goal of scientists, who employed the term *Aufartung durch Ausmerzung* (physical renewal through elimination), was to improve the racial stock of the German people through the elimination of its inferior members and racial aliens dwelling in their midst.[4]

American Breeders' Association

In America, Luther Burbank's work on plant breeding in the 1890s and renewed interest in Mendel's theory of heredity created a need for an organization that would pool the interests and talents of animal breeders and genetic scientists. The success of Burbank's experiments with plants convinced James Wilson, secretary of the United States Department of Agriculture (USDA), and Willet M. Hays, director of the Minnesota Experiment Station, that an organization which combined genetics and animal breeding could achieve important scientific results. Hays and several of the other Americans who attended the first International Conference on Hybridization in London in 1899 returned to the States determined to form a permanent association dedicated to advancing knowledge about the laws of heredity and breeding.[5]

Wilson made plans for the proposed group to hold its first meeting in 1903 at the December session of the American Association of Agricultural Colleges and Experiment Stations (AAACES) in St. Louis. The forty to fifty people who showed up for the meeting named their new organization the American Breeders' Association (ABA) and elected Hays as its chairman. As the first national organization to promote research on genetics and human heredity in the United States, the new ABA sought to bring animal breeders and scientists together from across the country in order "that each may get the point of view of the other and that each appreciate the problem of the other."[6] Commercial breeders, professors at agricultural colleges and experiment stations, and USDA researchers formed the core of the membership.[7]

At the second meeting of the ABA in 1905, Hays announced that the association already had 726 members and proposed it reach a goal of several thousand as soon as possible. At the meeting a series of reports about the great success achieved in the selective breeding of plants and animals prompted delegates to ask why such techniques could not be applied to human beings.

The third ABA meeting in 1906 agreed to divide the work of the association into committees under three main categories—general subjects, animal breeding, and plant breeding. The fifteen animal breeding committees ranged from Poultry, Sheep and Goats, Swine, and several kinds of horses to Wild Birds, Wild Mammals, Fur Animals, Fish, and Bees and Other Insects. The creation of a committee on Human Heredity, or Eugenics, as it came to be called, launched the American eugenics movement in America.

Mrs. Edward Henry Harriman, widow of the railroad magnate, who felt there was a serious need for heredity research, contributed substantial funds that led to the establishment in 1910 of the Eugenics Record Office (ERO) at Cold Spring Harbor on Long Island in New York.[8] Poultry researcher Charles B. Davenport, a respected biologist and active ABA member, became its director.

American Eugenics Movement

Davenport, who quickly emerged as the leader of the movement in America, described eugenics as "the science of the improvement of the human race by better breeding."[9] He stressed the importance of people's genetic history and looked forward to the time when a woman would no more accept a man "without knowing his biologico-genealogical history" than a stockbreeder would take "a sire for his colts or calves who was without pedigree."[10]

Davenport and other eugenicists believed that social deviation was genetically determined and that criminality was the result of bad genes. Their proposed solution to social problems was to keep people who deviate from acceptable social norms from reproducing. They also favored a national immigration policy which would keep out individuals and families with a poor hereditary history. Davenport advocated examining the family history of all prospective immigrants so that people with "imbecile, epileptic, insane, criminalistic, alcoholic, and sexually immoral tendencies" could be identified and kept from entering the country. He also advocated compulsory sterilization of genetically defective people "to dry up the springs that feed the torrent of defective and degenerate protoplasm."[11] Davenport told one prospective patron that "the most progressive revolution in history" could be achieved if "human matings could be placed upon the same high plane as that of horse breeding."[12]

At the first National Conference on Race Betterment in 1914, Davenport urged his audience "to awaken an interest in heredity among our best stock, so that in marrying, the old ideals of marriage into good stock may be restored." He lamented the dying out of the old New England families through their failure to reproduce and urged good Americans to realize the "importance of marrying, marrying well, and having healthy effective children—and plenty of them."[13]

At the same conference Harvard professor Robert DeC. Ward stressed the need to keep certain kinds of foreigners out of the country, pointing out that the country was more selective about the breeds of cattle it imported than the immigrants it let in. He urged "every citizen who wants to keep the blood of the race pure" to support the establishment of a literacy requirement for immigrants. A few years later just such a literacy requirement became law.

Many of the American eugenicists were openly anti-Semitic. Madison Grant wrote in 1916 about the problem of "the Polish Jew, whose dwarf stature, peculiar mentality, and ruthless concentration on self-interest are being engrafted upon the stock of the nation." A colleague wrote to him that "our ancestors drove the Baptists from Massachusetts Bay into Rhode Island, but we have no place to drive the Jews."[14] Their proposed solution to the "Jewish problem" was realized with the immigration restriction laws of the 1920s.

Those laws had disastrous results for many European Jews in that they slowed immigration from eastern and southern Europe to a trickle. "Throughout the 1930s, Jewish refugees, anticipating the holocaust, sought to emigrate, but were not admitted," writes Stephen Jay Gould. "The legal quotas, and continuing eugenic propaganda, barred them even in years when inflated quotas for western and northern European nations were not filled....We know what happened to many who wished to leave but had nowhere to go. The paths to destruction are often indirect, but ideas can be agents as sure as guns and bombs."[15]

Harry H. Laughlin, Davenport's right-hand man at Cold Spring Harbor, who also had experience manipulating the lives of animals, quickly became one of America's most prominent and active eugenicists. Son of a midwestern preacher and graduate of the Kirksville Normal School in Missouri, Laughlin became interested in agriculture in Iowa, where he held several school posts and took agriculture courses at the state college. In 1907 he returned to the Kirksville Normal School to head its one-man Department of Agriculture, Botany, and Nature Study. After he wrote to Charles Davenport for advice about breeding experiments he was doing on chickens (Davenport's specialty), Laughlin went to Cold Spring Harbor to attend a summer course, which he described as "the most profitable six weeks that I ever spent." The experience set him on the road to becoming a professional biologist specializing in heredity.

While Laughlin served as superintendent of the Eugenics Record Office, he earned a doctorate in biology from Princeton University, published papers on genetics, and achieved national professional recognition. His eugenics research established him as an authority on "feeble-mindedness" and the genetic characteristics of immigrants. Proud of his family lineage that went back to the American Revolution, Laughlin looked down on immigrants from southern and eastern Europe as biologically inferior. He became a congressional expert in Washington on the "biological" side of the immigration issue. He also became a strong advocate of compulsory sterilization, stating "it ought to be a eugenic crime to turn a possible parent of defectives loose upon the population."[16]

Family Studies

The Eugenics Record Office became the American center for eugenics research, especially research on "cacogenic" (bad-gened) families. It encouraged the public to send in genealogical information about their family's hereditary traits for a free analysis and trained field workers to go out and investigate cacogenic families. While the American eugenics movement produced a large body of studies on topics ranging from alcoholism to zoology, its family studies had the greatest influence.

The two most popular and influential of these studies were Henry H. Goddard's *The Kallikak Family: A Study in the Heredity of Feeble-Mindedness* (1912) and Richard L. Dugdale's *"The Jukes": A Study in Crime, Pauperism, Disease and Heredity*, originally published in 1877.[17] These family studies painted vivid pictures of degenerate hillbilly families living in filthy shacks and spawning endless generations of paupers, criminals, and imbeciles. The implicit and sometimes explicit assumption of these studies was that the cacogenic part of the population should be denied the right to reproduce. *The Hill Folk* (1912) warned that because paupers and the feeble-minded were multiplying rapidly, measures needed to be adopted to "control the reproduction of the grossly defective."[18]

The studies gave their subjects such demeaning nicknames as Rotten Jimmy, Crazy Jane, and Jake Rat, and accused them of sexual depravity ("debauchery," "fornication," "harlotry"). The studies also employed animal and insect imagery: they "mate" and "migrate," and they "nest" with their "broods" in "hotbeds where human maggots are spawned." Hill boys run around naked in summer "like little wild animals." A Hill wife looks "more like an animal than a woman," while members of the Dack clan have a "monkey-like instinct to steal and hide."[19] The family studies created the "white trash" myth that provided the eugenics movement with its central image and validated its main contention that social problems were primarily genetic in origin.

Eugenics had a strong influence on the emerging social disciplines—psychology, criminal justice, sociology, and social work—and inspired legislation that helped shape social policy with respect to crime control, education, marriage and birth control, liquor consumption, mental retardation, poverty relief, and sterilization. Leading American psychologists, sociologists, and other social scientists incorporated eugenic principles into their work. However, support for eugenics involved more than acceptance of the principle that traits and behaviors can be inherited. "It also laid an obligation on society to do something about controlling heredity," writes Carl Degler, "an obligation that usually translated into preventing the reproduction of mentally defective or criminally inclined people."[20] As one social scientist put it, society cannot rely on the self-restraint of "the neuropathic strain" of the population.[21]

Compulsory Sterilization

Sterilization began in America as a way to control crime. In 1887 the superintendent of the Cincinnati Sanitarium published the first public recommendation for the sterilization of criminals, both as a punishment and a way to prevent further crime. The first method authorities used to sterilize male criminals was the same method farmers used on male animals not selected for breeding—castration. Castration was used to sterilize male criminal offenders until 1899, when vasectomy was adopted as a more practical method.

The first American institution to perform sterilizations as official policy was the Indiana State Reformatory. In a single year the reformatory's Dr. Harry Sharp performed vasectomies on several dozen boys in hopes that they would keep them from masturbating. He realized the eugenic value of what he was doing only later when "it occurred to me that this would be a good method of preventing procreation in the defective and physically unfit."[22]

Indiana passed the first state sterilization law in 1907. It stated that "confirmed criminals, idiots, imbeciles, and rapists" could be sterilized against their wills if a committee of experts considered procreation inadvisable. Other states quickly followed Indiana's example. By 1915 thirteen states had authorized the sterilization of criminals and mentally ill people in state institutions. By 1930 more than half the American states had passed such laws.[23]

Eugenics became an accepted part of America's progressive agenda, with California leading the way with more than sixty percent of the country's 12,000 forced sterilizations by 1930. The United States became the model for other countries that wanted to sterilize their "defectives." Denmark was the first European country to pass such a law in 1929, followed in rapid succession by the other Scandinavian nations. Germany passed its sterilization law in 1933, shortly after the Nazis came to power.[24]

In the United States a challenge to the Virginia law, which allowed its state institutions to sterilize patients diagnosed as suffering from a "hereditary form of insanity or imbecility," reached the United States Supreme Court in 1927. The case (*Buck* v. *Bell*) involved a young woman, Carrie Bell, whom the state had diagnosed as "feebleminded," as it had also diagnosed her mother and daughter. Justice Oliver Wendell Holmes, who wrote the eight-man majority decision that upheld the Virginia law, defended the eugenic principles behind the sterilization law. He wrote that "experience has shown that heredity plays an important part in the transmission of insanity, imbecility, etc." He argued that if a state has the right to compel a young man to serve in the armed forces in time of war, then it certainly should be able "to call upon those who already sap the strength of the state for lesser sacrifices in order to prevent our being swamped with incompetence."[25]

Holmes concluded his opinion with reasoning not unlike the reasoning the Nazis were soon to use to justify their own eugenic measures. "It is better for all the world," he wrote, "if instead of waiting to execute degenerate offspring for crime, or to let them starve for their imbecility, society can prevent those who are manifestly unfit from continuing their kind. The principle that sustains compulsory vaccination is broad enough to cover cutting the Fallopian tubes. Three generations of imbeciles are enough."[26]

By the early 1930s compulsory sterilization had widespread support in the United States, with college presidents, clergymen, mental health workers, school principals, and many others among its strongest supporters.

Eugenics in Germany

German scientists were impressed by America's eugenic progress. After Alfred Ploetz, the founder of German eugenics, returned from the First International Congress for Eugenics in London in 1912, he informed the *Berliner Tageblatt*, one of Germany's largest newspapers, that the United States was the world's undisputed eugenics leader. The following year another leading German eugenicist praised the "forceful and decisive" American: "After he recognizes the importance of heredity in determining mental and physical traits for the entire population, he does not hesitate to proceed from theoretical reflection to energetic practical action and to enact legislation which will lead to ennoblement of the race".[27]

In the years following World War I, eugenics established deep roots in German medical and scientific circles where it came to be known as "race hygiene." In 1920 two respected academics—Karl Binding, a widely published legal scholar, and Alfred Hoche, a professor of psychiatry with a specialty in neuropathology—published *Die Freigabe der Vernichtung lebensunwerten Lebens* (*Authorization for the Destruction of Life Unworthy of Life*). Addressing the question of institutionalized patients, they argued that German law should permit the mercy killing of patients who were *lebensunwert* ("unworthy of life"), that is, people who suffered from "incurable feeblemindedness" and whose lives were "without purpose" and a burden to their relatives and society.[28] The terms they used to describe these patients ("human ballast," "semi-humans," "defective humanity," "mentally dead," and "empty shells of human beings") later became part of Nazi terminology.[29]

Hoche did not agree with the traditional notion that doctors should do no harm and dismissed the Hippocratic oath as a "physician's oath of ancient times." He extolled the educational value of killing mentally

handicapped patients because their corpses would provide new opportunities for scientific research, especially brain research.

After World War I, which found the Americans and Germans on
opposite sides of the conflict, Charles Davenport led the effort to rein-
tegrate German eugenicists back into the international movement.
Relations between German and American eugenicists were back on
friendly terms by 1925 when Germany rejoined the international
eugenics movement.[30]

German eugenics journals reported regularly on developments in
the United States, especially the progress Americans were making in
translating racial theory into laws that supported sterilization, racial segregation, and immigration restriction. Fritz Lenz explained somewhat
defensively that Germany lagged behind the United States in terms of
eugenic legislation because "the Germans are more disposed toward scientific investigation than toward practical statesmanship."

Beginning in the 1920s, American foundations provided extensive
financial support for eugenics research in Germany. The Rockefeller
Foundation, which was by far the largest contributor, financed the
research of leading German eugenicists and established and supported
the Kaiser Wilhelm Institute for Psychiatry, the Kaiser Wilhelm Institute
for Anthropology, Eugenics, and Human Heredity, and other major scientific institutions in Germany. During the Weimar era German eugenicists expressed their admiration of American eugenics accomplishments
and warned that if Germans did not make progress, America would
become the world's undisputed racial leader.[31]

The Third International Congress of Eugenics, held in New York in
1932 less than a year before the Nazis came to power, had as its theme
"A Decade of Progress in Eugenics." The congress issued a press release
to newspapers that proudly declared that "to a greater extent than ever
before the evolution of the lower organisms is under our control."[32]

By the time the Nazis came to power, more than twenty institutes
for racial hygiene had already been established at German universities.
The goal of racial hygiene, as Friedrich Zahn, chairman of the German

Statistical Society, described it, was the prevention of inferior life and genetic degeneration by "the targeted selection and promotion of superior life and an eradication of those portions of the population which were undesirable."[33] By 1932 racial hygiene had already established itself as scientific orthodoxy in the German medical community. It was taught in the medical faculties of most German universities and was the primary research goal at such prestigious institutions as the Kaiser Wilhelm Institute for Anthropology in Berlin (1927–45) and the Kaiser Wilhelm Institute for Genealogy in Munich (1919–45). "The major expansion in this department occurs before Hitler comes to power," writes Robert Proctor. "Most of the dozen or so journals of racial hygiene, for example, were established long before the triumph of National Socialism."[34]

Sterilization became the first "racial cleansing" project of the new Nazi government. On July 14, 1933, it issued the Law on Preventing Hereditarily Ill Progeny, which required the sterilization of patients suffering from mental and physical disorders in state hospitals and nursing homes. The new sterilization law covered congenital feeblemindedness, schizophrenia, manic-depressive psychosis, hereditary epilepsy, hereditary St. Vitus's dance, hereditary blindness, hereditary deafness, and severe hereditary physical deformity.[35]

Some Nazis wanted Jews included in the new law. Before the Nazis came to power, Arthur Gutt (later of the Ministry of the Interior) had advocated the mass sterilization of Jews, especially Eastern European Jews. By 1935 the Reich medical chief Gerhard Wagner was advocating that the law also apply to Jews, but the plan soon became unnecessary when the Nazis moved beyond it to their more radical solution to the "Jewish problem."[36]

To implement the sterilization law the Nazi government set up 181 genetic health courts and appellate genetic health courts throughout Germany, most of them attached to local civil courts. Two doctors and a lawyer, one of whom had to be an expert on "genetic pathology," presided over each hereditary health court. German doctors were required to register every case of genetic illness they knew about and were fined if they didn't. All doctors were also required to take a training course in genetic pathology at a racial institute. However, the Nazis had a good deal of catching up to do. When they embarked on their sterilization program in 1933, the United States already had sterilized more than 15,000 people, most of them while they were incarcerated in prisons or homes for the mentally ill.[37]

The American-German Partnership

America's sterilization laws, racial segregation, and immigration restriction made such a favorable impression on Hitler and the Nazis that Nazi Germany looked to the United States for racial leadership. Otto Wagener, who headed the Nazi Party's Economic Policy Office from 1931 to 1933, reported that Hitler took a special interest in eugenics developments in the United States. According to Wagener, Hitler said, "Now that we know the laws of heredity, it is possible to a large extent to prevent unhealthy and severely handicapped beings from coming into the world. I have studied with great interest the laws of several American states concerning prevention of reproduction by people whose progeny would, in all probability, be of no value or be injurious to the racial stock."[38]

In his unpublished autobiography, Leon Whitney, secretary of the American Eugenics Society, told a story that illustrated Hitler's keen interest in American eugenics. In 1934 Whitney received a letter from one of Hitler's staff members requesting that he send the Führer a copy of Whitney's recently published book, *The Case for Sterilization*. Soon after Whitney sent the book to Germany, he received a letter of thanks signed by Hitler. Later when Whitney showed Madison Grant the letter, Grant smiled, opened a folder on his desk, and showed Whitney a letter also from Hitler. The German dictator's letter thanked Grant for writing *The Passing of the Great Race*, telling him "the book was his Bible."[39]

The Germans took special interest in America's sterilization laws. *Folk und Rasse* commended the decisions of the United States Supreme Court that legalized compulsory sterilization. In 1939 the Nazi race publication *Archiv für Rassen- und Gesellschaftsbiologie* wrote that since the passage of the first American sterilization laws, the United States had "achieved something great." However, some German eugenicists considered some of America's sterilization practices too "radical" and expressed their disapproval of the arbitrary way American states enforced sterilization laws, as well as the way some states used sterilization as a form of punishment. They proudly pointed to the elaborate decision-making process conducted by their hereditary health courts, as required by German law.[40]

American eugenicists noted with pride the fact that the German law, which the Nazis were able to pass only six months after they came to power, was based on the California sterilization law and the Model Eugenic Sterilization Law, which Harry Laughlin had developed in 1922. Although the German law followed Laughlin's basic guidelines, it did not include the sterilization of criminals, alcoholics, and economically dependent people, which Laughlin's model law called for. Yet, the German law was close enough to the American model that the American publication *Eugenic News* was able to conclude that "to one versed in the history of eugenic sterilization in America, the text of the German statute reads almost like the American model sterilization law."[41]

In 1935 a representative of an American health committee, who visited Nazi Germany to consult with officials of the sterilization program and judges of the hereditary health courts, reported: "The leaders in the German sterilization movement state repeatedly that their legislation was formulated only after study of the California experiment as reported by Mr. Gosney and Dr. Popenoe. It would have been impossible, they say, to undertake such a venture involving some one million people without drawing heavily upon previous experience elsewhere."[42]

Gosney was president of the Human Betterment Foundation, the main eugenics organization in California. In a cover letter he sent to the administrator of a German Protestant social welfare organization, Gosney praised the fact that "with the adoption of a eugenic law by Germany, more than 150 million civilized people are now living under such a law." Popenoe declared that the German law encompassed "the largest number of persons who had ever been included in the scope of such legislation at any one time." He saw the German sterilization law as the fulfillment of California's eugenic principles and said it was superior to the sterilization laws of most American states.[43]

Nazi Germany's efforts quickly surpassed those of the United States. Although no exact figures are available, estimates of the total number of Germans sterilized under the Nazis range from 300,000 to 400,000.[44] However, for some racial hygienists that wasn't enough. Fritz Lenz, one of Germany's most prominent advocates of Nordic supremacy, argued that ten to fifteen percent of the population of Germany was defective and ought to be sterilized.[45]

The Nazis drew on the family studies that American eugenicists had used to justify their sterilization of "degenerates." The Germans, who had first translated and published Goddard's book about the Kallikaks in 1914, put out a second edition in November 1933, after the Nazis took power. The introduction to the second edition stated that the Kallikak study confirmed the necessity of the Nazi sterilization law that had passed in July. The *Zeitschrift für Rassenkunde* praised William Dugdale's earlier study of the Jukes as the first study to prove the hereditary character of "inferiority."[46]

America's immigration laws, which barred people with hereditary diseases and people from non-Nordic countries, also impressed the Germans. In 1934 the German race anthropologist Hans F. K. Gunther told an audience at the University of Munich that American immigration laws should serve as a guideline and inspiration for Nazi Germany.[47]

German race scientists also admired America's segregation and miscegenation laws. Nazi theorists complained that German race policies lagged behind America's, pointing out that in certain southern states a person with 1/32 black ancestry was legally black, while in Germany, if somebody was 1/8 Jewish or in many instances 1/4 Jewish, that person was considered legally Aryan. Germans studied America's miscegenation laws carefully, with German medical journals providing charts showing the current status of race relations in the United States and indicating states where blacks could or could not marry whites, could or could not vote, and so forth.

In 1939 Germany's leading race journal, *Archiv für Rassen- und Gesellschaftsbiologie*, reported approvingly that the University of Missouri refused to admit black students. Several months later the same journal reported, again with approval, the refusal of the American Medical Association (AMA) to admit black doctors to its membership. Since German doctors had recently prevented Jews from practicing medicine, except on other Jews, German race scientists were able to make the point that Germany was not the only country trying to preserve its racial purity.[48]

American Support for Nazi Eugenics

American eugenicists were the strongest foreign supporters of Nazi race policies. In 1934 *Eugenic News* proclaimed that in "no country of the world is eugenics more active as an applied science than in Germany" and praised the Nazi sterilization law as an historic advance:

> ...it remained for Germany in 1933 to lead the great nations of the world in the recognition of the biological foundations for national character. It is probable that the sterilization statutes of several American states and the national sterilization statute of Germany will, in legal history, constitute a milestone which marks the control by the most advanced nations of the world of a major aspect of controlling human reproduction, comparable in importance only with the states' legal control of marriage.[49]

In Virginia, where *Buck* v. *Bell* had originated and which ranked second behind California in the number of sterilizations performed, Dr. Joseph S. DeJarnette, leader of the state's eugenics movement, complained in 1934 that Virginia was not sterilizing enough people. He urged the state to expand the scope of its sterilization law to make it correspond more closely to that of Nazi Germany, telling the state lawmakers, "The Germans are beating us at our own game."[50]

Rassenpolitische Auslandskorrespondenz, a publication that monitored international reaction toward Germany's race programs, published eleven reports on American eugenic activities, four of them about the support of the American eugenics movement for Nazi race policies.[51]

American eugenicists were heartened by the widespread coverage the American media gave to eugenic developments in Germany. Leon Whitney saw American newspapers' in-depth coverage of Hitler's plan to sterilize 400,000 Germans as the main reason for the marked increase in interest in eugenics by the American public. He was grateful that Hitler's ambitious plan was generating discussion "among thousands of persons [in the United States] who may never before have taken any real interest in the subject."[52]

Harry Laughlin, an enthusiastic supporter of Nazi Germany, had collected newspaper clippings about the Nazis even before they came to power in 1933. On the margin of one of the clippings about the opening of a Nazi race bureau for eugenic separation, Laughlin wrote, "Hitler should be made an honorary member of the ERA [Eugenics Research Association]!" Laughlin used his position as superintendent of the Eugenics Record Office to disseminate the Nazi eugenics message to the American public.

Laughlin was especially impressed by the power of film as a tool to spread the eugenics message. He obtained an English version of *Erbkrank* (Hereditarily Ill), one of five silent films about sterilization produced by the National Socialist Racial and Political Office (*NS-Rasse und Politisches Amt*) between 1935 and 1937. Hitler liked *Erbkrank* so much that he commissioned a sequel with sound, *Opfer der Vergangenheit* (Victims of the Past) and had it shown in all German movie houses in 1937.[53] The captions and commentaries of *Erbkrank* and other Nazi propaganda films about "hereditarily ill" people, describe them as "creatures," "beings," "existences," "life unworthy of life," "idiots," and "travesties of human form and spirit."

Some of the films equate mentally and physically handicapped people with animals. *Erbkrank* shows a young man with a shaved head eating handfuls of grass, while other Nazi films declare that the handicapped are below the level of animals, especially when contrasted with pedigree hunting dogs and racehorses often shown to illustrate the merits of selective breeding."[54]

Erbkrank shows an assortment of mentally handicapped people, with one of the film's English subtitles proclaiming that "many idiots are under the animal." The subtitle below the final scene, showing a man and woman planting, reads: "The farmer, who prevents the overgrowth of the weed, promotes the valuable." In the film's introduction, Walter Gross, director of the Racial Policy Office, sums up the film's message: "A people that builds palaces for the descendents of drunks, criminals, and idiots, and which at the same time houses its workers and farmers in miserable huts, is on the way to rapid self-destruction."[55]

Although the film claimed that Jews were especially prone to mental retardation and immorality, Laughlin insisted in *Eugenic News* that the film contained "no racial propaganda of any sort." Its sole purpose, he insisted, was to "educate the people in the matter of soundness of family-stock quality—physical, mental, and spiritual—regardless of race."[56]

Americans Visit

After the Nazis came to power in 1933, scores of American anthropologists, psychologists, psychiatrists, and geneticists visited Germany and were warmly received. Officials arranged high-level meetings with Nazi leaders and scientists and visits to racial hygiene institutes, public health departments, and hereditary health courts. When the Americans returned and reported on their visits in professional journals and newsletters, they lauded the German sterilization program and explained how the hereditary health courts guaranteed that "unfit" members of German society always got a fair hearing.

The awarding of honorary degrees from prestigious German universities was one of the ways the Nazi government cultivated support from foreign scientists. In 1934 the Johann Wolfgang von Goethe University in Frankfurt awarded an honorary degree to the famous American paleontologist, Henry Fairfield Osborn. Osborn, who was one of the earliest and most important figures in the American eugenics movement, had been president of the American Museum of Natural History in New

York for twenty-five years and founder of the biology department at Columbia University. He was also founder of the American Eugenics Society and had served as president of the Second International Congress for Eugenics in 1921. Honored by the prestigious academic award, Osborn traveled to Nazi Germany to accept the degree.[57]

The Nazis used the 550th anniversary of the University of Heidelberg to showcase Germany's new spirit of learning and science and to present honorary degrees to a number of eminent German and non-German scientists, among them the Americans Foster Kennedy and Harry Laughlin. Kennedy, a psychiatrist and member of the Euthanasia Society of the United States, was well-known for his public support for killing the mentally handicapped.[58]

Laughlin was one of the American eugenicists most admired in Nazi Germany. When Dr. Carl Schneider, dean of the faculty of medicine and professor of racial hygiene at the University of Heidelberg, wrote to Laughlin in May 1936 to inform him that Heidelberg wanted to award him with an honorary Doctor of Medicine, Laughlin was thrilled to receive such an honor from one of the world's most prestigious universities. Although he did not travel to Nazi Germany to receive the degree in person, he accepted it proudly on December 8, 1936, at the German consulate in New York City.

The honorary degree praised Laughlin as a "successful pioneer of practical eugenics and the farseeing representative of racial policy in America." He received congratulations from his eugenics colleagues and recognition in both the German and American press.[59] Three years later Professor Schneider, who had nominated Laughlin for the degree, became a scientific adviser to the Nazi euthanasia program that exterminated thousands of mentally and physically handicapped Germans in gas chambers.[60]

After World War II began, but before the United States entered it, American eugenicists continued to visit Germany. In the winter of 1939–40 the geneticist T. U. H. Ellinger traveled to Germany for a series of meetings with Hans Nachtsheim, a geneticist at the Kaiser Wilhelm Institute for Anthropology, Human Heredity, and Eugenics.

Ellinger also met with Wolfgang Abel, an anthropologist known for his research on Gypsies and African bushmen and a member of the SS. Abel discussed with Ellinger the results of German research on the "Jewish element" in the German population. When Ellinger returned to the United States, he explained in the pages of the *Journal of Heredity* that the treatment of Jews in Germany had nothing to do with religious persecution, but rather was "a large-scale breeding project, with the purpose of eliminating from the nation the hereditary attributes of the Semitic race." Ellinger reported that he was very impressed by the "amazing amount of unbiased information" that the Kaiser Wilhelm Institute had collected about the physical and psychological traits of Jews.[61]

When the well-known American anthropologist Lothrop Stoddard spent four months in Nazi Germany in 1940, the Nazis pointed proudly to the fact that he and other famous Americans were continuing to visit Germany even after the start of the war. Officially, Stoddard was in Germany as a journalist for the North American Newspaper Alliance, but it was his reputation as a famous eugenicist that gained him access to the highest levels of government and scientific research.[62]

In his most popular book, *The Rising Tide of Color Against White-World Supremacy*, published in 1920, Stoddard had written that progress and civilization were the result of "Nordic blood," which was "clean, virile, genius-bearing blood, streaming down the ages through the unerring action of heredity, which, in anything like a favorable environment, will multiply itself, solve our problems, and sweep us on to higher and nobler destinies." In *The Rising Tide, The Revolt Against Civilization*, and his other books, widely acclaimed throughout the western world, Stoddard warned against the threat to Nordic supremacy from the less civilized people of southern and eastern Europe and the colored peoples of Africa and Asia.[63]

Stoddard visited various German racial hygiene institutes and met with the country's leading scientists and government leaders, including Hitler and Himmler. Stoddard attended a session of the Hereditary Health Supreme Court in Berlin, which consisted of the two regular judges, a psychopatholgist, and a criminal psychologist. He wrote about the cases brought before the court: a mentally retarded girl; a deaf-mute with several "unfortunate" hereditary features in her family; a manic-depressive (Stoddard wrote "there was no doubt that he should be sterilized"); and an "apelike" man with a receding forehead and flaring nostrils who had a history of homosexuality, was married to a Jewish woman, and had three "ne'er-do-well children."

Stoddard left the session deeply impressed by the court's success at eliminating "inferior elements" and more convinced than ever that the German sterilization law was "being administered with strict regard for its provisions and that, if anything, judgments were almost too conservative." Stoddard assured his American readers that the Nazis were "weeding out the worst strains in the Germanic stock in a scientific and truly humanitarian way." As for the "Jews problem," it was "already settled in principle and soon to be settled in fact by the physical elimination of the Jews themselves from the Third Reich."[64]

Himmler, Darré, Höss

Like the Americans Davenport and Laughlin, Heinrich Himmler, head of the SS and a main architect of the Holocaust, began his journey to eugenics with animal breeding. His agricultural studies and experience breeding chickens convinced him that since all behavioral characteristics are hereditary, the most effective way to shape the future of a population—human or non-human—was to institute breeding projects that favored the desirable and eliminated the undesirable.[65]

Himmler's passion for farming and animal breeding began after he completed his *gymnasium* (high school) education and decided to train for a career in agriculture against his parents' wishes, even though he had no experience with farming. He enrolled in the Technische Hochschule in Munich where he studied agronomy and completed his practicum requirements with a two-month internship at a farm machinery company. During his final year of study in 1921–22, Himmler joined several agricultural associations. He wanted to find a position in Bavaria as a farm administrator, but he was too young and inexperienced.

In the mid-1920s, when Himmler became politically active as a sup-porter of the young NSDAP (Nazi) party, he gave speeches that extolled the virtues of German peasants and the role they were destined to play as the racial vanguard of the new Germany. From the outset, Himmler presented himself as an authority on agricultural matters. In a letter to a writer on farm subjects dated April 22, 1926, he wrote, "I am myself a *Bauer* [farmer] even though I don't have a farm." In the meantime, Himmler's operation of a chicken farm increased his obsession with eugenics and improving human as well as animal stock. As Fritz Redlich writes, "this interest in breeding and killing chickens was transferred to the breeding and killing of humans."[66]

Himmler became even more convinced of the benefits of race-con-scious breeding after reading a number of racist pamphlets. He believed the task of political leadership was to be "like the plant-breeding spe-cialist who, when he wants to breed a pure new strain from a well-tried species that has been exhausted by too much cross-breeding, first goes over the field to cull the unwanted plants."[67] After the war one of his SS officers testified that Himmler's farming background was behind his obsession with racial breeding. At each step of the way along the road to genocide, animal exploitation—breeding, culling, and slaughtering—paved the way.

In the early 1940s when Hitler and the other top Nazis were trying to come up with a solution to the troublesome issue of *Mischlinge* (German citizens who were part Jewish), Himmler as usual considered the issue from his animal breeding perspective. He wrote to Martin Bormann that "we must proceed along lines similar to those followed in the propagation of plants and animals." He urged mandatory racial screenings for descendents of families with mixed heritage for a mini-mum of several generations and recommended that "in cases of racial inferiority, individuals must be sterilized and prevented from continuing the race."[68]

Himmler was in a position to apply the principles and methods of animal breeding to humans in a way no American eugenicist was ever able to do.[69] Jochen von Lang writes, "After his commercial failure as a chicken breeder, Himmler elected to become a breeder of human beings."[70] Racially pure SS men were to be the breeding bulls, and those deemed unfit or troublesome were to be culled. "It must be a matter of course that the most copious breeding should be by this [SS] Order, by this racial elite of the Germanic people," Himmler proclaimed. "In twenty to thirty years we must really be able to furnish the whole of Europe with its leading class."[71] According to his biographer, Richard Breitman, Himmler didn't consider his victims human, so he was not at all concerned about their suffering or their fate. "They were like the pests and vermin that any farmer had to dispose of if he was going to sustain himself and his family."[72]

Like Himmler, Richard Walther Darré, the Nazi Party's chief agricultural expert and one of its earliest and most important ideologists, had studied agriculture and knew about breeding livestock. Darré, who had the title "Reich Minister of Food and Reich Leader of the Peasantry," believed that the peasantry was the nation's treasury of racial strength and that the principles of animal breeding should direct Nazi population policy ("a people can only reach spiritual and moral equilibrium if a well-conceived breeding plan stands at the very centre of its culture").[73]

Darré convinced Himmler that Germany needed a racial elite and helped him turn the SS into an Aryan vanguard. Himmler in turn made Darré an honorary member of the SS. Like Himmler, Darré believed in improving the nation's racial stock by eliminating its undesirable elements.[74] "Our nation's only true possession is its good blood. All eugenic progress can only begin by eliminating inferior blood."[75]

Rudolf Höss, the commandant of Auschwitz, was another strong supporter of eugenics with a farming background. Höss had been acquainted with Himmler since 1921 or 1922 and knew him well after 1930. "They were both enthusiasts of farming," writes Breitman, "they had much to talk about."[76] In the early days when Auschwitz was still only a small camp, the two men made plans to build a network of satellite camps and turn the complex into a major agricultural center. Höss later wrote in his autobiography that, because he was a farmer, Himmler's bold plans thrilled him. "Auschwitz was to become the agricultural research station for the eastern territories. Opportunities were opened up to us, which we never before had in Germany. Sufficient labor was available. Huge laboratories and plant nurseries were to be set out. All kinds of stockbreeding was to be pursued there."[77]

However, Höss soon learned of other plans for the camp. "In the summer of 1941 Himmler summoned me to Berlin to inform me of the fateful order that envisaged the mass extermination of Jews from almost every part of Europe, and which resulted in Auschwitz becoming the largest human slaughterhouse that history had ever known." By the summer of 1942 Auschwitz hit its stride as a full-service eugenics center for the improvement of Germany's human and animal populations, complete with stockbreeding centers and the Birkenau extermination facility for the culling of Jews, Gypsies, and other "sub-humans."

Germany's T-4 Program and the Invention of the Gas Chamber

Germany's eugenic campaign entered a new, deadly phase in 1939 with Hitler's order that, in the words of Yisrael Gutman and Michael Berenbaum, "initiated the systematic murder of mentally retarded, emotionally disturbed, and physically infirm Germans who were an embarrassment to the myth of Aryan supremacy."[78] In 1929 Hitler had told the annual Nazi Party convention in Nuremberg, "If Germany every year would have one million children and eliminate 700,000–800,000 of the weakest, the end result would probably be an increase in [national] strength."[79]

In 1935, when Hitler was finally in a position to do something about it, he told Dr. Gerhard Wagner, the Reich medical chief, that he wanted to rid the nation of its handicapped population. But since he feared an unfavorable response from public opinion in Germany and abroad, he thought it better to wait for war "when the attention of the entire world is turned on military operations and when the value of human life in any case counts for less." Then it will be easier to "free people from the burden of the mentally ill."[80] Michael Burleigh writes that the secretly drawn-up draft law "envisioned killing people suffering from serious congenital mental or physical 'malformation,' because they required longterm care, aroused 'horror' in other people, and were situated on 'the lowest animal level.'"[81]

Hitler put Philip Bouhler, head of the Chancellery of the Führer, and Karl Brandt, his personal physician, in charge of what the U.S. Military Tribunal indictment at the postwar Nuremberg medical trial described as "the systematic and secret execution of the aged, insane, incurably ill, or deformed children and other persons by gas, lethal injections, and diverse other means in nursing homes, hospitals, and asylums."[82]

The killing of German children began in October 1939 at the Görden state hospital in the Prussian province of Brandenburg and continued at twenty-one additional wards set up throughout the Reich. Once the children were identified and institutionalized, doctors and nurses either starved them to death, or gave them lethal doses of luminal (a sedative), veronal (sleeping pills), morphine, or scopolamine. If a child balked at swallowing the medication in tablet or liquid form, it was injected into the child's veins.[83]

The scope of the "euthanasia" program expanded greatly once it entered the next stage—the killing of handicapped adults. The progression from sterilization to extermination had been a logical one for the Nazis. First, the regime implemented compulsory sterilization to curb the birth of unfit infants. Then, it introduced euthanasia for children to eliminate any unfit infant or child whose birth had not been prevented by the sterilization program. The final step was the adult euthanasia program designed to rid the country once and for all of its mental and physical misfits.[84]

Like the children's program, the adult program was assigned to Hitler's Chancellery in Berlin. However, because of its larger scope, the Chancellery had to hire additional staff and move its operation to new quarters in a confiscated Jewish villa at 4 Tiergartenstrasse. That address gave the program its name—Operation T4, or simply T4. The selection of patients for "treatment" was put in the hands of a board of medical experts, consisting of forty specially appointed doctors, nine of whom were university professors of medicine. However, T4 psychiatrists were in charge of the actual killings. Unlike children killed on the wards, adult patients had to be transported from the "surrendering institution" to the place of execution.[85]

There had been much discussion about the most effective way to kill the patients, with most T4 doctors and technicians favoring the use of carbon monoxide gas. Binding had recommended gas twenty years earlier, vouching for its effectiveness based on experience with running automobile engines and malfunctioning stoves. When Brandt discussed the matter with Hitler, Hitler accepted his recommendation that gas be used. The chemist Albert Widmann had recommended releasing the gas into the hospital wards while the patients were asleep, but T4 managers concluded that this would be too impractical. Rather than bring the gas to the patients, they decided to transport the patients to gassing centers. Widmann tested the gassing on mice and rats before he recommended it for humans.[86]

In the winter of 1939–40 the Germans conducted a gassing demonstration over a two-day period at a SS-built installation in the city of Brandenburg. After eight male patients were satisfactorily killed in a test run, T4 set up six gassing facilities: Brandenburg and Grafeneck, which opened in January; Hartheim and Sonnenstein, which opened in May and June; and Bernburg and Hadamar, which replaced Brandenburg and Grafeneck at the end of 1940. Although the Nazi government officially stopped its T4 campaign to eliminate the mentally and physically unfit in August 1941, the killing of the "unfit" continued unofficially for the rest of the war. It is estimated the official T4 program killed between 70,000 and 90,000 patients. However, since the killing of the mentally ill was not confined to the T4 program and continued well beyond 1941, the total number of victims was close to twice that number.[87]

In 1942, not long after German psychiatrists sent the last of their patients into the gas chambers, the *Journal of the American Psychiatric*

Association published an article that called for the killing of retarded children ("nature's mistakes").[88]

From Animal Exploitation to Mass Murder

After the official close of the T4 program in August 1941, much of its technical expertise and equipment and at least ninety of its personnel were sent to Poland to set up and operate extermination camps. The technique already developed to transport, deceive, and kill T-4 patients became the procedure for the mass murder of Jews. Henry Friedlander describes the contribution of the T4 program to the Final Solution:

> ...The killing technique was the most important contribution made by the T4 euthanasia program to the final solution. This technique involved both the hardware and software of the killing process. It encompassed not only gas chambers and crematoria, but also the method developed to lure victims into these chambers, to kill them on an assembly line, and to process their corpses. These techniques, including the extraction of teeth and bridgework containing gold, were developed by T4 and exported to the East.[89]

"The euthanasia program was probably not consciously devised as a training ground for staff to carry out the Final Solution," writes John Roth, "but it cannot be sheer coincidence that personnel from Schloss Hartheim and other centers regrouped in Poland to officiate at the death camps."[90]

The euthanasia killings were the opening chapter of Nazi genocide. "The mass murder of the handicapped preceded that of Jews and Gypsies; the final solution followed euthanasia," writes Friedlander. "The killers who learned their trade in euthanasia killing centers of Brandenburg, Grafeneck, Hartheim, Sonnenstein, Bernburg, and Hadamar also staffed the killing centers at Belzec, Sobibor, and Treblinka."[91]

The cradle of American and German eugenic thinking—animal agriculture—produced a number of key T4 personnel, including many of those later sent to Poland to staff the death camps. Victor Brack, T4's chief manager, received a diploma in agriculture from the Technical University in Munich, and Hans Hefelmann, who headed the office that coordinated the killing of handicapped children, had a doctorate in agricultural economics.[92] Friedrich Lorent, chief of the T4 *Haupwirtschaftsabteilung* (Central Finance Office), had trained at an agricultural institute before he began working for the Nazi Party full-time. Jacob Woger, the son of a farmer who managed T4's Grafeneck killing center, would have been transferred east in 1941 with other T4 personnel to work at a death camp in Poland, but a serious traffic accident cut short his career.[93]

Before spending more than two years at the Hartheim killing center in Austria, Bruno Bruckner had worked as a porter in a Linz slaughterhouse.[94] Otto Horn, who worked at both Sonnenstein and Treblinka, had been an agricultural worker and a male nurse before T4 recruited him. Werner Dubois had studied agriculture and worked on a farm near Frankfurt on the Oder before working for the Nazis, first as a driver with a SS motor unit at the Sachsenhausen concentration camp and then as a driver of T4 buses which transported patients to their deaths at Grafeneck, Brandenburg, Hadamar, and Bernburg. He also transported corpses and urns, and then he became a T4 stoker whose job it was to remove bodies from the gas chambers, extract gold teeth, and burn corpses. His final job was at the Belzec death camp where he operated the gas chamber's diesel engine.

Willi Mentz, an especially sadistic guard at Treblinka, had been a milker of cows in 1940 when the agricultural labor exchange in Munster hired him to work as a milker at the Grafeneck killing center. T4 put him in charge of cows and pigs first at Grafeneck, then at Hadamar. After he was transferred to Treblinka in July of 1942, his first job was to burn bodies in the upper camp where the gassings took place. His next job was at the Lazarett, the fake infirmary where he shot mothers and young children. Another T4 worker sent to Treblinka,

August Miete, had gotten his job at the Grafeneck through his local chamber of agriculture.[95]

Kurt Franz, Treblinka's last commandant, trained with a master butcher before joining the SS. Karl Frenzel, who worked as a stoker at Hadamar before being posted to Sobibor, had also been a butcher.[96] Gitta Sereny, who interviewed Franz Stangl, the commandant of Treblinka, called Franz, Miete, and Mentz "the three worst murderers amongst the SS." They were the guards the prisoners most wanted to execute had the revolt of August 2, 1943 succeeded.[97]

For T4 personnel and death camp workers sent to Poland to exterminate the Jews, experience in the exploitation and slaughter of animals proved to be excellent training.

CHAPTER FIVE

WITHOUT THE HOMAGE OF A TEAR

Killing Centers in America and Germany

We have now discussed how the domestication/enslavement of animals was the model and inspiration for human slavery, how the breeding of domesticated animals led to such eugenic measures as compulsory sterilization, euthanasia killings, and genocide, and how the industrialized slaughter of cattle, pigs, sheep, and other animals paved the way, at least indirectly, for the Final Solution.

Throughout the history of our ascent to dominance as the master species, our victimization of animals has served as the model and foundation for our victimization of each other. The study of human history reveals the pattern: first, humans exploit and slaughter animals; then, they treat other people like animals and do the same to them.

It is significant that the Nazis treated their victims like animals before they murdered them. As Boria Sax writes, many Nazi practices were designed to make killing people seem like slaughtering animals. "The Nazis forced those whom they were about to murder to get completely undressed and huddle together, something that is not normal behavior for human beings. Nakedness suggests an identity as animals; when combined with crowding, it suggests a herd of cattle or sheep. This sort of dehumanization made the victims easier to shoot or gas."[1]

During the twentieth century two of the world's modern industrialized nations—the United States and Germany—slaughtered millions of human beings and billions of other beings.[2] Each country made its own unique contribution to the century's carnage: America gave the modern world the slaughterhouse; Nazi Germany gave it the gas chamber.

Although the two twentieth-century killing operations under discussion here differ with respect both to the identity of the victims and the purpose of the killings, they have several features in common.

Streamlining the Process

At killing centers speed and efficiency are essential for the success of the operation. Just the right mix of deception, intimidation, physical force, and speed is needed to minimize the chance of panic or resistance that will disrupt the process. At the Belzec death camp in Poland everything proceeded "at top speed, so that the victims would have no chance to grasp what was going on. Their reactions were to be paralyzed, to prevent escape attempts or acts of resistance. The speedy process was also intended to increase the center's killing capacity. In this way, several convoys could be received and liquidated on the same day."[3] Friedlander describes the streamlined operation at T4 facilities: "From the moment they arrived at the killing center, patients were inexorably moved through a process to make their murder smooth and efficient."[4]

Making the process as smoothly efficient as possible also helps suppress the emergence of moral scruples on the part of the killers. Neil Kressel writes that organizers of genocides try to make the acts of mass murder as routine, mechanical, repetitive, and programmed as possible. "By reducing the need for thinking and making decisions, the routinization of the massacre diminishes the chance that participants will recognize the moral dimension of their acts."[5] At Union Stock Yards in Chicago, Jurgis Rudkus was struck by the "cold-blooded, impersonal way" the slaughterhouse workers swung the hogs up "without a pretence at apology, without the homage of a tear."[6]

By the time the Germans seized Hungary in 1944 and began transporting its large Jewish population to Auschwitz, the vast human slaughterhouse had reached the peak of its efficiency. Long trains transported Hungarian Jews to the annex camp of Birkenau on a three-track siding that went right up to the new crematoria working at full capacity, making it possible for a train to arrive immediately after the previous one had been unloaded. As the last corpses were being removed from the chambers and dragged to the incineration ditch behind the crematorium, those scheduled to be gassed next were undressing in the big room.[7]

While the American meat industry has had more than a century to streamline its operations, the acceleration of line speeds in the last twenty-five years has greatly increased the pace with which the meat and poultry industries slaughter animals. While previously government inspectors would stop the line when they found defective meat or animals who had not been properly stunned, today the slaughter line does not stop for fear that even a minute of "down time" will hurt profits. As one slaughterhouse worker said, "They don't slow that line down for nothing or nobody."[8]

United States Department of Agriculture (USDA) inspectors quickly learn the hazards of doing their job. According to Tom Devine of the Government Accountability Project (GAP), "Inspectors who have attempted to stop the line have been reprimanded, reassigned, physically attacked by plant employees and then disciplined for being in fights, had their performance appraisals lowered, been placed under criminal investigation, fired, or been subjected to other forms of retaliation that were necessary to 'neutralize' them."[9]

Workers are under constant pressure to keep the line moving at top speed. "As long as that chain is running," one worker says, "they don't give a shit what you have to do to get that hog on the line. You got to get a hog on each hook or you got a foreman on your ass."[10] Any worker who allows even a momentary lapse in the flow of animals—called a "hole in the line"—puts his job at risk. "All the drivers use pipes to kill hogs that can't go through the chutes. Or if you get a hog that refuses to go into the chutes and is stopping production, you beat him to death. Then push him off to the side and hang him up later."[11]

Chute/Funnel/Tube

At killing centers the last part of the passage that takes victims to their deaths is called variously a "chute," "funnel," "tube," or "kill alley." In

Sioux Falls, South Dakota, the nearly block-long underground passage used to drive livestock from the stockyard to the Morrell meatpacking plant is called the "Tunnel of Death."[12]

In his book about meatpacking and livestock raising in the United States, Jimmy Skaggs describes the "chute" at the 14-acre IBP (Iowa Beef Packers) plant in Holcomb, Kansas. Every day "cowpunchers push 3,700 head of cattle into a chute that feeds its disassembly line with raw material." Once a steer enters the chute, his fate is sealed. When he emerges out of the chute into the plant, he's immediately "zapped by a pneumatic gun that fires a yellow pellet into its skull" (with Skaggs the steer is always an "it" or a "beast"). After the steer "stumbles to its knees, glassy-eyed," workers tie his rear hoof with a chain. A pulley then yanks the "comatose beast" up off the platform so that he struggles upside down as he swings out over the kill floor where "men stand in gore with long knives slitting each steer's throat and puncturing the jugular vein."[13]

Another IBP facility calls the ramp which workers use to drive cattle single-file into the plant a "cattle funnel." According to Donald Stull, a social scientist at the University of Kansas, the ramp "gradually narrows as it winds upward to the knock box high above the killfloor." Two knockers with stun guns take turns shooting steel pistons point-blank at the arriving cattle to fracture their skulls and knock them unconscious, or at least stun them so they can't thrash around. Once a steer is hooked and chained, he "falls forward and down onto a mechanized overhead trolley and swings out onto the floor, hanging upside down from its left hind foot."[14]

At Belzec, Sobibor, and Treblinka, the "tube" was the final passage that led to the gas chambers. At Sobibor the tube consisted of a path, three or four yards wide and 150 yards long, which was fenced in on both sides with barbed wire intertwined with branches. SS men and their auxiliaries drove their naked victims through the tube to the gas chambers.[15] The head of the camp's administration, Hans-Heinz Schutt, said, "Once they were inside the so-called tube, which led from the hut to the extermination camp, there was no longer any escape."[16]

At Treblinka the "tube," which was eighty to ninety yards long and five yards wide, led from the "disrobing rooms" in the lower camp to the gas chambers in the upper camp. After going about thirty yards toward the east side of the camp, the tube made a sharp, almost ninety-degree turn and went straight up to the central opening of the gas chamber building in the upper camp. Barbed-wire fencing, thickly camouflaged with wood, bushes, and trees, enclosed the tube and kept it hidden from view. Guards used fists, whips, and rifle butts to force their naked victims to run four and five abreast with their arms raised through the tube.[17]

At Treblinka and Sobibor the SS called the tube the "Road to Heaven" (*Himmelfahrtsstrasse*).[18] At Treblinka the Germans placed a dark curtain they took from a synagogue over the entrance to the building that contained the gas chambers. On it was written in Hebrew: "This is the gate through which the righteous may enter."[19]

The same blend of mocking irony and self-exculpation is evident in the United States. Dr. Temple Grandin, an animal scientist employed by the meat industry, calls the ramp and double-rail conveyor she designed to funnel cattle to their deaths the "Stairway to Heaven." At the Swift meatpacking plant in Tolleson, Arizona, where she designed her first "Stairway to Heaven," she experienced her initiation when she killed her first animal. "When I got home, I couldn't believe I had done it," she said. "It was very exciting. I was scared that I'd miss, because it takes some skill."[20]

Processing the Sick, Weak, and Injured

At killing centers, those who arrive sick, weak, or injured interfere with the efficient running of the operation. Each center has to find ways to deal with those who can't keep up.

At Treblinka, after a camp staff member ordered the new arrivals to turn over their luggage and valuables and prepare themselves for the shower they would need to take before continuing the trip, the staff member told the old, the sick, the injured, and mothers with babies to go to the "infirmary," where they would receive medical attention. That reinforced the impression that the operation was what the Germans said it was—a journey of resettlement to a work camp farther east. So while guards drove those designated for gassing to the disrobing area, other guards led those destined for the "infirmary" up the path to the execution pit.

When they arrived at the pit, the inmates were told by the guards to undress and sit down together on a mound of dirt near the pit. The guards then shot them, at first with rifles, but later with pistols in the back of the neck. The German guards did most of the shooting, but when the traffic got heavy the Germans enlisted Ukrainian auxiliaries to help out.[21]

Animals who arrive sick, weak, or injured at American stockyards and meatpacking plants have long been a problem for the meat industry. Shortly after the Civil War, a *New York Times* editorial, which described the inhumane way animals were sent to slaughter, concluded that "the manner in which live cattle are dragged or driven to the shambles [slaughterhouse] is an outrage upon the natural feelings of anyone not utterly hardened by familiarity with cruelty in its most barbarous forms."[22]

Little has changed in that regard since 1865. Animals arriving at stockyards, auction houses, and slaughterhouses today are often too sick, weak, or injured to stand. Calves and pigs kept since birth in small crates and stalls have an especially hard time. After being confined in crowded trucks, the animals arrive only to be met with workers who hit, kick, and jolt them with electric prods. On the way down slippery ramps, animals fall, break bones, get trampled. Animals too weak or injured to get up are called "downers."

In 1989 Becky Sanstedt captured on film the plight of downed animals at the United Stockyards in South St. Paul, Minnesota. The scenes she filmed were not unlike those described 124 years earlier in the *Times* editorial: downed animals left in holding pens for days unable to reach food or water; injured cows dragged by their hind legs behind trucks with heavy chains tearing their sockets and breaking their bones; bulldozers scooping injured cows up off the ground and depositing them on "dead piles." In the winter Sanstedt saw injured cows and pigs frozen to the ground. After she collected forty hours of video documentation, Sanstedt publicized her findings. Her exposé eventually forced the stockyard to announce a new policy regarding downed animals.[23]

Since downers impede stockyard and slaughterhouse operations, workers usually leave them where they fall or drag them out of the way until they can deal with them later. If the downer is dead or looks dead, she gets dragged to a "dead pile." If it later turns out she is still alive, she will be killed for human consumption. If she's dead, she will go off to the renderer, where she will be stripped of her valuable body parts, with the rest of her going to make pet food. One worker says that because injured cows called "haulers" have to be dragged through the kill alley to the knocking box, they come out on line "covered with [cow shit]."[24]

Sick and injured pigs fare no better. One meat inspector who worked at a "distress kill plant" in the Midwest described the plant as the end of the line for worn-out, sick, and crippled pigs: "Most of these animals aren't that old, they're just abused—malnourished, frostbiten, injured. Lot of DOAs [dead on arrivals]. Sows with broken pelvises who pull themselves around with their front legs, scooting along on their rumps for so long they get emaciated. They call them 'scooters.'"[25] The meat from these distress kill plants that passes inspection gets used for sausages, hot dogs, pork by-products, and ham, while condemned animals get rendered into animal feed, cosmetics, plastics, and assorted household and industrial products.

One worker explained that on pig farms sows who are forced to live on concrete develop such painful conditions that they can't walk. "On the farm where I work," she said, "they drag the live ones who can't stand up anymore out of the crate. They put a metal snare around her ear or foot and drag her the full length of the building. These animals are just screaming in pain. They're dragging them across the concrete, it's ripping their skin, the metal snares are tearing up their ears."[26] Worn-out sows are dumped on a pile, where they stay for up to two weeks until the cull truck picks them up and takes them to renderers who grind them up to make them into something profitable.[27]

Perhaps no animal is more "downed" and vulnerable than a female giving birth. Sue Coe witnessed a birth at the Dallas Crown Packing plant in Texas, which kills 1,500 horses a day for the European market, mostly France. When she visited the plant, Coe noticed a white mare in distress in front of a nearby restraining pen. Coe recorded what she saw: "Two workers use a six-foot whip on the horse as she gives birth, to get her to speed up and go onto the kill floor. The foal is thrown into a spare parts bucket. The boss in his cowboy hat observes from the overhead walkway."[28]

Killing the Young

Since the meat industry sends animals to slaughter as soon as they have enough flesh on them (and not a day later), these very young animals live out only a small fraction of their natural lives. Broiler chickens, who are the overwhelming majority of animals killed and eaten, are only seven weeks old when they are slaughtered. Since their natural life span is fifteen to twenty years, these artifically bloated infants get to live less than one percent of their natural lives. As Dr. Karen Davis, founder and president of United Poultry Concerns, says, "All the ones you see in the store are just baby birds with huge overblown bodies."[29] Pigs and lambs are sent to slaughter at five to seven months. Veal calves are four months old when they leave their crate and take their first walk to the truck that takes them to the slaughterhouse.

Robert Louis Stevenson once wrote, "Nothing more strongly arouses our disgust than cannibalism, yet we make the same impression on vegetarians, for we feed on babies, though not our own."[30] Some of the animals people feed on are "babies" in the most literal sense. Baby suckling pigs, killed and sold intact, minus only their innards, weigh between twenty and thirty-five pounds, while bottle-fed baby lambs, considered a "delicacy," are only one to nine weeks old when they are slaughtered. The youngest of the veal calves—called bob or bobby veal—is the closest human beings come to robbing the cradle. These baby calves are only one to five days old when they are killed and eaten.

Even the female animals whom the dairy and egg industries exploit for their milk and eggs live out only a small part of their natural lives before their usefulness ends and they are sent to slaughter. Dairy cows who could live twenty-five years in a healthy environment are usually slaughtered for ground beef after three or four years, while hens used for egg production live less than one tenth of the time they would live ordinarily.

Killing the young can sometimes be a problem for slaughterhouse workers. One English observer writes, "It is interesting what still reaches a slaughterman's calloused heart—calloused, that is, by the job of work he's commissioned to do by the consumer. For one man it is goats. 'They cry just like babies.' For a veteran blood-and-guts disposal man, it is carrying three-day-old calves to the shooting box and destroying them with a captive bolt."[31]

One American worker reported that to kill the calves faster, they would put put eight or nine of them in the knocking box at the same time. "As soon as they start going in, you start shooting, the calves are jumping, they're all piling up on top of each other," he said. "You don't know which ones got shot and which ones didn't get shot at all, and you forget to do the bottom ones." They're hanged alive and go down the line, wriggling and yelling. "The baby ones—two, three weeks old—I felt bad killing them so I just let them walk past."[32] However, he did those baby calves no favor by letting them "walk past," since it meant that the calves were fully conscious when the workers farther down the line hanged, bled, and cut them up.

In England Dr. Alan Long, who regularly visits slaughterhouses as a research adviser of the Vegetarian Society of the United Kingdom, has noticed a certain squeamishness among some of the workers about killing young animals. Workers have confided to him that the hardest part of their job is killing lambs and calves because "they're just babies." Long says it's a poignant moment "when a bewildered little calf, just torn from its mother, sucks the slaughterman's fingers in the hope of drawing milk and gets the milk of human unkindness." He calls what goes on in slaughterhouses "a relentless, merciless, remorseless business."[33]

Long often talks with workers during their breaks. "I've often gone with the gang of slaughtermen to their hut, when they are all bloody and disheveled from the slaughtering. I try to find out as much as I can and get their point of view. The sort of revealing remark that they'll make is, 'Well, it's legal, isn't it?' And I always think that in that remark there is a suggestion that they are perhaps a little bit surprised themselves."[34]

Long discovered that when it comes to baby animals, some workers have "sentimental quirks." He says, "sometimes a ewe will give birth in the slaughterhouse, and they won't slaughter the baby lamb; they'll feed it, make a pet of it. But then, there isn't much point in slaughtering a lamb that size because there's hardly any meat on it; it's nearly all bone. So what the slaughtermen do is make a pet of it and then ultimately they give it to a farmer. It comes back a bit later on, unrecognized, and it is slaughtered just like all the others."[35]

Dr. Gordon Latto describes a similar incident: "In a lunch session in a slaughterhouse, a lamb jumped out of its pen and came unnoticed up to some slaughtermen who were sitting in a circle eating their sandwiches; the lamb approached and nibbled a small piece of lettuce that a man was holding in his hand. The men gave the lamb some more lettuce and when the lunch period was over they were so affected by the action of the lamb that not one of them was prepared to kill this creature, and it had to be sent away elsewhere."[36]

Most of the members of the *Einsatzgruppen* (German mobile killing squads) found killing children more difficult than killing men, or men and women. That is why many units enlisted locals to shoot the women and children, or just the children. In the Ukraine, for example, *Einsatzkommando 4A* gave the job of shooting the children to its Ukrainian auxiliaries, while it killed the men and women.

One of the reasons shooting children was more problematic than killing adults was that it was done up close. According to testimony at the 1965 trial of Albert Rapp, head of *Sonderkommando 7a*, who was accused of shooting Gypsy women and children in the Smolensk region in March 1942, mothers had to carry their babies to the ditch prepared as a mass grave. There the executioners snatched children from the arms of their mothers, held them at arm's length, shot them in the neck, and then tossed them into the ditch. According to witnesses, the shooting was done with such haste that many of the victims fell or were thrown into the ditch while they were still alive. "The tangled pile of bodies in the ditch kept on moving and rose and fell."[37]

SS-Mann Ernst Göbel, who was in charge of one such killing operation, objected to the brutal way one of his men killed children: "Abraham got hold of some of the children by the hair, lifted them from the ground, shot them through the back of their heads and threw them into the grave." Göbel said that after a while he could not watch it anymore, so he told Abraham to stop. "What I meant was he should not lift the children up by the hair, he should kill them in a more decent way."[38]

Some Germans balked at their assignments. After the war SS-Mann Ernst Schumann testified that when he expressed his misgivings to Untersturmführer Täubner before one of the mass shootings, Täubner called him a coward. Schumann told him he did not come to Russia to shoot women and children. "I myself had a wife and children at home."[39]

Since the success of German killing operations depended on the ability of their members to do their job without wavering, commanders in the field were constantly on the lookout for signs of distress and for ways to ease the strain. Holocaust historian Raul Hilberg writes that the Nazis expended much research on developing "devices and methods that arrested propensities for uncontrolled behavior and at the same time lightened the crushing psychological burden on the killers. The construction of gas vans and gas chambers, the employment of Ukrainian, Lithuanian, and Latvian auxiliaries to kill Jewish women and children, the use of Jews for the burial and burning of bodies—all these were efforts in the same direction."[40]

In the Ukraine the discovery of a group of abandoned Jewish children caused an unexpected delay in one of the killing operations. Several German soldiers came upon the children in a building, guarded by a single Ukrainian guard. They reported their discovery to two German military chaplains stationed at a nearby field hospital. When the chaplains went to the building to investigate, they found ninety Jewish children, ranging from infants to seven-year-olds, crowded into two or three rooms. The children had had nothing to eat or drink for at least a day. Some were lying in their own urine and excrement; some were licking the walls.

Since the chaplains did not know upon whose orders the Ukrainian was acting, they reported the matter to the divisional Catholic and Protestant chaplains, who in turn informed the division's staff officer. The staff officer learned that a German *Sonderkommando* unit had shot the children's parents and that the children were also slated for extermination. He was told that the matter was in the hands of an SS lieutenant who had orders "from the highest authorities." The staff officer contacted the headquarters of Army Group South and requested a delay in the operation until the matter could be clarified. In the meantime, he arranged to have bread and water sent to the children.

At a meeting of the senior division officers, which the staff officer was asked to attend, the senior officers told him the liquidation of the Jewish children was urgently required and criticized him for delaying the operation. They issued an order for the killing to proceed, but rather than give the assignment to the *Sonderkommando* unit that had killed the children's parents, they borrowed a Ukrainian militia unit from the army to do the job.

After the war, SS Obersturmführer Hafner testified that the Ukrainians did not like their assignment one bit ("they stood around trembling"). He also told the court about one of the little girls, who shortly before she was shot reached out to him and took his hand.[41]

One of the Germans whom the Israeli psychologist Dan Bar-On interviewed for his book about "children of the Third Reich" spoke about his father, who told him about a child he had killed. "He came to me shortly before he died. He told me in his confession that, over the years, the brown eyes of a six-year-old girl had never let him rest. He was a Wehrmacht solider in Warsaw during the ghetto uprising. They were clearing the bunkers, and one morning a six-year-old girl came out of one of the bunkers and ran over to hug him. He could still remember the look in her eyes, both fearful and trusting. Then his commander ordered him to stab her with his bayonet—which he did. He killed her. But the look in her eyes followed him all those years. He had never told it to anyone before."[42]

Children were shown no mercy at death camps either. Yankel Wiernik describes how in the winter at Treblinka small children stood naked in the open, waiting for hours on end for their turn in the increasingly busy gas chambers. "The soles of their feet froze and stuck to the icy ground. They stood and cried; some of them froze to death." In the meantime, Germans and Ukrainians walked up and down the ranks, beating and kicking them. Wiernik said that one of the Germans, a man named Seep, took special delight in torturing children. When the women he pushed around begged him to stop because they had children with them, he would often snatch a child from the woman's arms and either try to tear the child in half, or grab it by the legs, smash its head against a wall, and throw the body away. Wiernik reported that such incidents were by no means isolated. "Tragic scenes of this kind occurred all the time."[43]

After the war Auschwitz survivor Perry Broad told of occasionally finding small children hidden in the huge piles of clothing he had to remove from the cloakroom in the summer of 1944 after each new transport of Hungarian Jews was sent to the gas chambers: "Sometimes the high-pitched voice of a forgotten child was heard from under a bundle. The child would be pulled out and held in the air, and one of the brutes who assisted the executioners would put a bullet through its head."[44]

One rare lapse in the usual procedure at the camps involved Simon Srebnik, a thirteen-year-old Jewish boy at the Kulmhof (Chelmno) death camp in eastern Poland. For some unknown reason, the SS spared the boy's life and kept him as a sort of mascot while they liquidated the 100,000 Jews of Wartheland. The boy sang Polish folk songs for them and in return they taught him German marching songs. However, the songs did not save him. When it came time to leave Chelmno, the Germans shot the boy in the head and left him for dead on a pile of corpses. A Pole found him and hid him in a pig sty, and he survived the war.[45]

Whatever qualms about killing children may have existed in their ranks, the Germans never changed their policy. On May 24, 1944, when SS and Gestapo chief Heinrich Himmler spoke to a group of German generals in Sonthofen, he revealed the reasoning behind the policy. On the audiotape of his talk that has been preserved, he can be heard telling the generals that the Jewish problem has been completely solved and then addressing the issue of killing children: "I consider that I did not have a right—this concerns the Jewish women and children—to allow the children to become the avengers who would kill our fathers and our grandchildren. I would have considered that to be cowardice. That is why the question was settled without compromise."[46]

Three years earlier Himmler had told SS troops on the eastern front to exact revenge against Jewish partisans. Since they were living in "an iron time," he said, they had to sweep with "iron brooms." Everybody has "to do his duty without asking his conscience first." As for Jewish babies? "Even the brood in the cradle must be crushed like a swollen toad."[47]

Animals in the Camps

Although the purpose of the German killing centers was the extermination of human beings, they operated in the larger context of society's exploitation and slaughter of animals, which to some extent they mirrored. The Germans did not stop slaughtering animals when they took up slaughtering people. Auschwitz, which its commandant Rudolf Höss called "the largest human slaughterhouse that history had ever known," had its own slaughterhouse and butcher's shop.[48] The other death camps likewise kept their personnel well supplied with animal flesh. Sobibor had a cow shed, pigpen, and henhouse, which were next to the entrance to the tube that took Jews to the gas chambers; Treblinka had a stable, pigpen, and henhouse located near the camp barracks of the Ukrainian auxiliaries.[49]

At first Sobibor used horses (as well as prisoners) to transport corpses and the sick and injured from the train to the ditches where they were shot and buried. Later when the camp built its new gas chambers, the installation of a narrow-gauge track and a small diesel locomotive, which pulled five or six wagons, made the horses no longer necessary.[50] Treblinka even had a "zoo." "We had any number of marvellous birds there," said its commandant Franz Stangl after the war.[51] Photographs from the album of Kurt Franz, who followed Stangl as camp commandant, show a small fenced-in enclosure that confined a couple of unhappy-looking foxes.[52]

The Germans trained their dogs to attack prisoners, and the threat of being torn apart by snarling German shepherds was a terrifying prospect, as former prisoners have testified.[53] The Germans trained the dogs with leather whips, which they also used on the prisoners.[54] Abraham Goldfarb, a prisoner at Treblinka, described how German guards stood with their dogs along the fence on both sides of the tube that led to the gas chambers: "The dogs had been trained to attack people; they bit the genitals and the women's breasts, ripping off pieces of flesh. The Germans hit the people with whips and iron bars to spur them on, so that they would press forward into the 'showers' as quickly as possible."[55]

At Treblinka Kurt Franz had a dog he called Barry (a mixed breed but with physical characteristics of a Saint Bernard predominating), which he trained to attack prisoners. Franz amused himself by spurring Barry to action with the command "Man, go get that dog!" By "Man" Franz meant his dog Barry, while "dog" referred to the prisoner he ordered Barry to attack. However, as one of the prisoners testified after the war, when Franz wasn't around, Barry "allowed himself to be petted and even teased, without harming anyone."[56]

Zeev Sapir described how early each morning at the Jaworzno camp prisoners went to work in the coal mines in groups of thirty, chained by their hands and guarded by four SS men and two dogs. "The Germans entertained themselves by setting the dogs on the prisoners," writes Sapir. "They would give the command '*Du Mensch, pass'an diesen Hund*'

('You human, beat this dog'), the dog would then attack the helpless chained prisoner, and the prisoner would arrive at his workplace bleeding and with clothes torn."[57]

The German preference for their dogs was not lost on a little girl in the Warsaw ghetto. "I would like to be a dog because the Germans like dogs, and I would not have to be afraid that they would kill me."[58] Actually, the Germans did not like *all* dogs, just their own. As Boria Sax explains, "A 'Jewish' dog might be shot, but a 'Germanic' dog would be treated with honor."[59] When the Germans marched into Austria during the *Anschluss*, they killed all the dogs they found in the homes of the Jews because they were "Jewish dogs." They also shot dogs in the Warsaw Ghetto for the same reason.[60] Sometimes the dogs didn't even have to be "Jewish" to get shot. In occupied Rotterdam, when a dog barked at a German patrol, the officer in charge immediately killed the dog and arrested the owner.[61]

The Decree Prohibiting Jews from the Keeping of Pets, issued in Germany on February 15, 1942,[62] forced Victor Klemperer and his wife Eva to end the life of their family cat Muschel, who had always been "a support and a comfort to Eva."[63] Rather than turn the cat over to "an even crueler death" at the hands of the Gestapo, they secretly took him to a vet. "She [Eva] took the animal away in the familiar cardboard cat box," wrote Klemperer in his diary, "she was present when he was put to sleep by an anesthetic that took effect very rapidly."[64]

Shooting animals was a popular pastime for many of the German mobile killing squad members and death camp personnel. A number of those who spent their working hours killing human beings liked to spend their free time killing animals. The diary entry on July 21, 1941, of Felix Landau, a member of an *Einsatzkommando*, reads: "The men had the day off today, some of them went hunting."[65] Members of Police Regiment 25 had to be reprimanded for hunting wild boars illegally.[66]

The German conquest of new lands early in the war meant many more animals became available for them to kill and eat. Special instructions from the General Quartermaster of the German Sixth Army in the Soviet Union, dated July 3, 1941, stated that it was "of primary importance that the troops, whenever possible, live off the land. Every opportunity should be exploited."[67] In Belgium, when members of a German unit closed up their camp before moving on, they helped themselves to whatever they could find in local cellars and barnyards. Martin Bormann, Hitler's personal secretary, who happened to be present, recorded laconically in his notebook: "huge slaughter of chickens and pigs."[68]

If a German got to send home one of the animals he killed, so much the better. In a letter that Eduard Wirths, one of the SS doctors at Auschwitz, wrote home in early 1945 about a recent hunt, he told his wife he shot six rabbits and kept one of them. ("You, my all, get that one tomorrow.")[69] This talent for killing rabbits came in handy, as suggested by a witness of the mass murder of Jews in the town of Brailov: "I would like to say that more than 500 Jews had been rounded up in the marketplace. Here too there were men, women and children. I saw children who tried to escape being shot as though they were hares and you could see a number of bloody children's bodies lying round this crowd of people."[70]

Hitler and Animals

Like many of his fellow human beings, Adolf Hitler used animal epithets to vilify other people. He often called his opponents "swine"[71] and "dirty dogs."[72] The Bolsheviks were "animals," and the Russians, a "bestial people," were a Slavic "rabbit-family" whom Stalin had molded into a totalitarian state.[73] After he conquered Russia, Hitler wanted "the ridiculous hundred million Slavs" to live in "pig-pens."[74] He called British diplomats "little worms,"[75] and as for the "half-Judaized, half-Negrified" people of America, they "have the brains of a hen."[76] Hitler also had contempt for his own people, referring to them as "the great stupid muttonherd of our sheep-like people,"[77] and as the defeats mounted late in the war, he blamed them for not having been up to the challenge. Hitler called his own sisters "stupid geese."[78]

Whatever deficiencies members of the Germanic *Volk* might possess, however, Hitler believed the Aryan/Nordic race was infinitely superior to the surrounding sea of sub-human "monstrosities between man and ape,"[79] as he made clear in a speech in Munich in 1927:

We see before us the Aryan race which is manifestly the bearer of all culture, the true representative of all humanity. Our entire industrial science is without exception the work of Nordics. All great composers from Beethoven to Richard Wagner are Aryans. Man owes everything that is of any importance to the principle of struggle and to one race which has carried itself forward successfully. Take away the Nordic Germans and nothing remains but the dance of apes.[80]

Hitler was fond of dogs, especially German shepherds (he considered boxers "degenerate"),[81] whom he liked to control and dominate. At the front during World War I, he befriended a white terrier, Fuchsl (Foxl), who had strayed across enemy lines. Later, when his unit had to move on and Fuchsl could not be found, Hitler became distraught. "I liked him so much," he recalled. "He only obeyed me." Hitler often carried a dog-whip and sometimes used it to beat his dog in the vicious way he had seen his father beat his own dog.[82] In the Führer headquarters during World War II, Hitler's female German shepherd, Blondi, offered him the closest thing he had to friendship.[83] "But with his dogs, as with every human being he came into contact with," writes Ian Kershaw, "any relationship was based upon subordination to his mastery."[84]

Although Hitler consumed animal products like cheese, butter, and milk, he tried to avoid meat to placate his "nervous stomach." He suffered from indigestion and episodic stomach pains that had troubled him since adolescence,[85] as well as from excessive flatulence and uncontrollable sweating.[86] The first evidence of his attempt to cure his stomach problems by controlling his diet appears in a letter he wrote in 1911 while living in Vienna: "I am pleased to be able to inform you that I already feel altogether well....It was nothing but a small stomach upset and I am trying to cure myself through a diet of fruits and vegetables."[87] He discovered that when he reduced his meat intake, he did not sweat as much, and there were fewer stains in his underwear. Hitler also became convinced that eating vegetables improved the odors of his flatulence, a condition that distressed him terribly and caused him much embarrassment.[88] He had a great fear of contracting cancer, which killed his mother, and believed that meat eating and pollution caused cancer.[89]

Nonetheless, Hitler never completely gave up his favorite meat dishes, especially Bavarian sausages, liver dumplings, and stuffed and roasted game.[90] The European chef Dione Lucas, who worked as a hotel chef in Hamburg before the war, remembers often being called upon to prepare for Hitler his favorite dish. "I do not mean to spoil your appetite for stuffed squab [fledgling pigeon about four weeks old]," she wrote in her cookbook, "but you might be interested to know that it was a great favorite with Mr. Hitler, who dined at the hotel often. Let us not hold that against a fine recipe though."[91] One of his biographers claims that Hitler's meat eating was confined mostly to sausages.[92]

Whatever his dietary preferences, Hitler showed little sympathy for the vegetarian cause in Germany. When he came to power in 1933, he banned all the vegetarian societies in Germany, arrested their leaders, and shut down the main vegetarian magazine published in Frankfurt. Nazi persecution forced German vegetarians, a tiny minority in a nation of carnivores, either to flee the country or go underground. A German pacifist and vegetarian, Edgar Kupfer-Koberwitz, fled to Paris and then to Italy where the Gestapo arrested him and sent him to the Dachau concentration camp (see Chapter 8). During the war Nazi Germany banned all vegetarian organizations in the territories it occupied, even though vegetarian diets would have helped alleviate wartime food shortages.[93]

According to the historian Robert Payne, the myth of Hitler's strict vegetarianism was primarily the work of Nazi Germany's minister of propaganda, Joseph Goebbels:

Hitler's asceticism played an important part in the image he projected over Germany. According to the widely believed legend, he neither smoke nor drank, nor did he eat meat or have anything to do with women. Only the first was true. He drank beer and diluted wine frequently, had a special fondness for Bavarian sausages and kept a mistress, Eva Braun, who lived with him quietly at the Berghof. There had been other discreet affairs with women. His asceticism was fiction invented by Goebbels to emphasize his total dedication, his self-control, the distance that separated him from other men. By this outward show of asceticism, he could claim that he was dedicated to the service of his people.[94]

In fact, Hitler was "remarkably self-indulgent and possessed none of the instincts of the ascetic," writes Payne.[95] His cook was an enormously fat man named Willy Kannenberg, who produced exquisite meals and acted as court jester. "Although Hitler had no fondness for meat except in the form of sausages and never ate fish, he enjoyed caviar.[96] He was a connoisseur of sweets, crystallized fruit, and cream cakes, which he consumed in astonishing quantities. He drank tea and coffee drowned in cream and sugar. No dictator ever had a sweeter tooth."[97]

As for compassion and gentleness, these were anathema to Hitler, who believed that might makes right and the strong deserved to inherit the earth.[98] He had utter contempt for the vegetarian nonviolent philosophy and ridiculed Gandhi.[99] Hitler's most basic belief was that nature is ruled by the law of struggle.[100] He wanted young Germans to be brutal, authoritarian, fearless, and cruel ("The youth that will grow up in my fortresses will frighten the world"). They must not be weak or gentle. "The light of the free, marvelous beast of prey must once again shine from their eyes. I want my youth to be strong and beautiful."[101] Hitler once summarized his worldview in a single, short sentence: "He who does not possess power loses the right to life."[102]

The alleged fondness of Hitler and other top Nazis for animals, especially their dogs,[103] has been put into perspective by Max Horkheimer and Theodor Adorno. For certain authoritarian personalities, they write, their "love of animals" is part of the way they intimidate others. When industrial magnates and Fascist leaders want to have pets around them, their choice falls on intimidating animals such as Great Danes and lion cubs, intended to add to their power through the terror they inspire. "The murderous Fascist colossus stands so blindly before nature that he sees animals only as a means of humiliating men. The Fascist's passionate interest in animals, nature, and children is rooted in the lust to persecute." In the presence of power, no creature is a being in its own right. "A creature is merely material for the master's bloody purposes."[104]

We Live Like Princes

The greatest number of animals who found their way into the German camps were the animals killed, cut up, cooked, and served at meals. Around-the-clock killing and butchering at the huge stockyard and slaughterhouse in Dresden kept the Wehrmacht and SS supplied with butchered animals shipped in from the occupied eastern territories. From the Russian area of Kursk alone, the Germans took 280,000 cattle, 250,000 pigs, and 420,000 sheep and shipped them to Dresden, where the pace of the slaughter became so intense that prisoners from the occupied territories had to be brought in as slave laborers. The constant traffic of cattle cars between Germany and the occupied territories helped provide the necessary cover for the transportation of Jews to the death camps.[105]

Judging from letters and diaries of the killers in the camps, eating animals was one of their greatest pleasures. In a letter to his wife (September 27, 1942) SS-Obersturmführer Karl Kretschmer, leader of *Sonderkommando 4A*, complains about nearly everything except the food. After grumbling about the "Jewish war" he has to fight and about how he is feeling down ("I am in a very gloomy mood. I must pull myself out of it. The sight of the dead—including women and children—is not very cheering"), his tone suddenly shifts. "Once the cold weather sets in you'll be getting a goose now and again when somebody goes on leave. There are over 200 chattering around here, as well as cows, calves, pigs, hens and turkeys. We live like princes. Today, Sunday, we had roast goose (1/4 each). This evening we are having pigeon."[106]

A couple of weeks later, Kretschmer tells his wife about how his unit is rewarded after its morning work (shooting people): "There is always good food for lunch—a lot of meat, a lot of fat (we have our own live-stock, pigs, sheep, calves and cows)." In the same letter Kretschmer reacts again to the "chattering" he hears outside: "At the moment there are 600 geese making a terrific racket in the yard. Your Christmas goose (geese?) are, I hope, amongst them. If things work out I'll bring them myself. If not, I'll make sure that you receive them in good time."[107]

In his next letter home to "Dear Mutti, dear children" sent four days later "so you don't think Papa has forgotten you," Kretschmer describes the importance of eating well:

> On Sunday we had a feast. There was roast goose. I had roast goose for breakfast, for lunch, and (cold) for tea. Then in the evening I had fish. Even the best roast does not go on tasting good indefinitely. Anyway you need not worry that we are living badly here. We have to eat and drink well because of the nature of our work, as I have described to you in detail. Otherwise we would crack up....Your Papa will be very careful and strike the right balance. It's not very pleasant stuff.[108]

This same appreciation of good food as compensation for "not very pleasant stuff" can be seen in the diary of Untersturmführer Johannes Paul Kremer, a SS doctor assigned to Auschwitz in the fall of 1942. Although the camp was every bit as bad as he had been told (he calls it *anus mundi*—"the asshole of the world"), it had its compensations, which for Kremer were good meals at the SS officers' mess and a regular supply of human bodies for his medical experiments.

His entry for August 31 reads: "Food in the officers' mess excellent. This evening we had pickled duck's liver."[109] Two days later he writes: "3.00 a.m. attended my first *Sonderaktion* [mass execution of Jews]. Dante's Inferno seems to me almost a comedy compared to this. They don't call Auschwitz the extermination camp for nothing!" His September 6 entry reads: "Today Sunday, excellent luncheon: tomato soup, half a chicken with potatoes and red cabbage, dessert, and wonderful ice-cream." After Kremer attends his sixth and seventh

Sonderaktion, he writes, "In the evening, at 20.00 hours, dinner with Obergruppenführer Pohl in the officers' mess, a real feast."[110]

During the rest of Kremer's stay at Auschwitz, his diary records the executions he attends, his medical research, and meals. His entry for October 11: "Today, Sunday, there was roast hare for lunch—a real fat leg—with dumpling and red cabbage." Kremer was especially interested in the executions because they supplied him with fresh human body parts for his research on starvation. His entry for October 17: "Attended 11th *Sonderaktion* (Dutch) in cold wet weather this morning, Sunday. Horrible scenes with three naked women who begged us for their lives."[111] The November 14 entry reads: "Today, Saturday, variety show in the communal house (really big!). Particularly popular were the dancing dogs and the two bantams which crowed to order."[112] Another SS doctor at Auschwitz, Eduard Wirths, wrote newsy letters home to his wife about the various gala social occasions he attended, such as "a special dinner in the *Führerhaus* for department heads, with half a wild duck for each."[113]

Franz Stangl, the commandant of Treblinka, told Gitta Sereny in an interview that every day for lunch "we usually had meat, potatoes, some fresh vegetables such as cauliflowers." He was especially proud of the bakery he built at the camp. "We had a wonderful Viennese baker. He made delicious cakes, very good bread."[114]

Although leftover parts of animals the Germans killed and ate sometimes found their way into prisoner meals, they were definitely not choice cuts. A Jewish woman at a slave labor camp described the fare: "The bread was hard and barely palatable. At noon there was a soup which we called 'sand soup.' They made it with potatoes and carrots which they did not bother to clean. Into this soup they threw one or two cow heads with teeth, hair, and eyes."[115]

Humane Slaughter
One bitterly ironic feature of killing operations is their attempt to make the killing more "humane." By "humane," the operatives mean they want the killing to be done more efficiently and to be less stressful on

the killers. The truth is, of course, they're not really interested in being "humane." If they were, they wouldn't be killing in the first place.

As Nazi Germany began implementing its eugenic policies, both Hitler and Himmler wanted the policies to be "more humane." Hitler believed it was more humane to kill defective children: "The exposure of the sick, weak, deformed children, in short their destruction, was more decent and in truth a thousand times more humane than the wretched insanity of our day, which seeks to preserve the most pathological subjects."[116] During his 1939 meeting with Karl Brandt, whom he appointed head of the T4 program, Hitler used the expression again when they talked about the best way to kill mentally ill Germans. When Brandt told him about the various options under consideration, including the use of carbon monoxide gas, Hitler asked him, "Which is the more humane way?" Brandt recommended gas, and Hitler gave his authorization.[117] In the Political Testament Hitler wrote in his bunker in Berlin the day before he committed suicide, he spoke about the "humane" method that had been used to exterminate the Jews.[118]

In August 1941, during his visit to Minsk in German-occupied Russia, Heinrich Himmler told Artur Nebe, the commander of *Einsatzgruppe B*, that he wanted to watch a liquidation up close to see what it was like. So Nebe ordered his men to round up about 100 Jews. As the shooting proceeded, Himmler became uneasy, dropping his eyes after each volley. After the liquidation was over, SS Obergruppenführer von dem Bach-Zelewski, who had also been present, said to Himmler, "Look at the eyes of the men in this Kommando, how deeply shaken they are! These men are finished for the rest of their lives. What kind of followers are we training here? Either neurotics or savages!"

In his talk to the men to boost their morale, Himmler conceded that the duty they were performing was "repulsive," but he reminded them that it was their duty as German soldiers to carry out their orders unconditionally. He told them that he assumed full responsibility before God and Hitler for everything that was happening and that the job they were ordered to do was obeying "the highest law."

Accompanied by Nebe and von dem Bach-Zelewski, Himmler next went to inspect a nearby mental asylum, which he also found disturbing. He told Nebe to end the inmates' suffering as quickly as possible. Then, after Nebe's men shot the patients, Himmler told Nebe to try to find another way of killing that was "more humane."[119]

Dr. Wilhelm Pfonnerstiel, professor of hygiene at the University of Marburg and a SS lieutenant colonel, reported after the war on his wartime visit to the Belzec extermination camp. "I wanted to know in particular if the process of exterminating human beings was accompanied by any act of cruelty." He admitted the operation had not been as humane as he would have liked. "I found it especially cruel that death did not set in until eighteen minutes had passed." He was also concerned about the welfare of the SS men doing the killing.[120]

During his trial after the war, Anton Kaindl, the former commandant of the Sachsenhausen concentration camp, declared in his depositions that Richard Glücks, the inspector of concentration camps, ordered the camp commandants to have gas chambers built on the model of those at Auschwitz. Exterminations at Sachsenhausen had been carried out by shooting or hangings until 1943, when Kaindl introduced gas chambers because "the existing facilities were no longer sufficient for the exterminations planned." The head doctor assured him that the use of prussic acid led to instantaneous death. "This is why I considered the installation of gas chambers suitable, and also more humane, for mass executions."[121]

Those who kill "humanely" often contend that their victims suffer minimally or not at all. This contention helps ease their guilt and makes the continuation of the killing more acceptable. Robert Jührs of the SS, whose job at Belzec was to shoot the arrivals who were no longer able to walk, said that because of the poor condition of the Jews after their long journey in indescribably overcrowded freight cars, he looked on shooting them "as a kindness and a release. I shot the Jews with a machine gun from the edge of the ditch. In each case I aimed for the head, so that each one died instantly. I can say with absolute certainly that not one of them suffered."[122]

In 1958 the United States Congress passed the Humane Slaughter Act to make the slaughter of farm animals "more humane."[123] The law required that animals whose meat is sold to the federal government or its agencies be "rendered insensible to pain" by means of "a single blow or gunshot or an electrical, chemical or other means that is rapid and effective, before being shackled, hoisted, thrown, cast, or cut."[124]

At committee hearings on the bill prior to its passage, one witness recommended wider use of a stunning mechanism then in use in some places that had already been tested on calves, lambs, and pigs. Originally proposed by John Macfarlane of the Massachusetts Society for the Prevention of Cruelty to Animals, the device had been developed by Remington Arms, a weapons manufacturer working in conjunction with the American Meat Institute and the American Humane Association. The witness demonstrated to the committee how the stunning mechanism worked. "Contact of this trigger rod with the animal's head discharges the cartridge," he explained, "forcing this out and striking the animal's head."[125]

Nearly five centuries earlier Leonardo da Vinci had predicted that "the time will come when men such as I will look upon the murder of animals as they now look upon the murder of men," but that time had obviously not yet arrived in America. At no point in the hearings did anyone question or object to killing animals. All parties concerned with the bill, animal welfare groups included, were interested only that the animals be killed "humanely."

The fact that the final law exempted religious ritual slaughter led some people to criticize Jewish ritual slaughter as "inhumane" because it requires that the animal must be conscious when he or she is killed. However, as Brian Klug points out:

> I have witnessed the slaughter of animals at a number of slaughterhouses. None of it, whether performed by religious or secular methods, impressed me as being anything other than a pitiful way to treat one's fellow creatures. Singling out Muslim and

Jewish methods in the name of the animals strikes me as invidious. Dignifying other methods with the word "humane" is, to my mind, adding insult to the ultimate injury.[126]

In 1978 Congress amended the Humane Slaughter Act so that its provisions covered all federally inspected slaughterhouses, not just those that sold meat to the federal government. Once again, humane and animal welfare groups, as well as the meat industry, voiced their support.[127] John Macfarlane returned to the second set of hearings to testify on behalf of the proposed amendments. In the intervening two decades, Macfarlane had left his post at the Massachusetts Society for the Prevention of Cruelty to Animals to become a livestock handling consultant and a member of the board of directors of the Livestock Conservation Institute.

Several spokespersons from the humane community stressed that the slaughter method that rendered animals unconscious made the operation more efficient, economical, and less stressful for those who did the killing. Emily Gleockler of Humane Information Services spoke of support for the bill by meatpackers who "found humane slaughter practices more efficient in labor utilization and resulting in lower costs." She assured the committee that the bill would "not impose any significant burden on the government which enforces it, on the livestock industry, the meat-packing industry, or consumers." What burden it might impose on the animals being slaughtered she did not say. Another spokesperson from the animal welfare community emphasized that "humane slaughter in the long run saves money for packing plants" and helps avoid "labor difficulties." By "difficulties" she presumably meant mental and emotional stress on slaughterhouse workers.[128]

Holocaust historian Raul Hilberg's observation about German attempts to find more humane ways to conduct their killing operations is relevant here: "The 'humaneness' of the destruction process was an important factor in its success. It must be emphasized, of course, that this 'humaneness' was evolved not for the benefit of the victims but for the welfare of the perpetrators."[129]

III

HOLOCAUST ECHOES

Take sides. Neutrality helps the oppressor, never the victim.
Silence encourages the tormentor, never the tormented.

—*Elie Wiesel*

Our grandchildren will ask us one day: Where were you during the
Holocaust of the animals? What did you do against these horrifying
crimes? We won't be able to offer the same excuse for the second time,
that we didn't know.

—*Helmut Kaplan*

CHAPTER SIX

WE WERE LIKE THAT TOO

Holocaust-Connected Animal Advocates

In this third and final part of the book the focus turns to bearers of opposed memories—Jewish and German—whose advocacy of animals has been influenced and in some cases shaped by the Holocaust.

This chapter profiles Holocaust-connected activists who possess a sensitivity to the suffering of others that characterizes many Holocaust survivors and their families. Leo Eitinger, a retired professor of psychology at the University of Oslo and himself an Auschwitz survivor, has concluded that former prisoners of the camps possess a more heightened sensitivity toward other people and a greater capacity for empathy.[1] Many children of survivors, seeking to achieve—insofar as possible—a repair of the world (*tikkun olam*), have pursued careers in the helping professions, for example, as teachers, marriage and family therapists, mental health counselors, psychiatrists, psychologists, and social workers.[2]

The activists profiled here have been able to extend their concern and compassion beyond the species barrier to those whom Henry Spira, himself a Holocaust-connected animal activist, called "the most defenseless of all the world's victims."

Combatting a Mental Aberration

Anne Muller remembers going through photograph albums when she was a child. Her mother would point to "some of the most beautiful and beautifully dressed people I had ever seen and tell me, 'That is your tante so and so and she was killed in a concentration camp.'" In one family photograph of about twelve people "she pointed to each person, told me the name, gave me a brief bio, and ended with he (or she) was killed in a concentration camp."

The loss of family members left a deep impression on Muller. "When you grow up learning about how your family was killed by a government and by people who thought they were worthless, or worse, and who had absolute power over them and exercised it with brutal force, taking everything, even their lives, you can't help but feel deeply for those who are in that predicament. Animals are weak, they have no voice, they can't help each other or themselves. We were like that too."

Muller and her husband, Peter, who live in New Paltz, New York, head two animal protection groups—Wildlife Watch, which includes the Coalition to Prevent the Destruction of Canada Geese, and the Committee to Abolish Sport Hunting.³ Muller says that when she first learned about hunting, it caused a deep visceral response. She was horrified to learn that "hunters were killing legally with the support and encouragement of state and federal government."

Muller is struck by the fact that there were so few people who helped the Jews during the Holocaust and that people lived their lives as usual in Germany and Poland while the ashes spewing from the stacks of the crematoria snowed down on nearby cities. "For most of the society, life was lived as if none of this was happening. People had regular jobs, concentration camp workers went off to work in the morning and came home at night to loving families, a home-cooked meal, a warm bed. It was a job for them as it is for the animal experimenter, the trapper, game agent, furrier, or the factory farm worker."

When Muller first heard about the Cambodian "boat people," she contacted Catholic Charities to find out how she could help. The result was that "we had three Cambodians living with us for months." Muller and her husband also sponsored four students they taught when they were in China, two of whom lived with them for a year. "Yes, we care about people," she says. "But nothing compares to the suffering that animals endure. So few of us are doing anything about it. But I've heard it only takes ten percent to make a revolution."

Muller ends her e-mail messages with a quotation from Albert Schweitzer: "The time will come when public opinion will no longer tolerate amusements based on the mistreatment and killing of animals. The time will come, but when? When will we reach the point that hunting, the pleasure in killing animals for sport, will be regarded as a mental aberration?"[4]

Survivor Voices

Muller first became aware of Marc Berkowitz when she began appearing on local call-in radio shows on behalf of Canada geese, whom a Rockland county town supervisor wanted to round up and kill, either with gas or poison. Muller says that whenever Berkowitz called in, he always came to the defense of the animals and to her defense.

"Marc is an amazing man. At Auschwitz, he watched his mother and one of his sisters being marched to the gas chamber, and he couldn't show emotion because he knew that if he did he would be killed and wouldn't be able to save the people he did end up saving." After Josef Mengele selected Berkowitz and his twin sister, who were twelve, for his twin experiments, he forced them to undergo experimental spinal surgery. Today Berkowitz strongly opposes forcing animals to undergo similar experiments.

At a public meeting at the Helen Hayes Center for the Performing Arts in Rockland, which Muller organized to defend Canada geese, Berkowitz joined movie actor Alec Baldwin as one of the speakers. "I dedicate my mother's grave to the geese," he told the audience of 400 people, with every major local TV and radio station in attendence. "My mother doesn't have a grave, but if she did I would dedicate it to the geese. I was a goose too."[5]

*   *   *

The identity of one survivor activist—known only as "The Hacker," or simply "Hacker"—may never be known because he was a member of the Animal Liberation Front (ALF), an underground network of people who risk arrest to rescue animals. Hacker worked closely with "Valerie" (also a pseudonym) in 1981 on the planning and implementation of the ALF raid at Dr. Thomas Gennarelli's head injury lab at the University of Pennsylvania. There researchers bashed baboons in the head and then measured the force of the blows with a device cemented to their skulls, research the federal government was funding to the tune of one million dollars a year. When the ALF broke into the lab and seized videos of the experiments that the researchers themselves had made and then released them to the media, public reaction was so strong that the experiments were stopped and the lab shut down.

> Valerie had first met Hacker at a vegetarian Thanksgiving dinner in Queens: Now in his sixties, Hacker had grown up in Nazi Germany. The cruelty he had seen and experienced there as a little boy was still as real to him as the tattoo that marked his stay in a concentration camp [Auschwitz]. He had come to the United States in his teens and been apprenticed into the meat trade. He had been adopted by the owner of a New York neighborhood butcher shop and had ended up running it himself, until an escalating revulsion toward slaughterhouse horrors finally drove him out of the business. A widower with two grown sons, Hacker was now a health food advocate.

Hacker told Valerie at the dinner, "I believe what Isaac Bashevis Singer wrote, 'In their behavior toward creatures, all men are Nazis.' Human beings see their own oppression vividly when *they* are the victims. Otherwise they victimize blindly and without a thought." Since neither Hacker nor Valerie was ever apprehended, their real names will probably never be known.[6]

*   *   *

Animal advocate Anne Kelemen says it took her a long time to think of herself as a Holocaust survivor. She was born in Vienna where she was living in the 1930s, when several months after *Kristallnacht* her parents sent her to England as part of the *Kindertransport* that carried Jewish children to safety. Kelemen spent the war years in England not knowing what was happening to her parents. She only found out about the Holocaust firsthand after the war when she was a young counselor of child survivors of the Nazi camps who were brought to England. Kelemen did not learn about the fate of her parents until later. As the result of doing extensive research, she learned that her father and mother had been numbers 86 and 87 of a transport of 1,000 Jews the Austrians sent from Vienna to the Belzec extermination camp in April 1942.

Kelemen has lived in Israel and has worked for many years in New York City as a community organizer for senior citizens. She rescues stray animals, has attended animal rights demonstrations, and "doesn't eat anything that walks on all fours." Although her love of animals began as a child in Vienna, she says what she went through during and after the war makes her take the side of the underdog, "whether the underdog is a dog, cat, or person."[7]

*   *   *

In 1990 Susan Kalev was in Greenwich Village in New York City when she noticed that the woman walking in front of her was wearing a T-shirt that told the story of veal calves—how they are taken away from their mothers and kept in dark, narrow stalls until they're sent to slaughter. Kalev was so intrigued by what she was reading that she passed the woman so she could read more about the calves on the front of the T-shirt. She started up a conversation with the woman, which continued over coffee. When the woman told Kalev she was on her way to a veal demonstration at a nearby restaurant and asked her to come along, Kalev took part in her first animal rights demonstration. A few months later she went to Washington, D.C. to be part of the 1990 March for Animals.

Kalev, who was born in Hungary during the Holocaust, says she has a "rescue fantasy"—a strong need to save lives, which she says many survivors and their children have. After the Nazis seized control of Hungary, she lost her father, sister, and other family members. She survived only because her mother's brother-in-law was able to put her, her sister, and her mother on a list that got them sent to an internment camp rather than to Auschwitz. Later in Israel, where Kalev lived for six years, she made contact with the surviving members of her father's family.

After earning her Masters of Social Work degree from Yeshiva University in New York City in 1980, Kalev worked as a family and adoption caseworker and then for ten years as an oncology social worker at the Columbia-Presbyterian Hospital. Currently she counsels HIV+ and AIDS patients at the Karen Horney Psychoanalytic Institute and is a psychotherapist in private practice.

Because Kalev believes in the interrelatedness of all living beings, she is a vegan (does not eat meat, fish, eggs, or dairy products). She gives talks on health, vegetarianism, and humane living to Jewish and other groups in New York, and for three and a half years was a humane educator in the New York City public school system. Whenever she rescues or helps another living being, whatever the species, she says she feels she's living up to the Talmud teaching: "He who saves a life, saves the whole world."

For Kalev the mistreatment of people and the mistreatment of animals are connected. Her commitment to a non-violent way of living has become her life work. Because she and her family were helpless victims during the war, she is determined to make a difference. "Each time I can make a difference here today," she says, "it feels as if I am somehow righting a wrong done to our people in the past."[8]

* * *

Alex Hershaft, founder and president of the Farm Animal Reform Movement (FARM) in Bethesda, Maryland, spent part of his childhood in the Warsaw Ghetto. After he escaped from the ghetto, he spent the rest of the war hiding from the Nazis in rural Poland. The Germans killed his father, but his mother managed to survive and was reunited with Alex after the war. He spent five years in an Italian displaced persons camp before emigrating to the United States at age sixteen. "I know first hand what it's like to be treated like a worthless object, to be hunted by the killers of my family and friends, to wonder each day if I will see the next sunrise, to be crammed in a cattle car on the way to slaughter."[9]

Hershaft, who became a vegetarian in 1962, says, "I always felt that there was something ethically and aesthetically obscene about taking a beautiful, feeling animal, hitting him over the head and cutting him up into pieces and stuffing the pieces in my face." He later left his job as an environmental consultant (he has a doctorate from Iowa State University) to start FARM, which educates the public about animal agriculture and vegetarianism through educational campaigns such as the Great American Meatout (March 20), World Farm Animals Day (October 2—Gandhi's birthday), and the National Veal Ban Campaign (Mother's Day).[10]

"My experience led me to a lifelong pursuit of justice for the oppressed. I soon discovered that the most oppressed beings on earth are non-human animals and that the most numerous and most oppressed among them are farm animals."[11] Hershaft is a highly respected leader of the national animal rights movement; he organized and managed large animal rights conferences in Washington, D.C. in 1997, 2000, and 2001.

His experiences in Nazi-occupied Poland have made Hershaft conscious of parallels between the treatment of farm animals and how the Nazis treated Jews. In his review of Gail Eisnitz's *Slaughterhouse*, he wrote: "In the midst of our high-tech, ostentatious, hedonistic lifestyle, among the dazzling monuments to history, art, religion, and commerce, there are the 'black boxes.' These are the biomedical research laboratories, factory farms, and slaughterhouses—faceless compounds where society conducts its dirty business of abusing and killing innocent, feeling beings. These are our Dachaus, our Buchenwalds, our Birkenaus. Like the good German burghers, we have a fair idea of what goes on there, but we don't want any reality checks."[12]

Something Terrible

Lucy Kaplan, who wrote the Foreword, is a graduate of Princeton and the University of Chicago Law School. After working as a litigation associate for a corporate law firm in New York City, she got her first taste of animal protection work in the early 1980s as an Animal Legal Defense Fund volunteer. She and her husband moved to Oregon, where after a dramatic liberation conducted by the Animal Liberation Front at the state university campus in the town where they lived, Kaplan did legal work for the attorney who represented the sole activist charged in the raid. She went on to do more animal rights legal work and then served for many years as legal counsel to PETA's Investigations Division, specializing in the federal regulatory process ("something far more interesting to me than courtroom litigation").

Kaplan's parents met in a displaced persons camp in Austria in late 1945. Her father had been in seven different Nazi camps, including Auschwitz, before his liberation in 1945, while her mother had been a slave laborer for the Nazi SS. When Kaplan and her sisters were growing up, other adults would often remind them that their parents had been through "something terrible." Once when Kaplan launched into a tirade against her father, "our beloved housekeeper/nanny quietly sat me down and told me that my father had had two very young daughters who had been shot and killed by the Nazis as my father watched." Kaplan says she has "really been haunted by Holocaust images my whole life, and there is no question but that I was drawn to animal rights in part because of similarities I sensed between institutionalized animal exploitation and the Nazi genocide."

Another important influence was Isaac Bashevis Singer, whose work Kaplan began reading in the late 1970s when she was still practicing corporate law. "Already a vegetarian, I fell in love with Singer's worldview and was elated to read his blistering condemnations of animal exploitation." Kaplan finished reading all his works and is now ready to start all over again. "I'm stirred most by the unabashed way in which Singer equates the exploitation and suffering of animals at the hands of humans to some of the most horrible exploitation abuses that humans have experienced. For me, no one compares to Singer in his grasp of the parallel between the Holocaust and modern animal genocides."[13]

Three Commandments

David Cantor, who began working full-time in the animal rights movement in 1989, lost distant relatives during the Holocaust. "My great-grandmother's sister, her husband, and their three children, who had not emigrated to the United States early in the twentieth century when most of our family did, were never heard from again after 1939 and were most likely killed after the Nazis invaded Poland."

Cantor grew up in Philadelphia in a liberal family for whom human rights, the Bill of Rights, and the civil rights movement were frequent topics of conversation with him, his brother, and his parents. Although they were not religious Jews, Cantor says "a sense of being considered different from those around us, an understanding that recent history had devastated our people, and my own personal vision of current events as favoring the iconoclast, the folk artist, the peace activist, the irreverent Jew in a dominant WASP culture, the American citizen who exercised the First Amendment rather than let it atrophy—these experiences shaped much of my thinking. I have no doubt that they continue to do so."

Cantor thinks the mindset behind "animal experimentation and other atrocities sanctioned by officials, news media, and others who teach people what to think about officially sanctioned behavior" is reminiscent of the Nazi era. "Just as ordinary family men operated the machinery of the Holocaust in Europe," he says, "community leaders today in the United States regularly call for the mass murder of deer and geese merely for engaging in their natural behavior, and the holocaust against eight billion chickens a year comes to most people as advertisements for popular fast-food chains and TV appearances by celebrities."[14]

Cantor says one of the most impressive comments he ever heard broadcast on public airwaves was made by a founder of the Holocaust Museum in Washington, D.C., to the effect that he had been able to distill his study of the Holocaust into three commandments: thou shalt not be a perpetrator; thou shalt not be a victim; thou shalt not be a bystander. Cantor says he thinks about these commandments often. "If learned throughout society, those three commandments could help people see that choices we make determine the extent to which we are perpetrators, victims, or bystanders in a society that has long been carrying out a holocaust against animals and other beings and ecosystems while declining to recognize it as a holocaust." He says it seems to him that "the point of understanding the Holocaust in Europe is to prevent and halt other ones, not to remain narrowly focused on that particular one, traumatic though it was."[15]

X-Ray Vision

Barbara Stagno, northeast director of In Defense of Animals (IDA), a national animal protection organization headquartered in California, learned at an early age that the Nazis killed her grandparents. In 1939 her mother traveled alone at age thirteen from her home in Bialystok, Poland to the United States, sent by her parents whom she never saw again (they were gassed at Treblinka). "Basically, it was a story I grew up with," says Stagno. "It was always there—my mother's parents killed by something awful and evil. I had the sense that something terrible and incomprehensible had happened, even though my mother didn't get specific." She says her mother told her basically, "They were given a bar of soap and told to take a shower. The men were separated from the women. And then they were killed in a gas chamber."

Each year Stagno's mother burns two candles on what she believes to be the anniversary of her parents' death. "It's a date in the Jewish calendar, which is utterly foreign to me, so I couldn't tell you exactly when it is. It's sometime in August." A few years ago Stagno decided she would also light two candles each year to commemorate her grandparents. When she told her mother she was doing this, her mother seemed surprised, and Stagno could see she was pleased. "We didn't discuss it at length, but now she always calls me to tell me when the date is coming up."

Stagno says her parents always had a soft spot in their hearts for animals and allowed and even encouraged her at times to pursue her interest in animals. "I had the usual round of companion animals—a mouse, rabbit, guinea pigs—and got my first cat at age eight." When she was in high school, her father used to drive her around the city to help her rescue strays and bring injured animals to the vet. Once on one of these missions they had to have the car fumigated because a rescued dog vomited repeatedly. "My father was red with anger, screaming 'Never again!' as we're out on the FDR Drive cleaning dog vomit for yet another round." But her father kept right on helping her and even built an outdoor shelter for feral cats "that was really beautiful."

Stagno thinks the more involved one gets in fighting for animals, the farther away one feels from the rest of society. "When you travel the aisles of the supermarket, you don't see 'food,' you see the end product of factory farming and slaughterhouses. When everyone else is cooing over a box of kittens that a co-worker brings to work, you see the millions dying on the streets or receiving lethal injections of sodium pentobarbital in the shelters." She says it's as if you've acquired a kind of "x-ray vision."

Stagno says one of the most rewarding parts of being an activist is meeting and working with others who possess this special vision. Before she worked in the movement, she had few close friends who shared her vision of the world. Now she knows why. "Although I've lost many friends since coming to work in the animal rights movement, I've gained far more and richer friendships. I know and have met some wonderful, extraordinary people. All those people with 'x-ray vision' are by and large truly exceptional, wonderful people. Knowing such people restores my belief that there is goodness in the human spirit."

Although what her mother told her about what happened to her grandparents made little sense to her at the time, Stagno says it colored her view of the world. "My mother's story taught me from a very young age that this is a world in which evil and might can prevail, in which people can erect barriers between one another, and based on those barriers, can conduct heinous and hideous acts." She says that most children eventually learn that in school when they read about wars and such, but having it happen to family members—even those she had never met—made the lesson that much more personal. "Learning the story of the gas chambers and people, my grandparents included, being led off to die, left a deeply frightening impression on me. When I was very young, it made me feel that the world was not safe."

The most shocking part of it all for Stagno is "how massive numbers of people could desensitize themselves to extreme human suffering. Because that is the real lesson of the Holocaust, isn't it? That people could do everything and anything to those that they deemed 'sub-human.' Which is, of course, what we do to animals."[16]

Holocaust Images

To those with "x-ray vision," a Holocaust image can come to mind on any given day. A few years ago when humane educator Zoe Weil was driving along a Pennsylvania highway, she saw something that conjured up for her just such an image. In her capacity as Education Director of the American Anti-Vivisection Society (AAVS), an animal protection group in Jenkintown, Pennsylvania, she had just made a presentation on marine mammals to a sixth-grade class. The program had gone well, so she was in a good mood. All but two of the students wanted to start an animal/environmental club at school, and they all planned to write letters to Congress and the President before the end of the day. When they were asked to become part of a presidential committee to determine whether or not dolphins and whales should be captured and held in captivity, the entire class voted to ban their capture and display.

Weil's good mood was interrupted by a sight all too common on the highways of America. "I was driving back to the office, happy and optimistic, when I suddenly saw a mass of pink, fleshy bodies crammed into an open truck ahead of me." The long truck had metal bars that kept the bodies inside. "I felt sick to my stomach, transported in my mind to Nazi Germany, where trains carried Jews to death camps." She says her breath became short and her body felt damp with sweat. "I drove closer and saw the bodies—at least 100—stuffed together, side against side, face against rear. They were pigs."[17]

Knowing they were being trucked to slaughter, Weil drove alongside the truck for several miles, feeling angry and helpless. She looked alternately at the road and at the pigs, especially at the one pig who kept looking at her. "My mind raced, trying to figure out a plan of action when faced with the horror beside me. The pig kept staring at me, and I was doing nothing." When the truck turned off at an exit, Weil wondered if she should follow the truck to its destination and try to save the pigs. Doing nothing made her feel "traitorous and impotent."

She says that encountering the pigs on the highway broke through her defenses and left her struggling to understand what we can do differently to put an end to such unconscionable cruelty. She thought about the courageous people who engage in direct action to save animals and felt enormously grateful for them.

As she drove on and her tears dried, Weil realized how terribly important the work of educating young people is. She decided there was probably nothing she could have done to save the 100 pigs on the truck, "but I *can* do something for other pigs—I can teach people. I can try desperately to create a world in which people do not eat or exploit pigs, or any other animal, human or non-human." Remembering the children she had talked to earlier who were not strongly attached to traditions of exploitation and had few defense mechanisms to keep them following habits of cruelty and abuse, she made a promise to herself:

I'm sorry, pigs, that I did nothing to save you, that I couldn't do anything to get you off that truck. But I promise you that I will tell ten thousand people about you, and help them open their hearts and minds to a new world where we can all live in peace, and people won't eat you anymore.[18]

Today Weil is keeping her promise as co-founder and co-director of the International Institute for Humane Education and its program organization, the Center for Compassionate Living, in Surry, Maine.[19] The organization, which offers the only humane education certification program in the United States, provides training and empowerment workshops to "people who want to help the planet and all its inhabitants."

*   *   *

Gail Eisnitz, author of the highly acclaimed *Slaughterhouse: The Shocking Story of Greed, Neglect, and Inhumane Treatment Inside the U.S. Meat Industry*, did not lose any close family members during the Holocaust, but her work as chief investigator for the Humane Farming Association,[20] which takes her to places most Americans never see and never want to see, sometimes brings to mind images from the Nazi years.

One such image came to Eisnitz when she visited a huge pig producing plant "in a valley where warehouses stocked with crated sows and crowded piglets dotted the landscape as far as the eye could see." Amidst an eerie silence, the service vehicles moving from barn to barn "didn't betray the suffering that was taking place inside." She says it was a very weird feeling to stand outside these benign-looking barns and try to imagine the deprivation inside. "If you didn't realize that the vehicles were trucks making their rounds to pick up pigs who didn't survive the conditions, if you couldn't see that the dumpsters were overflowing with dead bodies, you wouldn't think anything was wrong or bad." The scene reminded Eisnitz of "what it must have been like to look at a concentration camp from a distance. The pastoral view outside completely belied the atrocities within."[21]

*   *   *

Stewart David, who advocates for a cruelty-free lifestyle with his wife Terri in Asheville, North Carolina, is another activist mindful of Holocaust parallels. In his review of *Schindler's List* for the publication of the North Carolina Network for Animals, he wrote, "As a Jew raised in a neighborhood full of Holocaust survivors and those who lost loved ones, I don't mean to trivialize their pain. But aren't the Auschwitzes of today the slaughterhouses, factory farms, and laboratories that are so carefully hidden from view? Pain, violence, and suffering are no more acceptable because they are inflicted upon innocent animals rather than on innocent people."[22]

When David was growing up in Chicago, he was very aware of the survivors, especially the parents of a good friend whose mother was missing an arm. He remembered his Yiddish-speaking grandmother spitting at his German-made Volkswagen Beetle ("I never quite understood the whole thing"). David became a vegetarian in 1986 and went to his first animal rights conference in 1988. Soon afterwards he met Terri, already a vegan, who was tabling for an animal rights group. They married in 1990 and moved to North Carolina "to try and live a simpler life and work for the animals."

The most rewarding part of their life in Asheville, Stewart says, has been getting to learn about and love different animals. "We have goats, turkeys, and dogs. As a nice Jewish boy growing up in Chicago, I never thought I would love and care for turkeys or goats! We recently were involved in a cow rescue, and I have a whole new love and respect for bovines." He says the animals "give us the strength to get through the day and are a constant reminder of what animal rights is all about."[23]

The most difficult part of advocating for animals, he says, is trying to reach seemingly kind, compassionate people who have complicity in horrific animal suffering but just won't take it seriously or just don't care. It's an indifference he wants to see changed. "If the public is allowed to remain detached from the suffering of the factory farms, animal laboratories, fur farms, steel-jaw leg hold traps, rodeos, circuses, and other atrocities, these atrocities will continue. We must make them feel the pain of the creatures whose screams are hidden behind the locked doors, out of sight, out of mind. Their language may not be understandable to others, but we know what they are saying."[24]

* * *

Jennifer Melton is an animal rights attorney who is now legal counsel for Rocky Mountain Animal Defense in Boulder, Colorado.[25] She's not Jewish, but ever since she was first exposed to the Holocaust in her world history class in tenth grade, she has tried to learn more about it and apply its lessons to the present. "I think the Holocaust is an excellent, yet terrible, example of man's ability to assume the role of God and be able to decide who shall live and who shall die. With regard to animals, that decision is made millions of times each day."

Melton sees a similar mentality at work today. "This general disrespect for life, lack of empathy, and the singular focus on a personal agenda without regard to the suffering of your victim is forced on diverse beings from prisoners of war to scared cattle awaiting slaughter while listening to the screams of their brethren being killed." Melton, who grew up around cattle ranching and hunting, "used to pray for the soul of the animal I was forced to eat at the dinner table."

"It seems that violence is more readily condoned if it is perpetrated on beings different from oneself," she says. She grew up in Texas and says she can picture a guy standing in a cowboy hat saying, "It's different, let's kill it." Melton also does children's advocacy work (abuse and neglect cases). "It's all connected," she says. "Violence is violence. It doesn't matter whether it takes place in a concentration camp or slaughterhouse."[26]

Soap and Shoes

In 1998 Sonia Waisman taught the first "Animals and the Law" course at California Western School of Law in San Diego and is also a co-editor of the first Animal Law casebook ever published.[27] She recalls that every year in Hebrew school the students read and talked about the Holocaust, and since then she has visited Yad Vashem and seen many documentaries. She says that one of the many atrocities that somehow stood out was that the victims' bones were used to make soap. It was not until years later "that I learned that tallow in soap is actually animal bone."

Waisman has always cared about animals and has been a vegetarian since she was fourteen, but the whole thing came full circle "when I learned about soap and came to the eye-opening realization that Hitler 'merely' treated humans as humans treat non-human animals." Besides using bones to make soap, she says she can think of other parallels—mass killings, experiments, and transportation in "cattle cars" ("something that never registered when I was younger").

Waisman, who grew up in a kosher home and regularly visits her family in Israel, would like Judaism (and other religions as well) to be more concerned about animals. "As a Jew and as a compassionate person, it is inexplicable to me that Holocaust survivors and Judaism as a whole could have gone through that and not become enlightened enough to make respect for animals a basic tenet of the religion. How can 'we' do to 'them' what was done to 'us' and not even recognize it?"

She says that even if it's unrealistic to expect the already divided Jewish community to come together on this, she's amazed that along with the Orthodox, Conservative, and Reform movements, "there is not an equally as large and established movement sensitive enough to the parallels between the Holocaust and human treatment of non-human animals to incorporate cruelty-free living into part of an enlightened religious way of life."[28]

*   *   *

Dr. Rhoda Ruttenberg, who works as a staff psychiatrist in a government mental health clinic in Washington, D.C., thinks that all branches of Judaism, as well as all the other major Western religions, are very backward when it comes to animals. She says her alternative (Jewish) group will go overboard for all human rights, including gay rights and Palestinian rights, even though these are unpopular positions, "but they are silent about animals. Not against, just silent."

Ruttenberg points out that at the U.S. Holocaust Museum in Washington, D.C., there's a poem called "We Are the Shoes" by the Yiddish poet Moyshe Shulshtayn (Moses Schulstein) on the museum wall near a huge pile of shoes taken from Jews killed at a death camp. "The gist of the poem is that the shoes are only inanimate objects, observers, and haven't suffered like their owners, but I have always found that strange, since of course they are mostly made of leather." Ruttenberg quotes from the poem:

> We are the shoes, we are the last witnesses.
> We are shoes from grandchildren and grandfathers,
> From Prague, Paris and Amsterdam,
> And because we are only made of fabric and leather
> And not of blood and flesh, each one of us avoided the hellfire

She asks, "Is that ironic or what?"[29]

A Fateful Encounter

Colorado activist Robin Duxbury, whose father lost sixty members of his family in the Holocaust, remembers an encounter that made a lasting impression on her. She says that she was in a pet shop to buy some bird seed, and since it was winter, she was wearing her rabbit fur coat. She stopped by a rabbit cage to pet some cute little pygmy rabbits, when from behind her she heard a very loud woman's voice say, "Don't you think you're a hypocrite petting that rabbit when you have Thumper's whole family on your back?" Everyone in the store looked at her. Duxbury says she was terribly embarrassed, but managed to defend herself by directing the "f" word at the woman. She felt humiliated, but she admits "that woman had quite an effect on me. I never wore that coat, or any other fur coat again."

Later after Duxbury returned to college, she took a course on the Holocaust "primarily because all of my father's relatives from his mother's side of the family perished in German concentration camps during World War II. Inasmuch as my father does not discuss the Holocaust openly with anyone, I pursued this course in an effort to bring myself emotionally closer to him."

Since then, Duxbury has worked for animal protection organizations, going back and forth from donating her services on a full-time basis to being a paid employee for groups such as Animal Rights

Mobilization (ARM!), which she headed when it was in Denver. Today Duxbury is mostly involved with horse issues as the volunteer Investigations Director of Project Equus, a national horse protection organization she founded with two others.[30] Although Duxbury currently makes her living as a horse trainer and two days a week works for a tack shop ("a lot of fun, as it gives me contact with horses, which I love"), she hopes that some day Project Equus will be able to pay her for her services.

Duxbury says her father came to the United States when he was seven years old. Although he did not know very well the members of his mother's family who were killed in Europe, the loss hung over him and over Robin's childhood like a dark cloud. "We have confirmation that forty-seven uncles, aunts, cousins, nephews and nieces, and one sister of my grandmother perished in concentration camps in Esterwegen and Flossenberg. We think that because of where the other relatives were living in 1933, the remainder may have died in Dachau."

Duxbury says that to this day she still cannot find adequate words to describe her horror over how some people could, morally speaking, drop to a depth so low. Over the years she has periodically tried to find an eloquent way to express her feelings, but she says out of concern for sounding clichéd or patronizing, she usually ends up saying nothing. "I think this is exactly how my father feels, and it is how I have come to feel about institutionalized exploitation of non-human animals."[31]

Third Generation Activists

Erik Marcus is one of the most widely traveled speakers in the vegetarian movement, having spoken to audiences in over 100 cities. He is also the publisher of Vegan.com, one of the most popular vegetarian-oriented sites on the Internet. His book, *Vegan: The New Ethics of Eating*, has over 25,000 copies in print and is now in its second edition.[32]

Marcus grew up in East Brunswick, New Jersey, where he learned at a very early age that his grandfather, who had been a successful businessman in Norway, perished in the Holocaust. The Gestapo arrested him in 1942 and sent him to Auschwitz, possibly helped by his Gentile business partner who wanted sole possession of the business. With help from the Norwegian underground, Marcus's grandmother and her family, including his mother, escaped to safety in Sweden. After the war the family learned that Marcus's grandfather had died of dysentery at Auschwitz.

In the last chapter of his book, Marcus describes what happened to him freshman year in college: "I was living in a dormitory, and the guys in the next room had a VCR and frequently rented movies. I dropped in on them one day while they were watching a movie that contained footage taken inside a slaughterhouse. The shot I saw was of a dying calf, looking right into the camera. I felt as if this animal, who was rapidly bleeding to death as the film rolled, was looking directly at me. I left the room deeply shaken." The experience planted a seed, and a few months later Marcus stopped eating meat.[33]

Marcus feels that his Jewish values and vegan values are very much in harmony. He says a high proportion of the vegetarian movement's leaders are Jewish, and "in many cases I believe they owe their activity to the Jewish values they learned at an early age." He thinks the fact that many Jews are actively involved in combatting violence and exploitation inspires many of them to become vegan and promote gentler eating habits.

Marcus likes to remind vegetarians who think that not eating meat is enough that every chicken who produces eggs and every cow who produces milk goes to the slaughterhouse. "So if you want to totally withdraw your support from animal-abusing industries, a vegan diet is really the only way to go."

What role did his family background play in shaping the direction of his life? "By the age of five I had learned about the Nazis' institutionalized, government-endorsed slaughter. Without question, this made me a lot more sensitive and ready to take action when, at the age of nineteen, I encountered footage of the inside of a slaughterhouse."

* * *

Dan Berger is an animal activist and a student at the University of Florida in Gainsville. "The Holocaust has always been a part of my life," he says, "in the sense that it's what my dad teaches and my grandma lived through. My grandma's left leg is deformed around the ankle, causing her to limp." A couple of years ago she made a tape of her experiences during the Holocaust, but Dan admits he hasn't looked at it yet "because I don't want to know what *my* grandma had to go through." Dan remembers when he was very young seeing two pictures of his grandfather, who died in the 1960s from a liver disease he contracted in the camps. One was of a healthy man before the war, the other of the frail survivor immediately following the war. "The Holocaust has affected me in the sense of a heightened awareness of cruelty and the depths of suffering that humans can inflict on one another."

Berger grew up in Syracuse, New York, where his father taught in the Jewish Studies Department at Syracuse University. He says friends turned him on to vegetarianism in his freshman year of high school. After seeing a video showing the slaughter of cows and chickens that a couple of local activists showed in the school library in observance of the Great American Meatout, he decided to go vegan.

Berger attended his first animal rights event at the local St. Patrick's Day Parade, where he passed out the leaflets for the Syracuse chapter of the Animal Defense League (ADL). He says he went to every protest and every meeting he could. "I thoroughly enjoyed being in that environment." After the family moved to Boca Raton after his father's appointment as Professor of Holocaust Studies at Florida Atlantic University, Berger started his own ADL chapter.

Asked about the influence on him of his family background, Berger says, "I think the Holocaust connection has certainly had an impact on my life (I don't see how it couldn't) and has given me a perspective on life and how to look at physical suffering, the difference perhaps being that I have taken this perspective and commitment to carry over to non-human animals."[34]

The Odd Couple

Two of the foremost leaders of the modern animal rights movement—Peter Singer and Henry Spira—grew up in the shadow of the Holocaust. The two men could not otherwise have been more different. Oxford-trained Peter Singer is an internationally known philosopher, author of many books, and professor of bioethics at Princeton University, while Henry Spira was a merchant seaman, auto worker, leftwing journalist, union reformer, civil rights activist, and New York City high school teacher before turning to animal activism at age forty-five.

Peter Singer, whose book *Animal Liberation* helped jump-start the modern animal rights movement, lost three of his grandparents during the Nazi era. After the German takeover of Austria, his young, newly married parents managed to escape from Vienna and emigrate to Australia, but his grandparents were not so fortunate. The Germans transported his paternal grandparents to Lodz in Poland (they were probably gassed at Chelmno), and his maternal grandparents to the Theresienstadt concentration camp, where his grandfather died but his grandmother managed to survive.

Singer did not go public with this information until the early 1990s when in lectures he gave in Germany he defended the use of euthanasia under certain conditions. Since enthanasia is a very touchy subject in Germany because of the Nazi euthanasia program, which killed tens of thousands of mentally and physically handicapped Germans, Singer's position sparked a heated controversy. When Singer's most vocal critics accused him of being a "Nazi," he revealed what the real Nazis had done to his grandparents.

When Singer was a boy in Australia, he used to take long walks along a riverbank with his father on weekends. He remembers his father would point out the fishermen sitting on the bank and the fish gasping next to them and say how cruel it was. "He didn't understand how people could think it was fun."[35]

At Oxford University where Singer went to study philosophy in 1971, his ethical vegetarian friends challenged him to think about the way society treats animals. "Like everyone else, I took it for granted that all human beings were equal, but I hadn't thought very hard about what this meant." It had never occurred to him that when people say all humans are equal, "we do more than include all human beings within the sphere of moral equality: we also exclude nonhuman animals from that sphere, thereby granting every member of our own species—psychopaths, infants, and the profoundly intellectually disabled included—a moral status superior to that of dogs, pigs, chimpanzees, and dolphins." His friends challenged him to explain why this should be so. "Why was it that it was all right to eat, or experiment on, nonhuman animals, when we would never think of doing the same to human beings?" After doing extensive reading, Singer concluded that there was no ethical justification for granting all humans a moral status superior to that of all nonhuman animals. So he became a vegetarian.[36]

In his review essay—"Animal Liberation"—which appeared in the *New York Review of Books* on April 5, 1973, and was the basis of the book of the same title, Singer argued that if a being suffers, "there can be no moral justification for refusing to take that suffering into consideration, and indeed, to count it equally with the like suffering (if rough comparisons can be made) of any other being."[37] Perhaps he was now speaking for those gasping fish whom his father used to point out to him? In an interview for *Psychology Today*, Singer said, "I've noticed that quite a lot of people who are prominent in the animal liberation movement are Jews. Maybe we are simply not prepared to see the powerful hurting the weak."[38]

Singer and Spira first crossed paths in 1974, when Singer was a visiting teacher at New York University. In addition to teaching undergraduate courses in the Department of Philosophy, Singer taught an evening adult education course about animal liberation that was open to the public. The course attracted about twenty students.

One man stood out from the others. He certainly wasn't a typical "animal person." His whole appearance was different: His voice had too much of the accent of the New York working class. The way he put things was so blunt and earthy that at times I thought I was listening to a character from a gangster movie. His clothes were crumpled, his hair tousled. In general, he stuck me as an unlikely type of person to enroll in an adult education course about animal liberation. But he was there, and I couldn't help liking the direct way he had of saying what was on his mind. His name was Henry Spira.[39]

Spira (whose Hebrew name was Noah) went on to become one of the most effective animal activists of the late twentieth century. Born in Antwerp, Belgium, he was six years old in 1933 when the Nazis came to power in neighboring Germany. Five years later, after his father went to Central America to try to set himself up in a new business, his mother took Henry and his sister to Germany to stay with her father, Samuel Spitzer, who was the chief rabbi of Hamburg (Spira's paternal grandfather was also a rabbinic scholar).[40]

While the family was in Hamburg waiting for word from Spira's father to set sail for Central America, the Nazis unleashed their massive pogrom against the Jews of Germany and Austria. On the night of November 9–10, known as *Kristallnacht* ("the Night of the Broken Glass"), the Nazis burned synagogues, destroyed Jewish property, and beat, killed, and arrested Jews, sending 30,000 of them to concentration camps. Spira and his mother and sister managed to get out of Germany and sail to Panama to join his father. The Nazi terror he witnessed as a boy made a lasting impact on him. He told Singer the fact that so many people stood by and allowed the evil to happen was what impelled him to be an activist—not to stand by and allow evil to be done.[41]

Spira later said it all began to gell for him during Singer's course.

Singer made an enormous impression on me because his concern for other animals was rational and defensible in public debate. It did not depend on sentimentality, on the cuteness of the animals in question or their popularity as pets. To me he was saying simply that it is wrong to harm others, and as a matter of consistency we don't limit who the others are; if they can tell the difference between pain and pleasure, then they have a fundamental right not to be harmed.[42]

As the course proceeded, Spira became a vegetarian, and when it was over, he asked the others if they wanted to continue to meet, "not in order to discuss more philosophy, but to see if they wanted to see if there was something they wanted to do about it."

Spira's first campaign targeted the American Museum of Natural History, where for eighteen years in the museum basement two psychologists had been conducting experiments on cats that involved cutting out parts of their brains to study their sexual behavior. The long campaign succeeded in stopping the research and closing the lab. It was the first time in more than a century of antivivisection efforts in the United States and Europe that a cruel animal experiment had actually been stopped. Spira's next campaign against the Draize test succeeded in getting Revlon and Avon to stop testing their new cosmetics in the eyes of rabbits.

During the last two decades of his life (he died in 1998), Spira focused primarily on farm animals, whom he called "the most defenseless of all the world's victims." He said he felt animal liberation was "the logical extension of what my life was all about—identifying with the powerless and the vulnerable, the victims, dominated and oppressed."[43] To the end of his life, Spira believed that "unless you believe in fascism—that might makes right—we do not have a right to harm others."[44]

What Made It Possible
Aviva Cantor, a journalist, Socialist Zionist, feminist, and animal advocate who believes that patriarchy is the root cause of human oppression, writes that "nowhere is patriarchy's iron fist as naked as in the oppression of animals, which serves as the model and training ground for all other forms of oppression."[45]

Cantor, who lost relatives on both sides of her family in the Holocaust, was raised in the East Bronx by parents who had immigrated to North America from Russia after World War I.[46] After attending the Ramaz Jewish Day School through high school and the Massad Hebrew-speaking summer camp, Cantor went to Barnard College and the Columbia School of Journalism, from which she received her Master's degree. She also studied history at Hebrew University in Jerusalem and at YIVO in New York City. She worked as a journalist for the London *Jewish Chronicle* and the Jewish Telegraphic Agency, co-founded the Jewish feminist magazine *Lilith*, and wrote the *Equalitarian Haggadah*. Since 1984, Cantor has been Vice President for Communications for the U.S.-based animal protection organization, CHAI (Concern for Helping Animals in Israel).

Cantor's father, an ardent Zionist who grew up in the *shtetl* of Vizneh in Byelorussia (Belarus), attended the famed Volozhin Yeshiva and became a Hebrew scholar fluent in seven languages. Her mother comes from a long line of businesswomen in Dubno in Russian Poland (now Ukraine). The Germans murdered her aunt and her family in Dubno and her paternal grandmother in Byelorussia.

In her feminist interpretation of Jewish history and culture, *Jewish Women/Jewish Men: The Legacy of Patriarchy in Jewish Life*, Cantor describes how from ancient times rabbis recognized that cruelty to animals breeds violence against other humans. "While the Five Books did not contain the concept of across-the-board animal rights and embodied the belief that animals could be used for 'legitimate human needs,'" she writes, "they did contain laws against what came to be called *tzaar ba'alei chaim*, causing animals pain and suffering, both physical and psychological."[47] In a story by the Yiddish writer Sholem Aleichem, a little boy decides a certain person cannot possibly be a Jew because he's cruel to animals. Cantor writes about an incident, recalled by Rabbi Michael Weissmandel, which took place in Slovakia during the war: "While being shoved onto a deportation train, a Jew named Itzik Rosenberg called out to his non-Jewish neighbors, who were watching the scene with glee, 'I beg you—go to my home and feed the geese. They have had nothing to eat or drink all day.'"[48]

Cantor believes the Holocaust is the ultimate expression of the principle of domination that defines power as power *over* others. "What made the Holocaust possible (and, some may argue, inevitable) is the fact that patriarchal values dominate our society. Men seek power over each other, over women, over children, over animals, over the natural world, and justify this on the grounds of utility. It is these values which have made the Holocaust possible."

In her book Cantor writes that the Holocaust goes to the very heart of the nature of patriarchy. "For not only was it planned—and overwhelmingly carried out—by men, but it emerged out of a masculinist value system that glorifies power, domination, violence, the annihilation of the 'useless' and the helpless, ravaging, exploitation, and cruelty." Under patriarchy, not only is the possession of power by one sex an abuse in and of itself, but sooner or later that power is likely to be abused even more. "In a world where male violence against human beings rendered powerless, against women, against children, against animals, against the environment, is as pervasive as the air, a mega-crime such as the Holocaust should never be unexpected."[49]

We Have Learned Nothing

Albert Kaplan, son of Russian Jews who immigrated to the United States in the early 1900s, advises European institutional investors for Laidlaw Global Securities, an investment banking firm in New York City.

He grew up in upper New York state where his father founded a small chain of department stores. Kaplan remembers vividly the unending supply of animal parts that showed up at mealtime—lambs, chickens, fish, and "always lots of steaks." One day in 1959 when an unusually thick slab of steak appeared in front of him, Kaplan began wondering from which part of the cow it might have come from—front? side? back? The unexpected train of thought took away his appetite, and he never ate meat again.

Kaplan doesn't eat cheese, eggs, butter, or milk either, nor does he wear animals—fur, leather, or wool, which he calls "lamb's fur." Once when he visited a Jain center on Staten Island, the monk offered him tea, milk, and honey. Kaplan accepted the tea, but declined the milk and honey. The priest asked him about it. After Kaplan explained, the monk told him, "You are a greater Jain than I."

Kaplan has lived in London, Paris, Luxembourg, and Israel, as well as in New York. In London, he was one of the early members of the Jewish Vegetarian Society, but he dropped his membership because he believes that "vegetarianism is not the answer. Veganism is." He tried to get the society to change its name from "vegetarian" to "vegan," but he was unuccessful. Nonetheless, he has fond memories of the organization. "They have a restaurant which is much fun, and not bad food. Their meetings can be hilarious. Largely elderly cranks attending lectures about constipation and other bowel movement problems. A great group."

Kaplan says the seven years he spent in Israel taught him that his own people are not free from inflicting cruelty. "Animal Auschwitzes are ubiquitous in Israel, some of which are operated by Holocaust survivors. There is a massive industrial vivisection laboratory near Ashkelon where animals are tortured for a fee. This laboratory will conduct any 'experiment' on any animal you name."[50] He tells of a visit he made to a kibbutz Holocaust museum near Haifa. "Around two hundred feet from the main entrance to the museum is an Auschwitz for animals from which emanates a horrible odor that envelops the museum. I mentioned it to the museum management. Their reaction was not surprising. 'But they are only chickens.'"

When Kaplan traveled to the Soviet Union to visit his parents' villages near Minsk, he learned that not a single member of his mother's family, which she estimated to number more than one hundred members, survived the Holocaust. His father's somewhat smaller family was not entirely destroyed, so Kaplan was able to meet several of them, including a first cousin who was a partisan and survived Auschwitz.

Kaplan wants the lessons of the Holocaust to help Jews and non-Jews improve the way they treat animals, but he is not hopeful. "The vast majority of Holocaust survivors are carnivores, no more concerned about animals' suffering than were the Germans concerned about Jews' suffering. What does it all mean? I will tell you. It means that we have learned nothing from the Holocaust. Nothing. It was all in vain. There is no hope."[51]

CHAPTER SEVEN

THIS BOUNDLESS SLAUGHTERHOUSE

The Compassionate Vision of Isaac Bashevis Singer

One of the most powerful pro-animal voices of the twentieth century was the Yiddish writer Isaac Bashevis Singer (1904–91), winner of the Nobel Prize in Literature in 1978.[1] Although Singer survived the Holocaust by following his older brother Joshua to the United States in 1935, his mother, younger brother, and many members of his extended family who remained in Poland were killed. Although Singer's later stories and novels set in America are mostly about Holocaust survivors and refugees from Europe, he did not write about the Holocaust directly. Nonetheless, it was the ever present lens through which he viewed the world, especially when it came to the exploitation and slaughter of animals, which upset him greatly.

The Eleventh Commandment

Singer was born in the small Polish village of Leoncin where his father was a Hasidic rabbi. Although he only lived there until the age of three, Singer remembered that their house had very little furniture, but many books. He also remembered the animals. "Every week there was a market, and many peasants would come to the town bringing livestock. Once I saw a peasant beating a pig. Maybe it had been squealing. I ran in to my mother to tell her the pig was crying and the man was beating it with a stick. I remember this very vividly. Even then I was thinking like a vegetarian."[2]

After the family moved to Warsaw where his father served as a rabbi in a poor Jewish neighborhood, Singer took to catching flies and removing their wings. He would then place the wingless fly in a match box with a drop of water and a grain of sugar for nourishment. He did this until he finally realized he was committing "terrible crimes against those creatures just because I was bigger than they, stronger, and defter." This realization bothered him so much that for a long time he thought about little else. After he prayed for forgiveness and took "a holy oath never again to catch flies," his thinking about the suffering of flies "expanded to include all people, all animals, all lands, all times."[3]

His experience catching flies appears in his autobiographical novel, *Shosha*, which is set in Warsaw.[4] When the narrator and Shosha pass the street where they both grew up, Shosha tells him, "You stood on the balcony and caught flies." The narrator tells her not to remind him. When Shosha asks him why not, he tells her what becomes a constant refrain throughout Singer's writings: "Because we do to God's creatures what the Nazis did to us."[5]

Another of Singer's early memories is of Yanash's market in Warsaw where people brought chickens, ducks, and geese to be slaughtered. "The butchers began to pluck their feathers even while those creatures were still alive and wallowing in their own blood."[6] The scenes of slaughter Singer witnessed there made a deep and lasting impression on him. *The Family Moskat*, the first novel he wrote after he came to America, has a slaughterhouse scene: "Slaughterers stood near blood-filled granite vats, slitting the necks of ducks, geese, and hens. Fowl cackled deafeningly. The wings of a rooster, its throat just slit, fluttered violently."[7]

The narrator of *Shosha* describes the slaughterhouse at Yanash's market: "The same blood-splattered walls, the hens and roosters going to their deaths shrieking with the same voices: 'What have I done to deserve this? Murderers!' Since it is evening, the harsh light of the lamps reflects off the slaughterers' blades. Women push forward, each with her fowl to be killed. Porters load baskets with dead birds and carry them off to the pluckers. This hell made mockery of all blather about humanism." Deeply disturbed by what he has seen, the narrator makes a decision: "I had long considered becoming a vegetarian, and at the moment I swore never again to touch a piece of meat or fish."[8]

The main question that haunted young Singer was why there was so much bloodshed in the world. He did not receive satisfactory answers from his father, mother, or the morality books he read in Hebrew and Yiddish translation. "I had studied in the book of Leviticus about the sacrifices the priests used to burn on the altar: the sheep, the rams, the goats, and the doves whose heads they wrung off and whose blood they sprung as a sweet savor unto the Lord. And again and again I asked myself why should God, the Creator of all men and all creatures, enjoy these horrors?" He also wondered about the wars and assassinations, pestilence and famine, bloodshed and exile described in the Bible. "One misfortune followed another until the Babylonians, the Greeks, and the Romans destroyed the Temple and drove the Jews into Exile, where for almost two thousand years they paid for the sins they themselves did not commit. How can a merciful God allow all this to happen and keep silent?"[9]

In *The Certificate*, another autobiographical novel set in Warsaw, the young narrator stops in front of a sausage shop and stares at the sausages hanging in the window.[10] He addresses them silently: "You were once alive, you suffered, but you're beyond your sorrows now. There's no trace of your writhing or suffering anywhere. Is there a memorial tablet somewhere in the cosmos on which it is written that a cow named Kvyatule allowed herself to be milked for eleven years? Then in the twelfth year, when her udder had shrunk, she was led to a slaughterhouse, where a blessing was recited over her and her throat was cut."[11]

The narrator wonders if anyone is ever compensated for his sorrows. "Is there a paradise for the slaughtered cattle and chickens and pigs, for frogs that have been trodden underfoot, for fish that have been hooked and pulled from the sea, for the Jews whom Petlyura tortured, whom the Bosheviks shot, for the sixty thousand soldiers who shed their blood at Verdun?"[12]

The narrator of another Singer novel, *Meshugah*, sees on the obituary page of a newspaper photographs of men and women who only the day before had lived, struggled, and hoped.[13] "Oh, what a dreadful world!" he thinks. "How indifferent was the God who created all this." At that very moment, Singer realized "thousands of people languished in hospitals and prisons. In slaughterhouses the heads of animals were being cut off, carcasses skinned, bellies ripped open. In the name of science countless innocent creatures were being subjected to cruel experiments, infected with harsh diseases." He asks, "How much longer, God, will you look on this inferno of yours and keep silent? What need have you of this ocean of blood and flesh, whose stench spreads across your universe?...Have you created this boundless slaughterhouse merely to show us your power and your wisdom? Are we commanded to love you with our hearts, our souls, for this?"[14]

When young Singer set out to become a writer in Warsaw, he purchased an account book in which he jotted down sketches, sayings, and ideas for stories, novels, and plays. One of his entries was about the Ten Commandments and how they might be improved. He wrote that the Sixth Commandment—"Thou shalt not kill"—should apply to all God's creatures, not just human beings.[15] As if to emphasize this point, Singer added an Eleventh Commandment: "Do not kill or exploit the animal. Don't eat its flesh, don't flail its hide, don't force it to do things against its nature."[16]

On to America

When Singer went to the dining room of the ship that took him from Cherbourg to New York in 1935, he requested a single table and saw his chance to make a decision he had been thinking about for some time. "Oddly, I had for years contemplated becoming a vegetarian. I had actually gone through periods during which I had eaten no animal flesh. But I often had to eat on credit at the Writers' Club, and I lacked the courage to demand special dishes. I had put it all aside for a time when I could act according to my convictions." So act he did. When the waiter came over to take his order, he told him, "I am very sorry, but I'm a vegetarian."

The waiter informed him that the ship didn't have a special vegetarian kitchen and suggested he join the kosher table. Singer explained that being kosher wasn't the same as being vegetarian. After overhearing his conversation with the waiter, the people at the surrounding tables started asking Singer questions in French, English, and German. Why was he a vegetarian? For health reasons? Doctors' orders? Did it have to do with his religion? Some of the men seemed annoyed that such a controversial subject had been introduced at mealtime. "They had come here to enjoy themselves, not to philosophize about the anguish of animals and fish. I tried in my mangled German to explain to them that my vegetarianism was based on no religion but simply on the feeling that one creature lacked the right to rob another creature of its life and devour it."

The other diners then proceeded to ignore him. "I don't know to this day if it was my vegetarianism that put them into a hostile mood or the fact that I chose to sit alone." The "vegetarian" meal that the waiter brought him consisted mostly of leftovers—stale bread, a chunk of cheese, an onion, and a carrot. When Singer realized the other diners wanted nothing to do with him ("I had committed the sin of isolating myself from others, and I had been excommunicated"), he decided to forego the dining room and eat alone in his cabin.[17]

One night he ventured below deck to a concert in the ship's salon. Standing at the door and watching the large crowd enjoying themselves, he felt like an outsider. "There had been a time when I envied those who took part in such recreations. I regretted the fact that I couldn't dance. But this urge evaporated within me. There reposed in me an ascetic who reminded me constantly of death and that others suffered in hospitals, in prisons, or were tortured by various political sadists. Only a few years ago millions of Russian peasants had starved to death just because Stalin decided to establish collectives. I could never forget the cruelties perpetrated upon God's creatures in slaughterhouses, on hunts, and in various scientific laboratories."[18]

In America, when Singer visited an upstate Yiddishist colony where socialist, anarchist, and Freudian followers discussed "ready-made remedies for all the world's ills," he was surprised and disappointed that "no one in the colony considered the evils perpetrated daily upon God's creatures by the millions of hunters, vivisectionists, and butchers."[19] Later, in a cafeteria in New York City, as he read newspaper stories about assorted "human idiosyncrasies and quirks," he thought, "A combination of a slaughterhouse, a bordello, and an insane asylum—that's what the world really was."[20]

A Horrid Form of Amusement

Hunting was as repulsive to Singer as slaughtering animals and eating them. Not long after his arrival in America, when he saw a painting of mounted hunters with a pack of hounds, he thought, "What a horrid form of amusement! First they go to church and sing hymns to Jesus, then they chase after some starving fox."

In *The Estate*, his novel set in late nineteenth-century Poland, Singer describes a Jewish dress ball at the Topolka estate irreverently held on the eve of the Ninth of Ab, a date sacred to Jewish memory because it commemorates the destruction of the Jerusalem temple. The Jewish and Gentile guests arrive early so they can hunt in a squire's forest nearby. Later, when they return to the estate "with their booty: several rabbits, a pheasant, a few wild ducks," they add them to the animals already butchered for the feast, including the pig roasting on a spit, an especially jarring desecration of the holy day. An old cow with a shrunken udder has also been slaughtered for the occasion, and the poultry population of Topolka has suffered "almost complete decimation." Preparations for the feast produce a vivid scene: "The garbage trench behind the kitchen was full of bloody heads, feet, wings, and innards of fowl and attracted hordes of flies."[21]

The Slave, another Singer novel set in Poland, links hunting to greed, gluttony, and cruelty. When Jacob enters the castle of the Pilitzkys, he is struck by the vast array of weapons and mounted animals. "Everywhere were trophies of the hunt: stags' and boars' heads staring down from the walls; stuffed pheasants, peacocks, partridges, and grouse, looking as if they were alive." The castle armory is full of swords, spears, helmets, and breastplates. Everywhere Jacob turns he sees crosses, swords, nude statuary, and paintings of battles, tournaments, and the chase. "The very air of the castle smelled of violence, idolatry, and concupiscence."[22]

At the end of Singer's posthumously published novel *Shadows on the Hudson,* the main character writes a letter from Israel in which he associates hunting with the seeds of fascism. "As long as the other nations continue going to church in the morning and hunting in the afternoon, they will remain unbridled beasts and will go on producing Hitlers and other monstrosities."[23] Singer says he was astonished to read about "highly sensitive poets, preachers of morality, humanists, and do-gooders of all kinds who found pleasure in hunting—chasing after some poor, weak hare or fox and teaching dogs to do likewise." He was also dismayed by people who said they wanted to go fishing when they retire, believing that fishing was a harmless pursuit that will launch a new period of peace and tranquility in their lives. "It never occurs to them for a moment that innocent beings will suffer and die from this innocent little sport."[24]

While still relatively new to America, Singer went into a cafeteria on 23rd Street in New York City where he read news stories in a newspaper somebody had left on a table. He imagined things he would do to change the world if he had the power. "I was taking revenge for Dachau and Zbonshin. I gave back the Sudetenland to the Czechs. I founded a Jewish state in Jerusalem. Since I was the ruler of the world, I forbade forever the eating of meat and fish and made hunting illegal."[25]

Satan and Slaughter

Singer's horror at the killing of animals is clearly evident in the slaughter scenes in his first novel, *Satan in Goray.*[26] The scenes revolve around the novel's two ritual slaughterers—Reb Zeydel Ber, the uncle of the novel's main female character, and Reb Gedaliya, who assumes the messianic leadership in Goray in the last half of the novel.

Reb Zeydel Ber does his slaughtering in a courtyard where there is always a wooden bucket full of blood and where feathers constantly fly about, as butcher boys in red-spattered jackets move about with knives, shouting coarsely. Slaughtered chickens throw themselves about on the blood-soaked earth, furiously flapping their pent wings, as if trying to fly off. Doomed calves writhe on the ground in their final moments, until their eyes glaze and life ebbs from them.[27]

When Reb Gadeliya becomes Goray's ritual slaughterer, the people welcome his arrival since "beasts and fowls could be purchased cheaply in the nearby villages, and all the people of Goray longed for meat." After Reb Gedaliya requests that no expense be spared for the approaching Passover, which he promises will be the final one before redemption, Goray fills with "a great abundance of beasts and fowls." From early morning until late at night, Reb Gadeliya stands in front of a blood-filled pit and tirelessly cuts with his long butcher's knife into warm, distended necks, "slaughtering innumerable calves and sheep, hens, geese, and ducks." As he does his slaughtering in the courtyard, he is surrounded by a tumultuous throng of women and girls with their raised hands clutching pent fowl. "Wings fluttered and beat, blood spurted, smearing faces and dresses." Reb Gedaliya joked constantly, "for he hated sadness, and his way of serving God was through joy."

The people of Goray cannot remember a time when meat was so plentiful, as early each evening butcher boys drive herds of calves, sheep, and goats to the slaughterhouse where Reb Gedaliya rushes about with his knife, "expertly slashing at the shaven necks, and recoiling from the spatter of blood" and the butchers chop off the heads of still breathing animals, "dexterously stripping hides, tearing bodies open, and dragging out red satin lungs, half-empty stomachs, and intestines." They blow through the windpipe of the slain animal to inflate the lungs and slap the distended organs and spit into the flaps to see if there are any vents that would make the animal unclean. Reb Gedaliya stands in the middle with his knife, urging the butchers to finish their examination, shouting "Hurry! It's clean! It's clean!"

In Singer's work this craving for flesh symbolizes corruption and the close relationship between violence against animals and violence against people. As the critic Clive Sinclair writes, "there is a clear connection in *Satan in Goray* between the atrocities perpetuated by Chmielnicki's warriors and the work of butchers, represented by Reb Gedaliya and Reb Zeydel Ber."[28]

A Lust for Flesh

Singer's short story "Blood," set in rural Poland, is about an adulterous affair between Risha, who manages the large estate of Reb Falik, her elderly husband, and Reuben, the ritual slaughterer she hires after she convinces her husband they should raise cattle and open a butcher shop in the nearby village of Laskev.[29] Risha builds a slaughtering shed on the estate for Reuben, buys him fine clothes, and sets him up in an apartment in the main house so that he can eat his meals at Reb Falik's table.

Reuben does most of his slaughtering at night after Reb Falik retires, so that he and Risha can be alone together in the shed. "Sometimes she gave herself to him immediately after the slaughtering." Whether they make love on a pile of straw in the shed or on the grass just outside, "the thought of the dead and dying creatures near them whetted their enjoyment." Soon when Risha joins in the slaughtering, she takes such pleasure in it that she ends up doing it all herself.

The Laskev butchers, who have been forced out of business by Risha's success, enlist a young man to spy on her, so one night he goes to Reb Falik's estate and watches through a large crack in the wall of the slaughtering shed. He sees Risha take off all her clothes and stretch out on a pile of straw in the middle of animals bleeding to death. By now the lovers have become so fat that their bodies can barely join. "They puffed and panted. Their wheezing mixed with the death-rattles of the animals made an unearthly noise."

When the young man returns to Laskev and reports what he has seen, an angry crowd armed with bludgeons, knives, and ropes heads for the estate. When Reuben runs away, Risha decides he is a coward ("He was only a hero against a weak chicken and a tethered ox."). After Risha mobilizes the peasants on the estate to defend her against the mob, which returns to Laskev, Risha goes to the study house where Reb Falik is reciting the Mishna in his prayer shawl and phylacteries. When he sees Risha with a knife, he drops dead.

Risha converts to Catholicism, reopens her shops, and sells non-kosher meats to the Gentiles of Laskev and the peasants in surrounding villages who come to town on market days. At night she mumbles to herself and sings songs in Yiddish and Polish with meaningless phrases, "uttering sounds that resembled the cackling of fowl, the grunting of pigs, the death-rattles of oxen." In her dreams the animals get some small measure of revenge: bulls gore her with their horns; pigs shove their snouts into her face and bite her; roosters cut her flesh to ribbons with their spurs.

Singer's powerful indictment of religiously sanctioned slaughter ends several winters later when the people of Laskev are "terrified by a carnivorous animal lurking about at night and attacking people." When they finally catch and kill the mysterious beast, they discover to their amazement that the animal is Risha. "She lay dead in a skunk fur coat wet with blood....It was now clear that Risha had become a werewolf."

Meat and Madness

Another strong indictment of religiously sanctioned slaughter—"The Slaughterer"—is about the mental anguish of Yoineh Meir, a young rabbi who becomes the village slaughterer.[30] When the elders of Kolomir choose him, he protests ("He was soft-hearted; he could not bear the sight of blood"), but the elders, his wife, his father-in-law, and the new rabbi pressure him to accept the position.

The work is pure torture for him. Killing each animal "caused him as much pain as though he were cutting his own throat. Of all the punishments that could have been visited on him, slaughtering was the worst." Constantly immersed in blood and guts, Yoineh Meir becomes depressed and inconsolable. His ears are beset "by the squawking of hens, the crowing of roosters, the gobbling of geese, the lowing of oxen, the mooing and bleating of calves and goats; wings fluttered, claws tapped on the floor. The bodies refused to know any justification or excuse—every body resisted in its own fashion, tried to escape, and seemed to argue with the Creator to its last breath."

Yoineh Meir turns to the study of the Cabala to try to escape to where there was "no death, no slaughtering, no pain, no stomachs and intestines, no hearts or lungs or livers, no membranes, and no impurities," but the smell of slaughtered animals never leaves his nostrils. Even in bed at night, he's aware he is lying on feathers and down plucked from fowl.

Elul, a month of repentence which had once been a source of spiritual renewal for him, now becomes a burden. In every courtyard "cocks crowed and hens cackled, and all of them had to be put to death." The holidays that follow—the Feast of Booths, the Day of the Willow Twigs, the Feast of Azereth, the Day of Rejoicing in the Law, the Sabbath of Genesis—bring no relief. "Each holiday brings its own slaughter. Millions of fowl and cattle now alive were doomed to be killed."

Yoineh Meir has nightmares in which cows assume human shape, with beards and sidelocks, and skullcaps over their horns. In one dream the calf he slaughters turns into a girl. "Her neck throbbed, and she pleaded to be saved. She ran into the study house and spattered the courtyard with her blood." He even dreams he slaughters his wife instead of a sheep. In another dream, a goat, cursing in Hebrew and Aramaic, spits and foams at him, then jumps on top of him and tries to butt him. He wakes up in a sweat and gets out of bed to recite the midnight prayer, but his lips cannot utter the holy words. "How could he mourn the destruction of the Temple when a carnage was being readied here in Kolomir, and he, Yoineh Meir, was the Titus, the Nebuchadnezzar!"

Yoineh Meir becomes acutely conscious of the animals around him. He hears the scratching of a mouse and the chirping of a cricket. It seemed to him that "he could hear the worms burrowing through the ceiling and the floor. Innumerable creatures surrounded man, each with its own nature, its own claims on the Creator." A love wells up inside him "for all that crawls and flies, breeds and swarms. Even the mice—was it their fault that they were mice? What wrong does a mouse do? All it wants is a crumb of bread or a piece of cheese." He asks himself, how can one pray for life for the coming year, or for a favorable writ in

Heaven when one is robbing others of the breath of life? He sees no way the Messiah can redeem the world as long as this injustice continues to be done to animals. He thinks, "When you slaughter a creature, you slaughter God."

As Yoineh Meir stands at the pit all day, slaughtering hens, roosters, geese, and ducks, and the pit fills with blood, he wonders if he's losing his mind. "Feathers flew, the yard was full of quacking, gabbling, the screaming of roosters. Now and then, a fowl cried out like a human being."

That night Yoineh Meir wakes from a nightmare bathed in sweat. "I'll have none of your favors, God!" he shouts. "I am no longer afraid of your Judgment! I have more compassion than God Almighty—more, more! He is a cruel God, a Man of War, a God of Vengeance. I will not serve Him. It is an abandoned world!" He goes to the pantry and collects his knives and whetstone—his "instruments of death"—and takes them to the outhouse, where he throws them into the pit, knowing full well that he's blaspheming and desecrating the holy instruments. He is mad, but he no longer wishes to be sane. He sheds his prayer shawl and phylacteries. "The parchment was taken from the hide of a cow. The cases of the phylacteries were made of calf's leather. The Torah itself was made of animal skin."

Yoineh Meir heads toward the river, shouting defiantly. "Father in Heaven, Thou art a slaughterer! Thou art a slaughterer and the Angel of Death! The whole world is a slaughterhouse!" With each stride he feels more and more rebellious. "He had opened a door to his brain, and madness flowed in, flooding everything." He throws away his skullcap, rips off his prayer fringes, and tears off pieces of his vest, feeling the recklessness of somebody who has cast away all his burdens.

The butchers, hearing Yoineh Meir has gone mad, chase after him. As he runs toward the river, he imagines he's running into a bloody swamp: "Blood ran from the sun, staining the tree trunks. From the branches hung intestines, livers, kidneys. The forequarters of beasts rose to their feet and sprayed him with gall and slime." He knows he cannot escape. "Myriads of cows and fowls encircled him, ready to take revenge for every cut, every wound, every slit gullet, every plucked feather. With bleeding throats, they all chanted, 'Everyone may kill, and every killing is permitted.'" Yoineh Meir breaks into a wail that echoes through the woods. He raises his fist to God and shouts, "Fiend! Murderer! Devouring beast!"

Two days later they find Yoineh Meir's body in the river downstream near the dam. Since many witnesses testify that he acted like a madman in his final moments, the rabbi rules that his death was not a suicide, a ruling that allows Yoineh Meir to be buried next to the graves of his father and grandfather. The story ends on a bitterly ironic note: "Because it was the holiday season and there was danger that Kolomir might remain without meat, the community hastily dispatched two messengers to bring a new slaughterer."

Holy Creature

"The Letter Writer," the story in which Singer describes what animals suffer as an "eternal Treblinka," is about Herman Gombiner, who lost his entire family to the Nazis.[31] He is an editor, proofreader, and translator at a Hebrew publishing house in New York City, and he lives alone in a small uptown apartment crammed with books, newspapers, and magazines. For companionship, Herman corresponds with people who write letters to a periodical about occult matters to which he subscribes.

Each day Herman sets out a piece of bread, a small slice of cheese, and a saucer of water for a mouse who comes out of her hole at night, sometimes even when the light is on. "Her little bubble eyes stared at him with curiosity. She stopped being afraid of him." Herman gives her the Hebrew name of Huldah. Each morning before he goes to work, Herman pours out the stale water from the night before, refills the saucer, and puts out a cracker and small piece of cheese. Before he leaves, he says, "Well, Huldah, be well!"

After the publishing house closes and Herman loses his job, he gladly spends his first day of unemployment at home with his books. When twilight comes, he worries about Huldah until he hears a squeak and sees her come out of her hole and look cautiously around. Herman holds his breath. "Holy creature, have no fear," he thinks. "No harm will come to you." She approaches the saucer of water, takes one sip, then a second and a third. As she slowly starts gnawing on the piece of cheese, Herman marvels at her—"a daughter of a mouse, a granddaughter of mice, a product of millions, billions of mice who once lived, suffered, reproduced, and are now gone forever....She is just as much a part of God's creation as the planets, the stars, the distant galaxies." When Huldah raises her head and stares at him "with a human look of love and gratitude," Herman imagines she is saying thank you.

Herman grows weaker through the winter, but he manages to keep sending and receiving letters with the help of a woman on his floor who collects his mail and slips it under his door and who also mails his letters for him. Sometimes he thinks about the ways the dead continue to be present in the lives of the living and imagines that his relatives must be still living somewhere. He prays for them to appear to him. "The spirit cannot be burned, gassed, hanged, shot. Six million souls must exist somewhere."

As it becomes more difficult for Herman to get out of bed, he worries about what will happen to Huldah. One night when he remembers that she has gone without food and water, he tries to get out of bed, but he can't move. He prays to God: "I don't need help any more, but don't let that poor creature die of hunger!"

Herman is close to death with pneumonia when a lady by the name of Rose Beechman, with whom he has been corresponding, suddenly shows up. She was planning to come to New York in two weeks anyway, but her deceased grandmother contacted her from beyond the grave to alert her that Herman was deathly ill and that she should go to him immediately. She stays in his apartment and sleeps on a cot so she can nurse Herman back to health.

As Herman begins to recover, he remembers the mouse. "What had become of Huldah? How awful that throughout his long illness he had entirely forgotten her. No one had fed her or given her anything to drink. 'She is surely dead,' he says to himself." In despair, he prays for her: "Well, you've had your life. You've served your time in this forsaken world, the worst of all worlds, this bottomless abyss, where Satan, Asmodeus, Hitler, and Stalin prevail." Herman consoles himself that Huldah is no longer hungry, thirsty, or sick, but is at one with God. In a mental whisper he speaks a eulogy for the mouse who had shared a portion of her life with him and who, because of him, had left this earth.

> What do they know—all these scholars, all these philosophers, all the leaders of the world—about such as you? They have convinced themselves that man, the worst transgressor of all the species, is the crown of creation. All other creatures were created merely to provide him with food, pelts, to be tormented, exterminated. In relation to them, all people are Nazis; for the animals it is an eternal Treblinka.

Herman tells Rose Beechman about the mouse and asks her to pour some milk in a dish just in case she is still alive. Later, when Herman hears a noise, he sits up. "God in Heaven! Huldah is alive! There she stands, drinking milk from the dish!" A joy he had hardly ever known grips Herman and fills him with gratitude. He feels love for Huldah and for the woman, Rose Beechman, who understood his feelings and gave Huldah some milk. "I am not worthy, I am not worthy," he mutters. "It is all pure Grace."

Herman had not even cried when he received the news that his family had perished in the destruction of Kalomin, "but now his face became wet and hot. Providence—aware of every molecule, every mite, every speck of dust—had seen to it that the mouse received its nourishment during his long sleep." Herman watches Huldah lap the milk slowly, pausing occasionally, sure in the knowledge nobody would take away what was rightfully hers. Herman calls to her silently in his thoughts, "Little mouse, hallowed creature, saint!" and blows her a kiss. Huldah continues to drink, occasionally cocking her head and glancing at Herman. When she finishes, she goes back to her hole. The story ends with the first rays of a new day making the windowpanes rosy and bathing Herman's books in a purplish light. "It all had the quality of a revelation."

Vegetarian Protest

Singer, who became a vegetarian permanently in 1962, often said that not eating meat and fish was his protest against the way men treated God's creatures. "For years I had wanted to become a vegetarian. I didn't see how we could speak about mercy and ask for mercy and talk about humanism and against bloodshed when we shed blood ourselves—the blood of animals and innocent creatures."[32] In his novels and stories, most of the main characters either are vegetarians, become vegetarians, or think about becoming vegetarians, with the Holocaust parallel always in the foreground.

Joseph Shapiro, the protagonist of *The Penitent*, is a secular New York Jew who becomes a vegetarian as part of the transformation that leads him to become an Orthodox Jew in Jerusalem.[33] The novel opens in 1969 at the Western Wall in Jerusalem where Joseph, with a beard and earlocks and dressed in long gaberdine and a velvet hat in the manner of the Orthodox, introduces himself to the narrator. Joseph has renounced the modern world and the secular life of modern Jewry and now lives in Mea Shearim, the ultra-Orthodox section of Jerusalem. He has a wife and three children and attends a yeshiva where he studies Torah. The day after Joseph meets the narrator at the Western Wall, he goes to the narrator's hotel and tells him his story.

Joseph, a descendent of rabbis in Poland, survived the war by fleeing the Nazis and wandering through Russia. After the war he returned to Poland and married his former girlfriend, Celia. They move to New York where Joseph prospers, but after he gets bored with Celia, he takes a divorcée named Liza as his mistress. One night, when he comes home early from Liza's, he finds his wife in bed with another man. Joseph goes to a Hasidic prayer house on the Lower East Side where he decides to turn his life completely around. Without even bothering to go home for his clothes, he boards a plane for Israel, where he is eventually taken in by a Hasidic family in Mea Shearim. He obtains a divorce from Celia and marries the young, shy daughter of his Hasidic host.

Joseph's decision to stop eating meat is one of the central themes of the novel. Early in the story when Joseph goes into a New York restaurant to eat breakfast, he sees someone at the next table eating ham and eggs. He thinks that "in order for this over-stuffed individual to enjoy his ham, a living creature had to be raised, dragged to its death, stabbed, tortured, scalded in hot water." Joseph had already come to the conclusion that "man's treatment of God's creatures makes mockery of all his ideals and of the whole alleged humanism." He thinks about the man enjoying his ham without the slightest concern that "the pig was made of the same stuff as he and that it had to pay with suffering and death so that he could taste its flesh. I've thought more than once that when it comes to animals, every man is a Nazi."

Joseph remembers the time he bought his mistress, Liza, a fur coat made from the skins of dozens of animals and "with what rapture and enthusiasm she stroked the fur of those butchered animals. How she poured out praises for skins torn from the bodies of others!" Joseph tells the narrator, "Everything that had to do with slaughtering, skinning, and hunting always evoked disgust within me and guilt feelings that words cannot describe."

Joseph also tells him about how both his wife and his mistress loved to watch gangster movies and laughed when the gangsters shot and stabbed each other. "I myself used to suffer terribly during those scenes. Violence and bloodshed have always made me shudder." He says they both also loved lobster. "I knew that a lobster is cooked alive in boiling water. But these supposedly delicate ladies didn't care that because of them a living creature was being murdered in a most horrible fashion."

Although Joseph had often thought about these things, he says that morning in the restaurant they hit him on the head like a hammer. He realized that in his business and personal life he had been deceiving others and himself and that living such a false life went against his deepest convictions. "I was myself a liar, but I hated lies and deceit of every kind.

I was a lecher, but I felt a revulsion against loose women and against wantonness in general. I ate meat, but a shudder ran through me each time I reminded myself how meat becomes meat. That morning I realized for the first time what a horrible hypocrite I was."

That day Joseph makes his first major, life-changing decision, which "had no direct bearing on religion, but to me it represented a religious decision." He vows to eat no more meat or fish, nothing that had ever lived and been killed. "I am absolutely convinced that so long as people shed the blood of God's creatures, there'll be no peace on earth. It's one step from spilling animal blood to spilling human blood."

Joseph's vegetarian commitment makes him something of a misfit among his new Orthodox brethren. They tell him the same thing his father did: "You must not pity creatures more than the Almighty does." Later, when his Hasidic host learns that Joseph doesn't eat fish or meat, even on the Sabbath, he is shocked. But Joseph holds his ground. "I was determined to live the way I wanted and the way I understood. If this meant that I had to alienate myself from all people, it would be no tragedy either. If one was strong, one could endure this as well." Joseph tells the narrator, "For me, thou shalt not kill includes animals, too." Since he was able to persuade his new wife to agree with his way of thinking, "we are a family of vegetarians."[34]

In the "Author's Note" that follows *The Penitent*, Singer writes that the major difference between himself and Joseph Shapiro is that he has not made peace with the cruelty of life and the violence of man's history. "Joseph Shapiro may have done so, but I haven't. I'm still as bewildered and shocked by the misery and brutality of life as I was as a six-year-old child, when my mother read to me the tales of war in the Book of Joshua, and the bloodcurdling stories of the destruction of Jerusalem."[35]

Treblinka Was Everywhere

Singer's observation that "every man is a Nazi" when it comes to animals is also found in *Enemies, A Love Story*, his first novel set in America.[36] Its protagonist, Herman Broder, is another Singer character who has lost his entire family in the Holocaust and sees the reality of might makes right triumphant all around him. The focus of the novel is Herman's struggle to cope with the complications of having three wives: Yadwiga, the Polish peasant who hid him from the Germans; Masha, his troubled mistress, also a survivor, whom he later marries secretly; and Tamara, his first wife who reappears in New York after it had been assumed she had been killed by the Nazis.

Herman lives with Yadwiga in Brooklyn, but he also rents a small room in the same Bronx building where Masha lives with her mother. The room has holes in the floor, and at night one can hear the mice scratching. Masha sets traps, "but the sound of the trapped creatures in agony was too much for Herman. He would get up in the middle of the night and free them."

When Masha takes Herman to the Bronx Zoo, he sees it as a depressing prison. The eyes of the lion "expressed the despondency of those who are allowed neither to live nor to die" and the wolf "paced to and fro, circling his own madness." To Herman, the zoo is a concentration camp. "The air here was full of longing—for deserts, hills, valleys, dens, families. Like the Jews, the animals had been dragged here from all parts of the world, condemned to isolation and boredom." Some of the animals cry out their woes, while others remain silent. "Parrots demanded their rights with raucous screeching. A bird with a banana-shaped beak turned its head from right to left as if looking for the culprit who had played this trick on him."

When Herman takes a trip to upstate New York with Masha, he thinks he can hear the screeching of chickens and ducks. "Somewhere on this lovely summer morning, fowl were being slaughtered; Treblinka was everywhere." When flies, bees, and butterflies fly in through the window of their bungalow, Herman refuses to take action. "To Herman these were not parasites to be driven away; he saw in each of these creatures the manifestations of the eternal will to live, experience, comprehend."[37]

Early one morning in Brooklyn, when Herman sees a sunlit bay "filled with boats, many of them just returned from early-dawn trips to the open sea," he thinks about the fish who had been swimming in the water only a few hours before, but now lay on the boat decks "with glassy eyes, wounded mouths, bloodstained scales. The fishermen, well-to-do sportsmen, were weighing the fish and boasting about their catches."[38] It reminds him of the same Nazi mind-set that killed his family. "As often as Herman had witnessed the slaughter of animals and fish, he always had the same thought: in their behavior toward creatures, all men were Nazis. The smugness with which man could do with other species as he pleased exemplified the most extreme racist theories, the principle that might is right."

When Herman spends the day and night before Yom Kippur eve at Masha's house, her mother buys two sacrificial hens for the ceremony of Kapparot, one for herself and one for Masha. The custom, which symbolically transfers one's sins to a fowl, requires the penitent to swing a live hen (for a female) or a rooster (for a male) by the legs in a circle above the head three times, while speaking the following words: "This is my exchange, my substitute, my atonement; this hen (or rooster) shall go to its death, but I shall go to a good, long life, and to peace."[39]

Masha's mother wants to buy a rooster for Herman, but he refuses. "For some time now he had been thinking of becoming a vegetarian. At every opportunity, he pointed out that what the Nazis had done to the Jews, man was doing to the animals." As he looks at the two captive hens, one white, one brown, lying on the floor, "their feet bound, their golden eyes looking sideways," he objects to the hypocrisy of killing hens for Yom Kippur. "How could fowl be used to redeem the sins of a human being? Why should a compassionate God accept such a sacrifice?" When Masha agrees with him and refuses take the hens to the ritual slaughterer, her mother takes them instead.[40]

Late in the novel when Herman finds himself reluctantly presiding at a Passover seder, he thinks again about the injustice and hypocrisy of it all: "A fish from the Hudson River or some lake had paid with its life so that Herman, Tamara, and Yadwiga should be reminded of the miracles of the exodus from Egypt. A chicken had donated its neck to the commemoration of the Passover sacrifice."

They Too Are God's Children

Singer's aversion to the slaughter and eating of animals is also present in *Shadows on the Hudson*.[41] Early in the novel, set in New York after World War II, Anna passes a fish store where fish with "bloodstained scales and glassy eyes" are put out on ice. Nearby a meat truck is parked outside a butcher shop where "big-bellied men carted raw sides of beef atop their heads. In the window, among the bloody chunks of meat, hung a whole lamb, its belly slashed open from neck to tail." Anna thinks this could happen to anyone. "They might easily have displayed me in the same way."

Henrietta Clark and her companion, Professor Shrage, eat "cheese, nuts, fruit, vegetables, and all sorts of cereals and crackers" purchased from a health food store. Henrietta wonders, "How could one hope for God's grace when one helped to kill the living and deprived souls of their bodies?" Believing one should stop eating cheese, milk, and eggs as well, she regards herself "as no more than a semi-vegetarian, because indirectly she was assisting the ritual slaughterers, the butchers."

When the novel's central character, Hertz Dovid Grein, enters a cafeteria and sees the cook bring out a roasting pan of meat from the kitchen, he thinks, "What about the creatures whose flesh he's carrying in here? A few days ago they were alive. They too have souls. They too are God's children. They were quite possibly made of better material than human beings. Since they were sinless, they were certainly more innocent. But day after day they are ritually sacrificed—angels in the shape of oxen, calves, sheep."

Later Grein enters a synogogue and puts on a prayer shawl and phylacteries the way his father used to do in Poland. He reads in the liturgy the Bible passage about the consecration of the firstborn of all creatures, which ends, "But every firstling of an ass thou shalt redeem with a lamb, and if thou wilt not redeem it, then thou shalt break its neck." Like so many of Singer's characters, Grein questions this religiously sanctioned cruelty: "In what way is the ass guilty? Why does it deserve to have its neck broken? How could God issue such commands?"

When Grein recites the part of the liturgy that says, "The Lord is good to all, and His mercy is over all He has created," he asks himself if that's really true. "Was God really good at all? Had He been good to the six million Jews in Europe? Was He good to all the oxen and pigs and chickens that people were slaughtering at this very moment? Could anyone really call such a God good?"

Concluding that the essence of Judaism is that "people should live in such a way that they did not build their happiness on the misfortune of others," Grein decides to do what other Singer characters do—return to God by making a vow to stop eating meat and fish. "How could one serve God when one butchered God's creatures? How could one expect mercy from heaven when one spilled blood every day, dragged God's creatures to the slaughterhouse, caused them terrible suffering, shortened their days and years? How could one ask compassion of God when one plucked a fish from the river and looked on while it suffocated, jerking on the hook?"

Grein decides that even consuming milk and eggs is killing cattle and birds because "one could get milk only by destroying the calves for which the milk was intended, and the chicken farmers sooner or later sold the fowl to the butcher." He thinks, "One could easily exist on fruit, vegetables, bread, cereals, oil—the products of the earth." He wonders how he can continue to wear leather shoes and woolen clothes. "They sheared the sheep only until they slaughtered them." And what about sleeping at night? "The mattress contained horsehair, the pillows were stuffed with feathers. Whatever one touched was made of some other creature's flesh, hide, hair, bones."

Grein questions God's ways: "Since God hated bloodshed, why had He created a world founded on murder? Could one keep the commandment 'Thou shalt not kill' and still wage wars? Could one apply that commandment only to people and not to animals?" Another character in the novel remarks, "I knew that the earth with all its green mountains and fertile valleys was nothing but a slaughterhouse. You want to flee to God, but God Himself is the worst murderer."

Toward the end of the novel, Anna is home alone in bed when she remembers a report "she had read in a Yiddish newspaper describing the great number of Jews whom the Romanian Nazis had driven into a slaughterhouse and butchered there."[42] She thinks, "Yes, such savagery *had* been perpetrated in this world, and whatever the future might bring, the record of these events would remain in perpetuity. No power could ever erase the appalling disgrace—not even God."

Affection for Animals

Although Singer was shy and quiet during his first years in America, his nephew Joseph remembers him as a playful man who often entertained him by running through the house, barking like a dog or quacking like a duck. "The whole family shares a tremendous love of animals," says Joseph. "Isaac is maybe a little nervous about them, but he really loves them."[43] In *The Family Moskat* Reb Dan is waiting at an inn to continue his journey with his family when he sees a goat in the courtyard. As the goat stares back at him, Reb Dan suddenly feels "a rush of affection for the creature....He felt like caressing the poor beast or giving it some tasty tidbit."[44]

In Singer's story "The Yearning Heifer" a young Yiddish writer from New York City, who rents a room for the summer on a farm upstate, urges the farmer to return a cow who is bellowing unhappily.[45] The farmer explains she is from a stable where there were thirty other cows and she misses them. "She most probably has a mother or a sister there." The writer goes with the farmer when he returns the cow to farmer from whom he bought her. Another story "Brother Beetle" is about an encounter with a beetle ("'Brother Beetle,' I muttered, 'what do they want of us?'").[46]

The rooster narrator of "Cockadoodledoo" tells the story of the rooster call.[47] Although roosters end up getting slaughtered ("the garbage dump is crammed with our heads and entrails"), the narrator promises that the rooster call will never be silenced: "The rooster may die but not the cockadoodledoo. We were crowing long before Adam and, God willing, we'll go on crowing long after all slaughterers and chicken-gluttons have been laid low. No butcher in the world can destroy that."

Singer was especially fond of birds. In *The Certificate*, when the young narrator visits an apartment in Warsaw, he meets a parrot perched on top of a large cage. "All at once the parrot, in what sounded very like a man's voice, said, 'Parrot monkey.' For some reason this moved me. Good Lord, I had no idea I had so much affection for birds."[48] "The Parrot" is about a man whose affection for his pet parrot lands him in prison after he throws his woman companion down a well for continually abusing his parrot and driving him out into a winter storm.[49] The narrator of *Shosha* dreams that, as he is strolling with Shosha in a forest, he encounters birds who are different from any he had ever known. "They were as big as eagles, as colorful as parrots. They spoke Yiddish."[50]

Singer's love affair with parakeets began in New York City in the 1950s on the day a yellow parakeet suddenly flew into his apartment. Dorothea Straus, the wife of Singer's publisher, described what happened: "One summer morning, as he was sitting at the kitchen table by the window open to the courtyard, he wished for a companion. Immediately, as if in answer, a parakeet flew inside. 'As soon as I saw him, I knew we would be friends. God had sent him to me. He was an old soul.'"[51] Singer named him Matzoth and went to a pet shop and bought him a female companion. He kept the door of their cage open so they could fly freely around his apartment. As Singer's biographer writes, "These birds loved each other and loved Isaac, and he loved them. They would sit on his head or his knee and coo. He would speak soft words to them in Yiddish or English."[52]

In *Enemies: A Love Story*, Herman buys Yadwiga two parakeets, a yellow male and blue female, whom she names Woytus and Marianna after her father and sister. Herman is fascinated by the way the pair communicates: "Woytus and Marianna seemed to have a language inherited from generations of parakeets. They obviously carried on conversations, and the way they would take flight together in the same direction, within a fraction of a second, indicated that they knew one another's thoughts."[53] One day when Herman is in the kitchen, he notices that "Woytus was delivering an avian lecture to Marianna, who was perched near him on the stand. Her head was bowed guiltily, as if she were being reprimanded for some inexcusable misdeed." When Woytus whistles and trills, Herman thinks "he was surely serenading Marianna, who rarely sang at all, but groomed herself all day plucking at the down under her wings." When the radio plays a song from a Yiddish operetta, the parakeets react "in their own fashion. They screeched, whistled, tweeted, and flew around the room."

When *Newsweek* reporters went to Singer's apartment in 1978 to interview him after it was announced he was to be awarded the Nobel Prize in Literature, Singer told them about his parakeets in the next room.[54] "Go in and you will see that they fly around. I have a great love of animals, and I feel that in them and from them we can learn a lot about the mysteries of the world because they are nearer to them than we are."

Singer's experience with parakeets came to a bad end the day the maid left a window open accidently and Matzoth flew out. Singer was disconsolate. He spent hours looking for Matzoth along Riverside Drive and in Central Park. He put ads in the newspapers and followed up on every answer, but he never got Matzoth back. Singer bought the female parakeet another mate, whom he called Matzi II, but the new parakeet accidently drowned in a vase of water. "They were a lot of joy," he said, "but they were also much trouble. I suffered so much when they suffered, when they got sick, got lost, or fell down, that in a way I am happy I don't have them anymore."[55]

After the parakeets, Singer spent more time feeding pigeons. Dorothea Straus wrote that he became "a familiar sight on upper Broadway, scattering grain, in the company of a congregation of bedraggled city pigeons."[56] He would feed them out of a brown paper grocery bag that contained seed he purchased in local stores. "The moment I come out with a bag of feed," Singer said, "they begin to fly toward me from blocks away."[57] Dorothea Straus described the scene:

"The birds cluster near him without fear, and he watches their minute flutterings and peckings with something close to love in his large, blue eyes. Only God knows what these creatures are feeling, he says to himself. The pigeons have found a friend, and Isaac Singer, in their midst, is not alone."[58]

Singer's longtime assistant, Dvorah Telushkin, writes that often on their work breaks Singer would get his bag of feed and they would go to Riverside Park. "Feeding the pigeons was an important ritual in Isaac's work."[59] She described one of the outings: "Isaac sat, bent way over the edge of a bench as he scattered seeds on the ground. The pigeons gathered near his feet, pecking vigorously as he looked on in silence. He threw a couple of handfuls toward a little sparrow and watched carefully as the tiny creature ate. 'This one to the left,' he suddenly said, sitting up. 'I am interested in this small one. The larger ones grab it all for themselves.'"[60] Always alert to those who were vulnerable, whatever the species, Singer had a special interest in cripples, giants, and other people society considered "freaks." "I cannot help it," he told Telushkin. "To me these are the real people. Frightened souls which no one sees."[61]

In *Enemies, A Love Story*, as Herman is walking through the snow drifts along Mermaid Avenue in Brooklyn, he sees a dead pigeon. "Well, holy creature, you've already lived your life," he thinks, and once again he questions God. "Why did you create her, if this was to be her end? How long will you be silent, Almighty sadist?"[62]

The Shadow of Imminent Destruction

Both parakeets and pigeons figure in "Pigeons," a story set in Warsaw in the 1930s that foreshadows the Holocaust.[63] The story opens: "When his wife died, Professor Vladislav Eibeschutz had only his books and birds left." Besides the books and manuscripts that he keeps in closets and trunks and on the floor-to-ceiling bookshelves of his library, the professor has about a dozen bird cages for parrots, parakeets, and canaries. Like Singer, the professor loves his birds and leaves their cage doors open so they can fly around freely. When Tekla, his half-blind Polish maid, complains about having to clean up after them, the professor tells her,

"Everything that belongs to God's creatures is clean." In his apartment the canaries sing, the parakeets twitter, talk, and kiss, and the parrots chatter, "calling each other monkey, sonny boy, glutton, in Tekla's village dialect."

Every day when the professor goes outside to feed the pigeons, flocks of them converge from all directions the moment he comes through the front gate. He tells Tekla the feeding of pigeons means as much to him as going to church or synagogue. God is not hungry for praise, he tells her, but the pigeons wait each day from sunrise to be fed. "There is no better way to serve the Creator than to be kind to His creatures."

Although caring for scores of birds who live in open cages and are free to fly around the apartment involves more effort and responsibility than feeding the street pigeons, "what joy these creatures gave Professor Eibeschutz in return for the few grains they ate!"

One of the parakeets who has learned many words and even whole sentences perches on the professor's bald spot, pecks at the lobe of his ear, and climbs onto a stem of his spectacles. Sometimes he stands like an acrobat on the professor's index finger as he writes. He thinks "how complicated these beings were, how rich in character and individuality. He could watch them for hours."

One day when the professor goes outside to feed the pigeons, they swoop down from all sides and become a jostling mass in the usual way. The pigeons perch on his shoulders and arms, fluttering their wings and pecking at him with their beaks. One bold pigeon even tries to land on the edge of the feed bag itself. Suddenly the professor feels something hit his forehead. He is startled and doesn't know what is happening until two more stones strike him on his elbow and neck. He has read in the newspapers about attacks on Jews by hoodlums in the Saxony Gardens and in the suburbs, but it had never happened to him. The pigeons scatter, and the professor retreats back inside where Tekla attends to the large bump on his head.

As the professor lies in bed, a Hebrew word he had long since forgotten comes to his mind: *reshayim*, the wicked. "It is the wicked who make history," he thinks, "their aim is always the same—to perpetuate evil, cause pain, shed blood." That evening, after Tekla cooks him some oatmeal, the professor falls asleep, but he wakes up in the middle of the night, feeling an ache on the left side of his chest and a sharp, violent pain shooting through his heart, shoulder, arm, and ribs. He tries to stretch his hand out toward the bell, but his fingers go limp before he can reach it. The last thought that runs through his mind is: what will happen to the pigeons?

Early the next morning when Tekla goes into his room and sees how grotesque he looks, she screams so loudly that neighbors come running. An ambulance arrives, but it is too late—Professor Eibeschutz is dead. The news of his death fills his apartment with flowers and well-wishers who want to pay their last respects. "The frightened birds flew from wall to wall, from bookcase to bookcase, tried to rest on lamps, cornices, draperies." Tekla tries unsuccessfully to shoo them back into their cages. "Some disappeared through the doors and windows left carelessly open. One of the parrots screeched the same word over and over in a tone of alarm and admonishment."

The next morning pallbearers come and carry the coffin out of the house. As the funeral cortege begins to move downhill toward the Old City, flocks of pigeons fly in over the roofs. "Their numbers increased so rapidly that they covered the sky between the buildings on either side of the narrow street and darkened the day as if during an eclipse. They paused, suspended in the air for a moment, then, in a body, kept pace with the procession by circling around it."

The delegations walking behind the hearse are amazed at this wondrous spectacle of pigeons darkening the sky as they circle above the hearse. Not until they reach the intersection of Furmanska and Marienstadt do the pigeons make one last circle and in a mass turn back—"a winged host that had accompanied their benefactor to his eternal rest."

The next day when Tekla goes out with a bag of feed, a few pigeons fly down and peck at the food hesitantly as they glance nervously around. During the night somebody painted a swastika on the professor's door. The Nazi era is at hand. "The smell of char and rot came up from the gutter, the acrid stench of imminent destruction."

A Way of Life

The importance of vegetarianism to Singer was evident in the interview he gave in his Manhattan apartment on August 9, 1964. After Singer and the two interviewers finished covering a wide range of topics, including Singer's early years as a writer in America, the art of translation, and world and Yiddish literature, one of the interviewers said, "I guess that's about it." But Singer was *not* finished. "Let me add that I am a sincere vegetarian. You may be interested to know that even though I don't have any dogma, this has become my dogma." He told the interviewers that as long as we are cruel to animals and apply to them the principle that might makes right, that same principle will be applied to us. "This is lately my kind of religion, and I really hope that one day humanity will make an end to this eating of meat and hunting of animals for pleasure."[64]

Singer told the *Newsweek* reporters who came to interview him about his Nobel Prize for Literature that the suffering of animals made him very sad. "I'm a vegetarian, you know. When I see how little attention people pay to animals, and how easily they make peace with man being allowed to do with animals whatever he wants because he keeps a knife or a gun, it gives me a feeling of misery and sometimes anger with the Almighty." He said it makes him want to ask God, "Do you need your glory to be connected with so much suffering of creatures without glory, just innocent creatures who would like to pass a few years in peace?"[65]

In another interview in the early 1980s when Richard Burgin asked him about his vegetarianism, Singer told him, "I really feel that sensitive people, people who think about things, must come to the conclusion that you cannot be gentle while you're killing a creature, you cannot be for justice while you take a creature who is weaker than you and slaughter it, and torture it." He said he had this feeling since childhood ("many children have it"), but his parents discouraged him from acting on it by telling him he should not try to be more compassionate than God. His mother warned him that if he became a vegetarian, he would die of malnutrition. As he got older, Singer felt he would be "a real hypocrite if I would write or speak against bloodshed while I would be shedding blood myself."

He told Burgin, "It is just common sense to me that if you believe in compassion and in justice you cannot treat the animals the very opposite simply because they are weaker or because they have less intelligence. It's not our business to judge these things. They have the type of intelligence they need to exist."

In the same interview Singer said, "I cannot call God merciful and I feel a great protest in myself against creation. I also see that man is merciless. The moment he gets a little power, other people's misfortunes are nothing to him." He said protest defined his relationship to God. If he ever tried to create a religion for himself, it would be a "religion of protest." He told Burgin he once wrote a book in Yiddish called *Rebellion and Prayer or The True Protestor*, but it was never translated. "It was written at the time of the Holocaust. It is a bitter little book and I doubt that I will ever publish it. I may be contradictory in many ways, but I am a true protestor. If I could, I would picket the Almighty with a sign: 'Unfair to Life.'" Singer ended the interview by telling Burgin, "The man who eats meat or the hunter who agrees with the cruelties of Nature, upholds with every bite of meat or fish that might is right. Vegetarianism is my religion, my protest."[66]

In the Foreword he wrote for Dudley Giehl's book on vegetarianism, published in 1979,[67] Singer asked what he considered the eternal question: "What gives man the right to kill an animal, often torture it, so that he can fill his belly with its flesh?"

We know now, as we have always known instinctively, that animals can suffer as much as human beings. Their emotions and their sensitivity are often stronger than those of a human being.

Various philosophers and religious leaders tried to convince their disciples and followers that animals are nothing more than machines without a soul, without feelings. However, anyone who has ever lived with an animal—be it a dog, bird or even a mouse—knows that this theory is a brazen lie, invented to justify cruelty.

The only justification for killing animals, Singer wrote, is "the fact that man can keep a knife or an ax in his hands and is shrewd enough and selfish enough to do slaughter for what he thinks is his own good." He praised Dudley Giehl for arousing people's consciences by telling them that by eating the flesh of animals and by hunting, they are committing murder. "All their nice talk about humanism, a better tomorrow, a beautiful future, has no meaning as long as they kill to eat or kill for pleasure." Although Singer wrote that he is aware that humanity's disregard for animals will not end soon, "it is good that there are some people who express a deep protest against the killing and torturing of the helpless."

Singer concluded his Foreword with a warning: as long as human beings go on shedding the blood of animals, there will never be any peace. "There is only one little step from killing animals to creating gas chambers à la Hitler and concentration camps à la Stalin....There will be no justice as long as man will stand with a knife or with a gun and destroy those who are weaker than he is."

When Singer died in 1991, the long obituary that appeared in the *New York Times* failed to mention that he was a vegetarian. However, the piece about him that appeared the following Sunday in the *New York Times Book Review* did not omit that part of his life:

He shied from chicken soup and became a devoted vegetarian. From childhood on he had seen that might makes right, that man is stronger than chicken—man eats chicken, not visa versa. That bothered him, for there was no evidence that people were more important than chickens. When he lectured on life and literature there were often dinners in his honor, and sympathetic hosts served vegetarian meals. "So, in a very small way, I do a favor for the chickens," Singer said. "If I will ever get a monument, chickens will do it for me."[68]

When Singer did have to attend a dinner where chicken was served, he would decline the main course. When a woman once asked if he avoided eating chicken "for health reasons," his answer was: "Yes, for the health of the chicken."

CHAPTER EIGHT

THE OTHER SIDE OF THE HOLOCAUST

German Voices for the Voiceless

This final chapter of the book is about people whose cultural heritage and experience of the legacy of Nazi Germany are quite different from those of the activists discussed in Chapter 6. Yet, despite their different experiences, both groups—Jewish and German—have comparable perceptions of and reactions to institutionalized violence against animals.

What follows are profiles of several German animal advocates—those who lived in Nazi Germany during the war as children before coming to the United States and those born after the war who now live in Germany or Austria. Although they come to the issue from a very different starting point from the activists discussed earlier, their recognition of the animals' "eternal Treblinka" and their determination to stop it make them allies in a common struggle.

From Wehrmacht to Animal Rights

In the early 1980s Dietrich von Haugwitz was in his 50s when he turned to animal rights after experiencing what he calls "that momentous intellectual breakthrough of recognizing the species barrier as morally and rationally untenable."[1]

Von Haugwitz's eventful life began in Silesia in eastern Germany where he grew up in an aristocratic family (hence the "von" in his name). He would have been tutored privately in the family castle in what is today Poland, but because Nazi law did not permit private tutoring, he attended elementary school with "commoners" until the age of eleven, at which time he was sent off to an exclusive upper-class boarding school. He remembers the distress his parents felt at the sight of their beloved country being run by "a bunch of vulgar thugs (as they viewed Hitler and his henchmen), and people all around them being drugged by this vile and immoral ideology which they abhorred." Von Haugwitz was too young to understand why they were so upset, "but I understand them now only too well because I am also very much out-of-step with what most people around me believe in and take for granted."

Von Haugwitz was drafted at age fifteen and a half into a pre-military anti-aircraft battalion, and then in the summer of 1944, at age seventeen, he received his draft letter commanding him to report for duty in the regular Wehrmacht on August 1. His father, a pacifist and staunch opponent of the regime, went to an old friend who was a military doctor. "Listen," he told him, "my son got his draft letter, but unfortunately he won't be able to make it because he has a bad case of appendicitis, you know (wink wink), so won't you please take out his appendix?" The doctor agreed, "so I was taken to the military hospital and they cut out my disgustingly healthy appendix."

When the next draft letter arrived for September 1, his father went back to his doctor friend and said, "Look here, we're all soooooo sad, but my son won't be able to start serving and fighting for our final victory, because he hasn't fully recovered from the surgery. So won't you please certify that and report it to the draft board?" The doctor did. When the next draft letter came, his father had to twist the doctor's arm and add a hefty bribe of some hard-to-get meat. So it went, until the doctor finally put his foot down and said, no, he couldn't continue to lie about this, that he'd be court-martialed and shot if he was found out. So young von Haugwitz finally had to report for duty, "but we had delayed the dreaded but inevitable draft for half a year, and that probably saved my life."

On January 14, 1945 von Haugwitz had a tearful farewell with his parents ("I'm sure they never believed they'd see me alive after that") and reported to an anti-aircraft unit in the port town of Wismar on the

Baltic Sea. He saw little action, but once he almost got killed when a small English plane swooped down on the cabin where he was cooking some food over an open fire with his shirt off because it was very hot. The machine gun fire shot the frying pan out of his hand and splattered boiling fat all over his chest. "There, that's how I got wounded in World War II!"

The British arrived in Wismar a few hours before the Russians, so von Haugwitz surrendered to the first British soldier he saw. "He said something like, 'I'm afraid I must ask you to regard yourself as my prisoner—do you smoke?' And he offered me a cigar! Honestly! I'm not making this up. Until then, the official image in Germany of the British was they were cruel, sadistic, blood-thirsty monsters. From that moment on, I realized that I was beginning to experience a world that was turned upside down, or rather right side up. And I fell in love with the English—a love affair that was to last forever."

The next day, as von Haugwitz was being marched with hundreds of other captured German soldiers through the countryside to a POW camp, he realized that once they locked him up in the camp, there would be no getting out. So when no British soldier was looking, he made a dash for it and ran to a nearby farm where he hid in a cattle barn for the next forty-eight hours. "For me this taste of freedom was the great turning point in my life. Everything I had taken for granted until then, everything that had controlled my life until then had come to an end."

Von Haugwitz spent May, June, and July making his way through Germany toward the village of Pockau in the Erzgebirge, a mountain range in central Germany (soon to be the Soviet zone, or "East Germany"), where his parents had gone after fleeing from the family castle as the Red Army approached. Earlier they had sent letters to his military address, and a couple of them had actually reached him. On his way to Pockau von Haugwitz survived mostly on the potatoes he dug up in the fields and whatever else he could find in the woods, fields, and villages through which he passed.

Von Haugwitz found Berlin in ruins, with a terrible stench in the air from the thousands of corpses still under all the rubble and floating in the rivers and canals. At the railroad station he managed to hop a ride on the roof of a train going south toward Leipzig and then caught a local train that took him to the village where his parents were supposed to be.

Having no idea if he would ever find them, he started walking down the main street when suddenly he saw his father walking toward him. "I ran toward him and called out excitedly, 'Dad—it's me!' I remember it as if it was yesterday. He stopped, stared, and shook his head. 'No, no. It's not true. My son is dead.' It took quite a while for him to realize it was me. He was so despondent that he had given up hope that I was still alive." What followed when they reached the attic where his mother, sister, and their beloved family dog were living was "a tearful, incredible reunion."

When it came time to leave the village, the family decided it would be best for them to split up, with Dietrich going west across the "Iron Curtain" to the British zone to escape the Russians, who were picking up young men and shipping them to labor camps. The plan was for his mother to go to Potsdam, near Berlin, where she had been a principal of a college before her marriage, and for his sister to go to Berlin, where they had relatives, in order to try to train as a nurse in a hospital, which would mean food, housing, and warmth for the coming winter.

"My father was the problem," says von Haugwitz. "He was so despondent we thought we'd 'park' him with distant relatives not too far from where we were. He'd stay there until my mother would send for him." He did stay there for a few weeks, until October 31, 1945—the eve of his birthday—when he walked out of that house and was never seen again. "We suspect that he decided to start walking back toward our home, since he blamed himself for having left. He felt he should have stayed with the estate that had been entrusted to him, by God I guess, sort of like the captain who must go down with his ship. A matter of honor. We don't know what happened to him, and at that time there was no authority in Germany to investigate this sort of thing."

Von Haugwitz made his way to the city of Braunschweig in the British zone, which was was sixty or seventy percent in ruins. There he lived as a penniless refugee in a bombed out cellar, a railroad car, and then finally a garage, while he studied piano at the local college of music. Although he graduated, gave some recitals, and played with some city orchestras, von Haugwitz decided to leave Germany. He had lost his home, and life was depressing, since most German cities were in ruins and crowded with other refugees from the East ("seven million displaced persons!").

But mostly, he says, he was disenchanted with the Germans. "They had cheered on the Nazis when things were going well, and they showed little inclination now to come to terms with the horrible past and their general complicity, even though we now had a free press that allowed the Germans, for the first time, to know what really happened. Germans wanted no great moral debate. What they all seemed to embark on was a headlong rush into crass materialism. Everybody just wanted to regain all they had lost—and then some. The positive aspect of that, of course, was what was then called the German 'economic miracle'—the re-building of the country and its infrastructure."

After years of writing letters trying to persuade some organization in America to sponsor him, a little country church in Minnesota finally picked up on it, and in 1956, "very excited and twenty-nine years old, I sailed on the *Queen Elizabeth*, from Southampton in England to New York." He stayed in Minnesota for only about nine months, directing the church choir, playing the organ, teaching piano, and giving piano recitals and talks in various towns. Then in 1957 he went to Hollywood, California, "where I had wanted to be all along." There he worked as a pianist, gave piano lessons, and did some acting on the side through friends he made in the movie industry. While acting in a German theater, he met a German woman named Eva and married her in 1960. ("I have been very happily married to her ever since.")

When he realized "I had started serious piano studies too late in life to ever become another Rubinstein or Horowitz or Ashkenazy, I decided not to settle for second best, especially because total dedication to nothing but music left a good part of my mind dissatisfied. I had too many other interests and inclinations."

In the 1960s, after studying computer programming, von Haugwitz worked at Southern California Financial Corporation (Great Western). He had always been an "animal lover," he says. He loved zoos, wildlife, animal films, and bird watching, and adored dogs and cats. "And of course I also loved my sausages." In California "we had some cats in our house, and we were the usual (meat eating) 'animal lovers.' "

That's when the first of three things happened to him that changed his life. He and his wife went on a short trip to Mexico, where they decided to do what one is supposed to do there—watch a bullfight. "When the first animal was killed, I broke down—emotionally and physically. I had never witnessed such unabashed animal torture before and simply couldn't believe what I saw—the suffering of the desperate animal *and* the blood lust of the cheering crowd! They couldn't wait to see the next animal brought in and tortured. I left, and the memory of what I saw haunted me for several years."

The second event happened in North Carolina where von Haugwitz worked as a computer programmer/systems analyst at Duke University Medical Center. His wife, Eva, who was a volunteer and board member at the local animal shelter, decided to educate the members of the Animal Protection Society by showing them a British film she leased, called "The Animals' Film." Von Haugwitz says the film, which is over two hours long, shows in graphic detail everything the animal rights movement is concerned about—hunting, trapping, vivisection, slaughterhouses, etc. "I fell apart. I had had no idea about any of this. I now realized that the torture of the bull I saw was just the tip of the iceberg."

He tried to resolve his mental conflict by reasoning as follows: "On an emotional level, all of this is terrible, agonizing, almost unbearable, if one is compassionate—and I'm proud to be compassionate rather than unfeeling. However, feeling is one thing, but reason is quite another. And reason tells me that this is the way it is, and it must be. Top of the food chain, hierarchy of values, that sort of thing. To my knowledge, there really were no truly rational arguments against the status quo—only emotional ones."

Then he happened to hear Professor Tom Regan speak. When he went up to Regan afterwards, he told him he was impressed and asked him if he had written anything. Yes, said Regan, he had just written a book called *The Case for Animal Rights*.[2] So von Haugwitz bought it and spent several months reading it, scribbling in the margins, thinking through all the arguments, trying unsuccessfully to shoot holes in them. That was the third and decisive event that turned him around. "The book changed my life. No book has ever affected me as profoundly as this one; no philosophical, social, or political theory has widened my horizon as much as this book. Here finally were the *rational* arguments that validated my feelings." The book was "an incredibly logical edifice of argumentation that demolished any argument defending the status quo—calmly and dispassionately. This appealed to my mind. I needed this approach. It was the only level on which I was reachable."

That began what von Haugwitz calls his third, unpaid career. In 1983 he joined the North Carolina Network for Animals, a statewide animal rights organization with local chapters. Since there was no chapter in Durham, he and Eva started one. Von Haugwitz led the chapter for six or seven years and was designated "Education Director" of the statewide organization. During that time he organized—or attended— demonstrations connected with vivisection, hunting, circus, rodeos, factory farming, and other animal issues and organized many other events, often educational in nature.

He gave talks on animal rights philosophy at schools and colleges around the state and in neighboring states, and appeared on TV and radio talk shows. He also wrote articles on animal rights themes and co-edited the North Carolina Network for Animals newsletter. He engaged in many hands-on activities as well, like relocating ducks from apartment complex ponds, or responding to homeowner associations where beavers were slated to be killed. "Currently we are fighting one battle in the state courts—the outlawing of pigeon shoots in the state. And we are working to force the Wildlife Commission to enforce the prohibition against canned hunting. This requires tenacious work with our attorneys."

"And, yes," he adds, "I've had to kick that addiction to those tasty sausages." As he has jokingly told Tom Regan often, he was determined to find logical flaws in his arguments, "so that I could go back to those wonderful German sausages with a good conscience, but dammit I never did succeed."

As for parallels with Germany during and after the war, von Haugwitz sees a similar mentality at work here in the United States. "I've always been upset about so many Germans I knew who, at the end of the war, said, in effect, 'But we had no idea! We really didn't know anything about Auschwitz and what happened to the Jews. There was no way of knowing. We weren't allowed to know those things. And if one talked about it, one would have been arrested,' etc. etc. etc."

"Baloney!" he says. "People knew very well that the Jews were systematically removed from everywhere and shipped off like cattle, and they lent a hand everywhere to the expulsion. As for the details of the extermination, people didn't want to know! And that is my main gripe. Rumors circulated, and some people knew some things, but most people said, in effect, 'If you know, please don't tell me. I don't want to know the details.' Because it would have been too upsetting." He sees the same denial operating today. "I have a large animal rights video collection, but it's hard to show people what goes on in slaughterhouses and in animal labs. They don't want to see it. It would spoil their appetite."

Revolted and Saddened

Peter Muller, a longtime activist with the Committee to Abolish Sport Hunting (CASH) in New York State, spent the first five and a half years of his life in wartime Germany.[3] He lived in Nuremberg where his father did radar research, but when the nightly Allied bombings became intense, the women and children were evacuated to small villages outside the city. Muller remembers the nightly bombings, the air raids, the chronic food shortages, and how families were arbitrarily assigned to people's apartments as subtenants because there was not enough housing. He remembers, "We had three families living with us as subtenants."

Muller had been born in Estonia to ethnic German parents on July 11, 1939, a couple of months before "all hell broke loose," as he put it. As a result of the pact between Hitler and Stalin that allowed the Soviets to annex the Baltic states and eastern Poland, Muller's family was "repatriated" to Germany, even though nobody in his family had ever been a German citizen, or had lived in Germany, or had even traveled there. "Germany was 'foreign' in every sense of the word, except that we spoke a variant of the local language."

Muller's family probably could have remained in Germany after the war if they had wanted to, even after the American occupying force officially declared them "stateless displaced persons." But the Germans were extremely xenophobic. "The locals considered us to be *Verdammte Auslander* ('damn foreigners'), which is really one word in the German language, even though there is a space in it." His parents decided it would have been extremely hard for Peter and his brother to have a decent future in that kind of atmosphere, so they applied for immigration. "We were all deliriously happy to be finally processed for immigration to the United States and allowed to immigrate in 1952."

The full significance of what Muller had lived through in Nazi Germany did not begin to sink in fully until his late teens when at Case Western Reserve University in Cleveland he started reading more about recent European history. "As I learned more about World War II and the Holocaust," he says, "I was revolted and saddened at the savagery of our species. I came to realize that humankind has a very thin veneer of civility on top of millions of years of evolution that evidently genetically predisposes us to brutality and senseless savagery directed to our own and other species."

When others learned that Muller had grown up in Nazi Germany during the war, they wanted to know the details. Muller says some of them simply did not believe some of the things he told them he had experienced firsthand. "For example, I had a geography professor who insisted that the Allies only bombed industrial targets and took great pains to avoid bombing civilian residential areas. That was my first live encounter with historical revisionism."

Muller says he has been a vegetarian on and off since he was about four or five. "Since early childhood I found the practice of the slaughter of animals and eating their dead bodies appalling and disgusting." Until he made a serious commitment to animal rights in 1976, "I would become vegetarian whenever I gave it some thought, but whenever I let the exigencies of life take over, I would revert back to meat eating."

After he graduated from college, he did graduate work in logic and the methodology of science at the University of California in Berkeley. Then he worked in the computer field as a programmer and systems analyst in California until 1967 when he moved to New York where he now works as a data-processing consultant and is adjunct assistant professor of computer science at New York University.

Muller became an animal activist through Luke Dommer, who had been with Friends of Animals (FOA), which at the time was headed by its founder Alice Herrington. One of the organization's committees was the Committee to Abolish Sport Hunting, which Luke headed under Alice's direction. However, Dommer and Herrington disagreed about how to take on the hunting establishment. "Luke wanted to proceed along scientific lines, pointing out the destruction of biodiversity and debilitation of ecosystems due to hunting. Alice wanted to adopt an approach that impugned hunters' sexual adequacy and presented hunting as a defense mechanism that hunters adopt to cope with their small penises and chronic impotence." Since Dommer didn't think much of that approach, he decided to leave FOA and take the Committee to Abolish Sport Hunting with him. Despite their disagreement, however, Dommer and Herrington remained lifelong personal friends.

In the early 1970s Dommer, who lived in Muller's neighborhood in Manhattan, invited Muller to go up upstate on first day of hunting to "kick some ass." Muller found the idea of confronting hunters in the woods "immediately appealing," and he has been a CASH activist ever since. Today his special interest is educating the public about the adverse effect of hunting and trapping on the environment.

When asked if his experiences growing up in Germany during and after the war had any effect on the animal rights direction his life took later, Muller says he doesn't think it was a major factor. "I know scores of people with a similar background and none of them have any understanding of animal rights. They consider me an oddball. I avoid them as much as I can. I think my animal rights disposition came from simply realizing that animal abuse is cruel and totally unnecessary for human survival or comfort." He does think that growing up as an "outsider" may have helped prepare him for his life as an activist, however. "Having had different experiences has made me skeptical of all mainstream assumptions."

Hitler's Baby

Shortly after Liesel Appel's birth in Nazi Germany in 1941, her father, Heinrich Steffens, a high-ranking education official in the government, arranged a Teutonic naming ceremony for her in the town hall of Klingenberg. For Liesel's parents, who were in their 40s and already had a son in the navy, Liesel was their miracle baby, specially conceived for their beloved Führer, who was urging all good Aryan Germans to have more children.

"My father brought a big picture of Hitler to the ceremony," says Liesel, "and I was proudly dedicated in front of all our family and friends."[4] One of those present was her father's best friend, Erich Koch, whom Appel knew as "Uncle Erich." Later in the war after Koch was appointed governor of Poland, he put Liesel's father in charge of the Polish education system.[5] After the war a court in Poland sentenced Koch to death for having planned, prepared, and organized the mass murder of 400,000 Jewish and Polish civilians.[6]

Appel says that, despite the war, she led a sheltered life as the pampered darling of her family and community. "I had a very, very happy childhood." One day Herr Steffens took his blond-haired pride and joy to the local school to show the students what a "perfect Aryan child" looked like. Appel remembers the long walks she took with her father in the nearby forest, where he taught her about nature and made up little songs and fairy tales which made her laugh. He also reminded her that she owed her life to Adolf Hitler and that it was her duty to make sure Germany stayed strong. "My father was my hero. I was convinced nothing bad could happen to me as long as he was around." In 1950 her father died suddenly of a heart attack while awaiting trial as a war criminal.

Liesel knew nothing about her parents' Nazi background, but in the spring of 1951 her innocence was shattered. She was outside playing hopscotch when a young, well-dressed stranger appeared and asked her in perfect German, "Little girl, where do you live?" Liesel smiled and pointed at her house. When the stranger nodded, Liesel noticed he was wearing a strange little cap on the back of his head. He told her he had lived in the house next door to hers and that a great man had saved his life during *Kristallnacht.*

Kristallnacht? When the stranger saw her blank expression, he explained that in November, 1938 Hitler ordered all Jewish property destroyed. He himself had been nine years old at the time. A mob broke into his house, killed his parents, and threw him off the second-story balcony. A neighbor came to his rescue and smuggled him to safety. "Now I live in Israel," the stranger said. "But I came back to thank the man who saved my life."

Liesel tried to understand what he was saying. This was the first she had ever heard of Israel, *Kristallnacht,* or people being killed next door. She suddenly became sure of one thing, however. "That man was my father!" she told him and grabbed the man's hand to take him home to meet her mother. When she arrived with the stranger in tow, she burst into the living room. Her mother was talking to Frau Lauder, who rented one of their rooms, but when they saw the man, they stopped talking and their expressions changed. Liesel saw the stranger stiffen and felt tension in the room. She had the feeling that her mother and the man had met before.

Liesel started to tell her mother about the wonderful thing her father had done, when her mother interrupted and told Frau Lauder to take Liesel to her room. Frau Lauder took her up to her room and locked her in. Liesel banged on the door and screamed, but nobody came to let her out. When she went to the window, she saw the stranger walking quickly away. Then she heard her mother come upstairs and unlock the door. Her face was red, and she was sputtering with rage. She shouted at Liesel, "Don't you ever bring people like that into our house again!"

Liesel felt deeply hurt and confused. "People like what?" Suddenly, she had an awful feeling that her parents were somehow connected with the stranger's terrible story. "Mutti," she asked slowly, "what did we do during the war? Did we not save this man?" Her mother grabbed her arms and shook her hard. "Your father was a good man! He believed right! Why should he have saved a Jew?"

Liesel now began to realize that her wonderful, loving parents were part of the evil stories people whispered about children being taken from their parents and burned in ovens. Liesel had never spoken up to her mother before, but now she glared at her. "You are murderers!" she screamed. "Don't you ever touch me again!" She pushed her mother out of her room and slammed the door. "It was the end of my childhood," says Liesel. "I never touched her or called her 'mother' again."

Liesel spent the rest of her childhood feeling shame, guilt, and resentment. She took long walks alone in the forest and spent endless hours in her room writing in her diary and reading everything she could about the Holocaust. She was horrified to know she was living among people who had committed such atrocities. "I was surrounded by evil. I would look at people I saw in school or the streets and wonder what they had done during the war. I wouldn't let anyone reach me."

Her mother hoped her daughter would get over her bitterness, but nothing helped. Once she took Liesel with her on a vacation to the island of Norderney in the North Sea. Their accommodation happened to be near the local slaughterhouse where every Monday trucks arrived and unloaded pigs, calves, cows, and sheep. On Monday, instead of going to the beach with her mother, Liesel went to the slaughterhouse. "I never forgot the cruel faces of the truck drivers and butchers, who kicked the animals and threw them off the trucks, breaking their legs and backs." She desperately wanted to save the animals, but she felt powerless and alone "as these cruel men laughed at me and told me their greatest joy was to 'hook knives into animal flesh.'" She cried and pleaded, "especially for the life of a beautiful calf, who was left as the last one to die." When she looked through the window, she saw the calf looking at her. "I sneaked into the building, as all the butchers were busy doing their terrible deeds. I touched the calf and was going to take him outside, but I was caught and given a beating."[7]

When Frau Steffens was unable to repair her relationship with her daughter, she sent Liesel to a boarding school in Düsseldorf. One night when Liesel was 17, she ran away from the school. She went to London where she changed her name to Lisa Scotland and married George Brown, a local black musician. "We were both running from our identities. He didn't like being black, and I didn't like being German."

In 1980 Liesel, George, and their two children moved to Palm Beach, Florida, where they opened a restaurant, but racial hatred made their life miserable and eventually forced George to return to England. Depressed about the end of her twenty-year marriage, Appel moved to California where she finally found the strength to confront her past and tell her children the truth about their family background.

Appel converted to Judaism in 1990 ("I felt like I was coming home"). After she married Don, a retired insurance agency owner, she returned to South Florida where she became active in Jewish community affairs. In 1995 she presented a two-hour testimonial videotape to the Holocaust Memorial in Miami Beach, and she has also spoken at other Holocaust memorial events. She has told her story to many groups, including B'nai B'rith, Hadassah, "Ort," and the Commission for Jewish Education, where she gave a ten-week workshop. When she speaks to young people, she says she tries to empower them "to speak up when necessary, even against their parents, if they see any injustice committed against any fellow man or creature."

In London Appel had been a crusader for racial justice for the emerging African nations and a passionate anti-apartheid activist. "I worked for Amnesty International in the 1950s and travelled to Africa many times. I remember when Nelson Mandela was arrested and we demonstrated in England. It is remarkable what I have seen in my lifetime, what committed people can do to abolish injustice. With apartheid gone, I went to my next project—animal rights."

Appel was managing the Christian Dior cosmetics counter at Bloomingdale's in Boca Raton when the store decided to set up a large fur department and sell fur coats for prices up to $100,000. She wrote to the store manager and the head of Bloomingdale's in New York, but she never received an answer. "I was outspoken, and when models were hired to walk around the store in these fur coats, they avoided coming anywhere near the cosmetics department. I was told they were afraid of me and didn't want a confrontation. I resigned. The fur is still there."

Growing up in Germany, Appel had never been allowed to care for an animal because her parents considered them "dirty." When she adopted "Snowball," a four-year-old mixed breed dog, from the local pound, he "opened my eyes to unconditional love and from the love of this one wonderful creature, my awareness of the plea of all animals was a natural progression."

Today Appel's "animal family" consists of two dogs (Fritz, a mutt from the local shelter, and Smokey, a formerly homeless husky) and three cats, two of whom, Lee and Dawn, were tiny babies when they were abandoned and going to be killed. "I fed them with a bottle. They are now strong and beautiful." Breana, the third cat, was a pregnant stray for whom "we set up a 'maternity ward' with classical music, lots of good food, and peace and privacy for the expectant mother." Four days later tiny Breana gave birth to seven kittens. "Having these babies raised under our roof was one of the most wonderful experiences of my life. Our dog Fritz groomed the tiny cats daily. He was so excited and even carried the kittens in his mouth. All seven found loving homes after being nursed for eight weeks, and we still keep in touch. Breana will always be with us."

Appel became a strict vegetarian (vegan) twelve years ago, and recently she and her son built a brand new, attractive restaurant/health store in Jupiter, Florida. She says her change of diet was "a natural progression from my love for animals and becoming a member of PETA [People for the Ethical Treatment of Animals]. After reading a PETA magazine, there was just no way I could eat meat again." She says she is determined to live as cruelty-free as possible out of a deep need "to make up for an unbelievable evil committed by my people." She says she became vegan overnight, "not once looking back and just wondering why the perversity of eating flesh and animal products had not come to me sooner."

Appel says she is proud to be part of all the animal rights groups, like PETA and the Animal Rights Foundation of Florida, where she's surrounded by people who understand the way she sees things. "I do see change in awareness. There is hope. I felt hopeless as a child and wanted to kill myself. I felt like a misfit, knowing in my heart what is right, but I couldn't get anyone around me to see it. It is remarkable what I have seen in my lifetime, what committed people can do to abolish injustice. If we wait long enough and are persistent, change will come for good."

The Meat Eaters Could Make It Happen Again

For his book about the children of Nazis,[8] the Israeli psychologist Dan Bar-On interviewed a former doctor at Auschwitz, who was tried and acquitted after the war. When Bar-On asked the doctor about the effect of his having been at Auschwitz, the former doctor said, "I didn't have any dreams. I had quite different experiences. It's not the actual horror, the terrible fate of people, that's not it, you understand. It's strange, but you get used to that. No, it's the fact of the selection that I think of, like when I'm in the garden digging, and there are snails. Not that I can't kill the snails, that's no problem. But then there's one that I miss, that I see and have to kill, to dig up and kill the last one. That's what's so unpleasant. Take this one snail out especially, and it's such a disturbing, phobic experience. The notion that selection is continuing, going on. Or when I see cattle being transported."[9]

He told Bar-On that he once spoke to Gitta Sereny, the British journalist who wrote a book about Franz Stangl, the commandant of Treblinka, based on seventy hours of interviews she had with Stangl in a Düsseldorf prison in 1971.[10] The doctor told Bar-On that during one of Sereny's interviews, Stangl told her about an experience he had in Brazil where he fled after the war. Once when he was on a trip, Stangl told her, his train stopped next to a slaughterhouse. "The cattle in the pens, hearing the noise of the train, trotted up to the fence and stared at the train. They were very close to my window, one crowding the other, looking at me through that fence. I thought then, 'Look at this: this reminds me of Poland; that's just how the people looked, trustingly, just before they went into the tins [gas chamber]....I couldn't eat tinned meat after that. Those big eyes...which looked at me...not knowing that in no time at all they'd all be dead."[11]

Later when Sereny asked Stangl's wife if he had ever spoken to her about this incident, she said, no, he never had. "But you know, he suddenly stopped eating meat at one point."[12] After the Auschwitz doctor finished telling Bar-On the story about Stangl, he said that for him "it's not the eyes, but rather the fact that something is being sacrificed, killed by hand. That's it."[13]

Robert Jay Lifton interviewed another Auschwitz doctor, whom he identified as Ernst B. "When you see a selection for the first time," said the doctor, "I'm not talking only about myself, I'm talking about even the most hardened SS people, you see how children and women are selected. Then you are so shocked...that it just cannot be described. And after a few weeks one can be accustomed to it." He tried to tell Lifton what it was like: "I think I can give you a kind of impression of it. When you have gone into a slaughterhouse where animals are being slaughtered...the smell is also a part of it...not just the fact that they [the cattle] fall over dead and so forth. A steak will probably not taste good to us afterward. And when you do that every day for two weeks, then your steak again tastes as good as before."[14]

Bar-On also interviewed the son of the former Auschwitz doctor whom he had interviewed earlier. He learned that the doctor had never talked to his son about Auschwitz. The son told Bar-On that he sees the potential for mass murder all around him. When he goes to his favorite bar, he talks with workers who seem to have no scruples about harming others. He believes there are many people who could do the exact same thing to other people even today. "I think a lot of people are capable of that, just from the way they talk. And if you get to know them a bit better, their character, then I have no doubt that they are capable of it."[15] He told Bar-On, "There are two kinds of people: meat eaters and plant eaters. The meat eaters are the dangerous ones."[16] Toward the end of his book, Bar-On remarks that the son "lives very much in the present tense, wary of the 'meat eaters' who could make 'it' happen again."[17]

Another one of the children of Nazis, whose father was put on trial for war crimes, told Bar-On that he can't stand the sight of blood. Seeing his own blood when he goes to the doctor is not a problem, he says, "but when someone else is bleeding, that's a terrible thing for me. Whenever I see animals being sent to the slaughterhouse, for a couple of days afterward I'm unable to eat any meat."[18]

Animal Brothers

Edgar Kupfer-Koberwitz was a vegetarian, pacifist, and conscientious objector whom the Nazis condemned for being a "strong autonomously thinking personality." He was born on April 24, 1906, in Germany near Breslau (now Wroclaw, Poland), but fled to Paris after the Nazis came to power. Three years later he went to the island of Ischia in the Bay of Naples in Italy where he worked as a tour guide until the Gestapo caught up with him in 1940 and sent him to the Dachau concentration camp.[19]

Kupfer-Koberwitz was a prisoner in Dachau from 1940 to 1945. During the last three years he had a clerical job in the camp storeroom, a position that allowed him to keep a secret diary on stolen scraps of paper. He buried the scraps, and when the Americans liberated Dachau on April 29, 1945, he collected them. The "Dachau Diaries" were published in 1956. From the notes he made during an illness in the camp, he wrote "Animal Brothers," an essay in the form of a series of letters to a friend explaining why he doesn't eat meat.[20]

He writes in the Preface: "The following pages were written in the Concentration Camp Dachau in the midst of all kinds of cruelties. They were furtively scrawled in a hospital barrack where I stayed during my illness in a time when Death grasped day by day after us, when we lost 12,000 inmates within four and half months."

Kupfer-Koberwitz begins by telling his friend he doesn't eat meat because of a firm promise he made to himself twenty years earlier. His reason is simple: "I eat no animals because I don't want to live on the suffering and death of other creatures." He explains, "I have suffered so much myself that I can feel other creatures' suffering by virtue of my own." He reasons that he is so glad when he is not persecuted, why should he persecute other creatures or have them persecuted? He is so glad when he is not captured, why should he capture other creatures or have them captured? He is so glad when nobody harms him, why should he harm other creatures or have them harmed? He is so glad not to be injured or killed, why should he injure or kill other creatures or have them injured or killed for his sake?

Just because these creatures are weaker and smaller than oneself, he writes, how can "any sensitive and noble-minded person derive from that a right to abuse their weakness and smallness?" He asks, should not the greater, stronger, and more powerful always protect weaker creatures, instead of killing and persecuting them?[21]

Kupfer-Koberwitz writes that his decision not to eat animals has made him think and feel in a new way. "You don't know in what a changed way I can face all creatures since twenty years ago, how freely I can look into the eyes of deer and dove, how much I feel myself brother to all creatures, loving brother to the snail, the worm and the horse, to the fish and the bird."[22]

Sensing that his friend will smile at his mention of "worm," Kupfer-Koberwitz writes, "Yes, it's true what I'm saying: even to the worm."

> I pick him up from the path where he might be stepped on and take him to a place where he will be safe—a spot of soil or lawn. It makes me happy, much more happy than I could be if my heel would crush him and leave him writhing in agony for hours to come. What does that little inconvenience matter—bending down and soiling the tips of my fingers? What does it matter,

compared with the blissful feeling of having entered the circle of Nature, the circle of fellow-creatures, with love—not as an instigator of terror and destruction. No, to bring Peace—as the older brother. But you don't persecute brothers—you don't kill brothers. Do you understand now why I eat no meat?

He goes on to discuss in some detail the heartlessness involved in slaughtering animals and in hunting and fishing. He mentions the soft, gentle voice of the woman who calls chickens, feeds them golden grain, and then grabs them by the throat and kills them. "Yes, I am afraid of those hands. Wouldn't they be capable of doing the same to humans?" Since he knows his friend will disagree, he writes, "You say no—I say yes! For everything begins on a small scale—everything is learned on a small scale—even killing."

He describes how pigs, horses, birds in cages, dogs, and other animals suffer. "I believe as long as man tortures and kills animals, he will torture and kill humans as well—and wars will be waged—for killing must be practiced and learned on a small scale. We should try to overcome our own small thoughtless cruelty, to avoid it, to abolish it. But all of us are still asleep in our traditions. Traditions are like greasy tasteful gravy, which lets us swallow our own selfish heartlessness without noticing how bitter it is."[23]

The Auschwitz Lie

Dr. Helmut Kaplan, who lives in Salzburg, Austria, is one of the leading thinkers of the animal rights movement in the German-speaking world. While he believes that "the important arguments and strategies concerning animal liberation stem predominantly from the modern animal rights movement," he often uses the Holocaust analogy in his speeches and writings "because it is—for speciesists—as politically provocative as it is ethically sound."[24]

At a demonstration against animal experiments conducted by the giant pharmaceutical firm Hoechst AG in Frankfurt, Kaplan told the demonstrators, "Ladies and gentlemen! You all know what the

Auschwitz lie is. It's the assertion that the concentration camps never existed. But what perhaps you do not know is that the concentration camps still exist! We are standing directly in front of one, an animal concentration camp. The assertion that the concentration camps were closed after the Second World War is the second Auschwitz lie!"

Kaplan then quoted Isaac Bashevis Singer about how human beings are Nazis when it comes to their treatment of animals. "If you don't believe it, then you should read reports of the experiments the Nazis carried out in their research labs on Jews, and then read reports on the experiments done today with animals. Then you'll lose your blindfold: the parallels are plain to see. Everything the Nazis did to Jews we are today practicing on animals. Our grandchildren will ask us one day: Where were you during the Holocaust of the animals? What did you do against these horrifying crimes? We won't be able to offer the same excuse for the second time, that we didn't know."

Since Kaplan was born in 1952, he did not experience World War II directly. At first, his father had been a supporter of National Socialism, but after the Nazis seized power in Austria, he became more and more negative and critical. As a radio operator during the war, he got to listen secretly to foreign radio broadcasts. When he returned to Austria after spending two years in the Soviet Union as a prisoner of war, he threw away his military decorations.

Kaplan says that when he was growing up, the sight of dead animals, such as halves of pigs being transported and fish displayed in stores, shocked and disgusted him. He became a vegetarian in 1963, at the age of eleven. "I sensed intuitively and was convinced that eating flesh has to be morally wrong." The conviction then grew within him that his belief about the immorality of eating meat could be proven concretely and rationally. After university studies in psychology and philosophy, Kaplan decided to dedicate his life to animal rights. Since 1986 he has written eight books and more than 200 articles on animal rights and vegetarianism. His most recent book is *Animal Rights: The Philosophy of a Liberation Movement.*[25]

In "Animals and Jews, or The Art of Repression" Kaplan writes that it is assumed that because the Holocaust was so horrible and unique, it can never possibly happen again and is therefore separate from the rest of human activity. "Uniqueness implies the comforting but fatal certainty that the worst is behind us. For whatever is unique and has already happened will not occur again, and therefore requires no precautions to prevent it."

Kaplan thinks that this repression is an obvious example of the ever present human tendency to trivialize. "Once there were these terrible crimes" is accompanied by another evasion, a geographical one: "Whatever happens 'down' there in Africa and 'over' there in South America may be bad enough, but that's what these people are like!"

"The crudest form of soporific human self-deception," he writes, "is the denial of those cruelties that are happening at this moment in our immediate surroundings: in testing laboratories, slaughterhouses, fur farms, etc. Because what happens here is exactly analogous to the Holocaust of the Nazis."

Animal Holocaust

Until recently Christa Blanke was a Lutheran pastor who served with her husband, also a minister, in a village near Frankfurt. She was born in war-ravaged Germany in 1948, and her mother insists she would not have survived without food parcels from CARE USA. "So at a very early stage in my life, I experienced what compassion is all about—it even extended to the former murderous enemy."[26]

Later when Blanke learned about the murder of six million Jews by Germans who belonged to her grandfathers' generation ("unbelievable for a teenager brought up to respect and honor the elderly"), she developed the strong conviction that if anything similar to that should ever happen in her lifetime, "I would fight with everything I had. These two decisions—to extend compassion to everyone in need and to fight a holocaust wherever I saw one—led me straight into the animal rights movement."

As a teenager, Christa conducted "pony vacations" and wrote a book, *Kleine Pferde, grosses Gluck* (*Small Horses, Big Joy*), which was published in German and Dutch when she was twenty. She went on to write many articles about animals for newspapers and periodicals. Then, after she was ordained, she set out to raise the consciouness of her church. In 1980 she conducted her first church service on behalf of animals, and since then she has conducted other animal church services in Germany, and one in Australia as well. In 1986 she co-officiated at a church service against animal experimentation in front of the pharmaceutical giant Hoechst AG ("Hoechst, erbarme dich!"—"Hoechst, have mercy!"). That same year she collected 30,000 signatures calling for "No eggs from factory farms in church institutions," which she presented to the state governing body of the Lutheran church in Hessen-Nassau.

On July 10, 1988, Blanke conducted the first live TV church service with animals—"Who is my neighbor?"—on German national television (ZDF). The program attracted thousands of domestic and foreign letters (ninety-six percent favorable) and hundreds of press articles. In 1989 Blanke and her husband Michael founded *Aktion Kirche und Tiere* (Action for Church and Animals) to mobilize other clergy, but their effort did not meet with much success. "As an ordained minister of the Lutheran Church, I tried to involve the church in helping animals in distress. So far I had done lots of charity work for the poor (soup kitchen, homeless, prisoners, addicts) with great support from my church, but now I found myself deserted by my fellow clergy."[27]

In 1998 Blanke founded the organization Animals' Angels, whose motto is *Wir sind bei den Tieren* ("We are with the animals").[28] "We specialize in fighting livestock transport throughout Europe. I strongly believe that the reason for me to take on this special issue of animal suffering is a direct result of all the studies I undertook to understand the Holocaust. Animals in transport go through tremendous suffering similar to what the Jews suffered when they were transported to the Nazi camps." Volunteer teams of Animals' Angels monitor animal transport trucks to slaughterhouses and animal markets. Teams following trucks transporting horses to slaughter have passed through both Treblinka and Auschwitz.

Blanke is very proud of her Angels, "mainly younger people whose sacrifices for the animals involved in the miserable live transport trade come from a caring nature and a well-founded professionalism." Teams of Animals' Angels have monitored animal transport trucks through France, Greece, Holland, Hungary, Italy, Lebanon, Lithuania, Morocco, Poland, Romania, and Spain. Blanke says their commitment to the hundreds of thousands of bulls, cattle, donkeys, horses, and sheep involved in the despicable animal transport trade fills her with pride. She says these young people represent the animals' hope for the future. "These dedicated young people, willing to sacrifice, to fight, to pour their hearts and souls into their work" give her hope and help keep her going.[29]

On November 8, 1999, the Hessian Social Welfare Ministry honored Blanke with the 1999 Animal Protection Prize from the State of Hessen at a ceremony at the Biebrich Castle "for her exceptional commitment to the protection of slaughter animals during transport and the exemplary personal commitment of this animal rights activist on behalf of agricultural work and slaughter animals." The Minister of Social Welfare, Marlies Mosiek-Urbahn, described the work of Animals' Angels: "Sixty volunteer teams escort international animal transports across all of Europe under the most difficult, psychologically and physically stressful, and sometimes even dangerous conditions, and show their presence at slaughterhouses and animal markets, at ports and loading stations. This involvement has led to the disclosure of numerous deplorable conditions and cruelties to animals, and often marked improvements for the animals were achieved. The experiences and knowledge are documented by the organization, utilized legally and journalistically, and have provided an important impetus for animal protection policy."

During a visit to Israel in July 24–28, 2000, organized by Yossi Wolfson of Anonymous for Animal Rights, Blanke held discussions with government representatives concerning the transportation of animals to and from Israel. Blanke says her focus on improving the transportation of animals is the first stage in an attempt to abolish the meat trade. "We are completely opposed to the slaughter of animals," she told the Israeli newspaper *Ha'aretz*, "but if they are fated to be slaughtered, then it should be done where they are raised, after which the frozen meat can be sent to other countries, thereby saving them the unnecessary suffering incurred during transport." Although she has not yet seen much change in the meat-eating habits of the public, she says they have seen surprising results with a number of the drivers who transport animals to slaughter. Some of them have left their jobs thanks to the influence of Animals' Angels and its education campaign throughout Europe.[30]

Blanke sees parallels between the Nazi era and what is being done to animals today. First of all, there is the decision to strip the animals of their dignity. Once there is no individuality left, then everything becomes possible. Secondly, there is the same kind of mind-splitting among the bystanders. Blanke says that during the Nazi period many Germans had some kind of "pet Jews," the ones who were really nice and not to be mixed up with the "ordinary ones." She says the same thing happens to the animals. There are pets like minipigs and riding horses, not to be confused with "slaughter pigs" and "slaughter horses." Blanke says this ethical schizophrenia is openly supported by governments and the meat industry, while the various media brainwash the public, as they did in Hitler's day.

Other similarities include: meeting points (*Sammelstellen*) where animals are loaded on trucks and railway cars, with no bonds of family or friendship respected; selections that take place according to "value," gender, and age; the use of ramps; numbers tattooed into the skin; language by drivers and butchers full of abuse and contempt ("German Jews were called *Judensau* [Jewish pig] and were treated accordingly"); and the use of euphemisms (to "euthanize" means to murder; "special treatment" refers to slaughter). Then, there is the need for lots of organization and paperwork to transport millions of animals over long distances and upon their arrival to murder them. A small number of people gain tremendous wealth from this horrific trade, says Blanke, and although everybody knows about it, only a few people are actively fighting against it.

Blanke points out that not only were Jews transported to the camps in cattle cars, but in some places the death journey started at exactly the same place where cattle were loaded on trucks or trains to be sent to slaughter.[31] As historian Marion Kaplan writes, "While some assembly points were in synagogues and other Jewish communal buildings, the Nazis cruelly located others in slaughterhouses."[32] After the Jews of Krefeld, for example, were rounded up and taken by train to the Düsseldorf central station about fifteen miles away, a Gestapo and SS escort marched them through the city streets to a slaughterhouse in Düsseldorf-Derendorf, ideal for its secluded location and long loading ramps. From there, the Jews were transported to a transit station called Izbica near Lublin and were then sent to either Auschwitz, Belzec, or Majdanek.[33]

On August 30, 1942, in the city of Wiesbaden, the Nazis took the city's last Jewish men, women, and children to the slaughterhouse behind the main railroad station and left them in the cattle pens for four days before loading them on cattle cars. The transport travelled on the special slaughterhouse track to Frankfurt and then on to Theresienstadt, the concentration camp in Czechoslovakia which served as a way station to Auschwitz.[34] Blanke points out that, during the Holocaust, the infrastructure of destruction did not change, only the identity of the victims.[35]

Blanke and her husband, who have three children (Ursula is reading law; Christopher is working in an old people's home in Berlin; Catriona lives at home), provide safety and shelter to various animals: four rescued elderly dogs, two abandoned cats, and a donkey in poor health after abusive treatment. The other animals (ponies and oxen) whom Blanke and her husband kept in Glauberg, where they lived and ministered for more than twenty years, have now been placed with the Animals' Angels Guardian program because the Blankes have less outdoor space in Mücke, where they moved in 1999.

In an article she wrote in the early 1990s—"That God Also Loves His Creatures Who Have Feathers and Fur, Claws, Horns and Quills:

Reflections on the Church and the Course of the World"—Blanke describes two items she received in the mail on the same day.[36] The first was a long, seventy-page report on the proceedings of a church synod conference held in Glauberg, at which church leaders in the course of discussing minor changes in church policy and procedures debated whether or not to insert a sentence or two stating that the Jews are chosen by God. After doing absolutely nothing to help Jews during the Holocaust, she writes, it is "grotesque" that "now the Christians in my church are quarreling over the addition of a sentence about Jews in church policy. Fifty years too late."

In the same mail she received a thick package with photographs and reports from Animals' Angels teams tracking animal transports across Europe. The fact that horses, cattle, sheep, pigs, and chickens are dying of thirst and hunger day in and day out as they are transported to slaughter prompts Blanke to ask, "When will my church raise its voice for the poor creatures who are shipped in rolling convoys across Europe for slaughter? Where is my church? Where is their outcry? They are too busy discussing better relations between Jews and Christians. Fifty years too late."

During a tour she took of a local slaughterhouse, Blanke was struck by the similarity of slaughterhouse language and the language of the Nazis. The veterinarian who conducted the tour explained that the slaughterhouse is divided into "pure" and "impure" zones. In the "pure zone," where business is conducted, the processed animals are under refrigeration, while in the "impure zone" the animals are kept in holding pens and then slaughtered. Since the killing is over for the day, the stalls are mostly empty. "Two groups of cows stare at us with their big dark eyes." Blanke sees pigs who have bloody rivulets running down their skin, who won't get any food or water before the slaughtering starts up again at four o'clock the next morning.

After the tour enters the "pure zone," where the meat marketing department and refrigerators are located, the vet tells them he has finished his work for the day. When he says proudly, "I carry out my duties wherever they tell me to," Blanke thinks, "Many things here are all too familiar. Words like 'ramp' and 'selection.' 'Suitable animals' are led into the stalls, while the 'unsuitable' ones are killed immediately in a special wing." The technical language depersonalizes victim and perpetrator—phrases like "delivery of goods," "shipments," "special processing" of sick animals, "procedures" of slaughtering, "utilization" of hair, bones, skin.

By the time Blanke leaves the slaughterhouse, she is sick to her stomach. "And we didn't even see the slaughtering itself. We didn't hear the fearful screams of the cows or the shrieks of the pigs. We didn't hear the machines drone or the firing of the bolt gun." What she did see, she writes, was "the degradation of the victim that always precedes a murder."

> We saw animals—who belong outside where the grass and trees grow, where the wind caresses them and the sun warms them, where their senses and their survival instincts are supported—crushed together, smeared in feces, standing fearfully behind iron bars on the cement floor of a large hall. There is no place to hide, no protection, nowhere to escape danger.

These animals "are living the final hours of their lives in the same city in which the church synod is having its convention, the synod that still cannot finish its business about changing church codes regarding relations between Jews and Christians." Blanke wonders if any of the synod members have ever been in a slaughterhouse. "Did any of them ever hear the victims of this daily holocaust screaming? I can't imagine it. But I can imagine that after all the speeches have been made and all the positions debated, the synod members will go to lunch and eat their lentil soup with beef sausage."

At home that night, as she feeds the animals, Blanke thinks how 130 years ago the church remained silent about the slave trade because they were only black people. Fifty years ago the church remained silent because they were only Jews. Today the church remains silent because they are only animals. "How many millions of animals must be slaughtered and exterminated, sparing only a few 'useful' groups, until the church discovers that God also loves those among His creatures who have feathers and fur, claws and hoofs, horns and quills?"

Blanke is aware that "the Holocaust comparison is not very popular in Germany and elsewhere, but to me it becomes stronger as I get more insights about the cruel trade with living animals." She also knows there is only so much she can do "because cruelty and greed always seem to get the upper hand." Still, she says she will do all she can. "I am absolutely dedicated to fight the contemporary holocaust of the animals as hard as I can."

AFTERWORD

In the United States where slavery and the eradication of most of the continent's native peoples are an indelible part of our history, institutionalized cruelty against the weak and defenseless is as American as apple pie. Although the U.S. eventually went to war against Hitler and helped defeat him, his worldview lives on in the land of the victors.

Hitler declared, "He who does not possess power loses the right to life." Nowhere has this belief found more fertile soil than in modern America, where every day millions of lambs, calves, pigs, chickens, cows, horses, and other animals, most of them very, very young and all of them innocent, are transported to killing centers to be slaughtered for the tables of the master species. Why? Because they can't fight back and defend themselves against those who would kill and eat them, and because there are so few people willing and able to take up the fight on their behalf. Fortified by denial, indifference, and mindless custom that stretches back to our primitive origins, our society's abuse and exploitation of animals seems hopelessly eternal.

The good news is that since a growing number of people are saying "no" to the slaughterhouse and all that it stands for, there is hope that someday these atrocities will come to an end. In the meantime, however, what about the killing of all those innocents that takes place in our midst mercilessly day after day? How long will we allow this socially condoned mass slaughter to continue without raising our voices in protest?

By way of conclusion, I say the sooner we put an end to our cruel and violent way of life, the better it will be for all of us—perpetrators, bystanders, and victims.

NOTES

1 THE GREAT DIVIDE

1. Sigmund Freud, "A Difficulty in the Path of Psycho-Analysis" (1917) in *The Standard Edition of the Complete Psychological Works of Sigmund Freud*, James Strachey, trans. (London: Hogarth Press, 1955), Vol. XVII, 140.

2. Freud, "Fixation to Traumas—The Unconscious" in Introductory Lectures on Psychoanalysis—Part III (1916–17), Lecture XVIII, *Complete Works*, Vol. XVI, 285.

3. Quoted in Colin Spencer, *The Heretic's Feast: A History of Vegetarianism* (London: Fourth Estate, 1990), 189.

4. Quoted in Matt Cartmill, *A View to a Death in the Morning: Hunting and Nature Through History* (Cambridge, MA: Harvard University Press, 1993), 88.

5. Carl Sagan, *The Dragons of Eden: Speculations on the Evolution of Human Intelligence* (New York: Random House, 1977), 13–17.

6. Richard E. Leakey and Roger Lewin, *Origins: What Discoveries Reveal About the Emergence of Our Species and Its Possible Future* (London: Futura, MacDonald and Company, 1982), 12–14.

7. Carl Sagan and Ann Druyan, *Shadows of Forgotten Ancestors: A Search for Who We Are* (New York: Ballantine, 1992), 363.

8. Ibid.

9. Edward O. Wilson, "Is Humanity Suicidal?" *New York Times Magazine* (May 30, 1993).

10. Jared Diamond, *The Third Chimpanzee: The Evolution and Future of the Human Animal* (New York: HarperCollins, 1992), 32. Montaigne pointed out that animals communicate by sounds and gestures little understood by people. "This defect that hinders communication between them and us, why is it not just as much ours as theirs? We have some mediocre understanding of their meaning; so do they of ours, in about the same degree." Quoted in Cartmill, *View*, 87.

11. Diamond, *Third Chimpanzee*, 364.

12. Allen W. Johnson and Timothy Earle, *The Evolution of Human Societies: From Foraging Group to Agrarian State* (Stanford, CA: Stanford University Press, 1987), 27.

13. Sherwood L. Washburn and C. S. Lancaster, "The Evolution of Hunting" in Richard B. Lee and Irven DeVore, eds., *Man the Hunter* (Chicago: Aldine Publishing Company, 1968), 303.

14. Barbara Ehrenreich, *Blood Rites: Origins and History of the Passions of War* (New York: Holt, 1997), 22.

15. Diamond, *Third Chimpanzee*, 55.

16. Sagan and Druyan, *Shadows*, 352.

17. Sagan, *Dragons of Eden*, 120.

18. Diamond, *Third Chimpanzee*, 32–3; see also Frederick E. Zeuner, *A History of Domesticated Animals* (London: Hutchinson, 1963), 15.

19. Karl Jacoby, "Slaves by Nature? Domestic Animals and Human Slaves" in *Slavery & Abolition: A Journal of Slave and Post-Slave Studies*, Vol. 15, No. 1 (April 1994), 90.

20. James A. Serpell, "Working Out the Beast: An Alternative History of Western Humaneness" in Frank R. Ascione and Phil Arkow, eds., *Child Abuse, Domestic Violence, and Animal Abuse: Linking the Circles of Compassion for Prevention and Intervention* (West Lafayette, IN: Purdue University Press, 1999), 40.

21. Jim Mason, *An Unnatural Order: Why We Are Destroying the Planet and Each Other* (New York: Continuum, 1997), 122; Jacoby, "Slaves by Nature?", 92.

22. Quoted in Peter J. Ucko and G. W. Dimbleby, eds., *The Domestication and Exploitation of Plants and Animals* (Chicago: Aldine Publishing Company, 1969), 107.

23. Ibid, 122–3. Castrating all males except those specially selected for breeding was the principle behind the Nazi sterilization and *Lebensborn* programs discussed in Chapter 4.

24. Sagan, *Dragons of Eden*, 230.

25. B. A. L. Cranstone, "Animal Husbandry: The Evidence from Ethnography" in Ucko and Dimbleby, *Domestication and Exploitation*, 254–6.

26. Ibid, 256–8.

27. Ibid, 259–60.

28. Philip Kapleau, *To Cherish All Life: A Buddhist Case for Becoming Vegetarian*, second edition (Rochester NY: The Zen Center, 1986), 11.

29. From Veg-NYC@waste.org email list (March 16, 1997).

30. For a critique of modern hunting, see Marti Kheel, "License to Kill: An Ecofeminist Critique of Hunters' Discourse" in Carol Adams and Josephine Donovan, eds., *Animals and Women: Feminist Theoretical Explorations* (Durham, N.C.: Duke University Press, 1995), 85–125.

31. For a discussion of the "distancing devices" of detachment, concealment, misrepresentation, and shifting the blame, see James Serpell, *In the Company of Animals: A Study of Human-Animal Relationships* (London: Basil Blackwell, 1986), 186–211.

32. Quoted in Serpell, "Working," 43.

33. Keith Thomas, *Man and the Natural World: A History of the Modern Sensibility* (New York: Pantheon Books, 1983), 46.

34. Mason, *Unnatural Order*, 176. Mason sees modern civilization's domination and exploitation of animals and nature manifest in two especially violent forms—animal experimen-

tation and industrial animal confinement and production, known as "factory farming." Jim Mason, "All Heaven in a Rage," in Laura A. Moretti, *All Heaven in a Rage: Essays on the Eating of Animals* (Chico, CA: MBK Publishing, 1999), 19.

35. At the end of Karl Jacoby's essay about the similar fates of domestic animals and human slaves, he asks, "Were the advances in civilization that the rise of agriculture made possible outweighed by the creation of new forms of domination over animals and fellow human beings?" Jacoby, "Slaves by Nature?" 97.

36. Aviva Cantor, "The Club, the Yoke, and the Leash: What We Can Learn from the Way a Culture Treats Animals," *Ms.* (August 1983), 27.

37. Jeremy Bentham, *Introduction to the Principles of Morals and Legislation* (1789). Quoted in Jon Wynne Tyson, ed., *The Extended Circle: A Commonplace Book of Animal Rights* (New York: Paragon House, 1989), 16.

38. Jacoby, "Slaves by Nature?" 94.

39. Ibid, 92.

40. Elizabeth Fisher, *Women's Creation: Sexual Evolution and the Shaping of Society* (New York: Doubleday, 1979), 190, 197; Stanley and Roslind Godlovitch and John Harris, eds., *Animals, Men and Morals: An Enquiry into the Maltreatment of Non-humans* (New York: Taplinger, 1972), 228; Mason, *Unnatural Order*, 199, 275; Jacoby, "Slaves by Nature?"

41. Fisher, *Women's Creation*, 190.

42. Ibid, 197.

43. Of all the animals exploited and killed in food production today, female animals—hens, pigs, dairy cows—fare the worst, with the egg industry "the most acute example of highly centralized, corporate exploitation of female animals." Lori Gruen, "Dismantling Oppression: An Analysis of the Connection Between Women and Animals" in Greta Gaard, ed., *Ecofeminism: Women, Animals, Nature* (Philadelphia: Temple University Press, 1993), 72–4.

44. Gerda Lerner, *The Creation of Patriarchy* (New York: Oxford University Press, 1986), 46.

45. Mason, *Unnatural Order*, 199.

46. Thomas, *Man and the Natural World*, 44.

47. Ibid.

48. Ibid, 44–5.

49. Winthrop D. Jordan, *The White Man's Burden: Historical Origins of Racism in the United States* (New York: Oxford University Press, 1974), 81.

50. Ibid, 82.

51. On one estate in the Caribbean the same letters are used to brand cattle today that were used to brand its slaves in the 1700s. Orlando Patterson, *Slavery and Social Death: A Comparative Study* (Cambridge, MA: Harvard University Press, 1982), 59.

52. Tzvetan Todorov, *The Conquest of America: The Question of the Other* (New York: Harper and Row, 1984), 137.

53. Kenneth M. Stampp, *The Peculiar Institution: Slavery in the Ante-Bellum South* (New York: Knopf, 1956), 210. In Europe local authorities subjected Gypsies to branding and mutilation and put iron rings around their necks. Donald Kenrick and Grattan Puxon, *The*

Destiny of Europe's Gypsies (New York: Basic Books, 1972), 43, 54. In the France of Louis XIV Gypsies were branded and their heads were shaved; in Moravia and Bohemia the authorities cut off the ears of Gypsy women. Isabel Fonseca, *Bury Me Standing: The Gypsies and Their Journey* (New York: Vintage, 1996), 229. During World War II, Germans tatooed and shaved Gypsies upon their arrival at Auschwitz-Birkenau. Kenrick and Puxon, *Destiny*, 155.

54. Stampp, *Peculiar Institution*, 188. In Jamaica it was legal to cut off the foot of a runaway. Jordan, *White Man's Burden*, 81.

55. Patterson, *Slavery and Social Death*, 59.

56. Stampp, *Peculiar Institution*, 188.

57. Ibid, 210, 188.

58. Herbert Aptheker, *Abolitionism: A Revolutionary Movement* (Boston: Twayne, 1989), 111.

59. Stampp, *Peculiar Institution*, 174. See also Marjorie Spiegel, *The Dreaded Comparison: Human and Animal Slavery*, revised edition (New York: Mirror Books, 1996).

60. Steven M. Wise, *Rattling the Cage: Toward Legal Rights for Animals* (Cambridge, MA: Perseus Books, 2000), 52.

61. "Neither the ancient Greeks nor Hebrews nor Christians had difficulty accepting that the end of everything in the universe was themselves," writes Wise. "But no scientific evidence today exists that other animals, or anything, were made for us." Wise recommends that those who hold such views "should put these childish things away." Ibid, 264–5.

62. Genesis 1:25–6.

63. Kapleau, *To Cherish All Life*, 21.

64. Quoted in Ibid, 21, 23.

65. Ibid, 1.

66. A single copy of the Gutenberg Bible, printed in the 1400s, required the skins of 170 baby calves, slaughtered while they were still milk-fed so that their hides could be turned into fine vellum. The initial 35 vellum copies of the Gutenberg Bible required the slaughter of close to 6,000 baby calves. Joyce E. Salisbury, *The Beast Within: Animals in the Middle Ages* (New York: Routledge, 1994), 23.

67. Milan Kundera, *The Unbearable Lightness of Being* (New York: HarperPerennial, 1999), 286. Albert Kaplan writes, "The suggestion that God gave the Jews, or anybody else, permission to murder animals and eat them is rubbish." Personal communication to author.

68. Andrew Linzey and Dan Cohn-Sherbok, *After Noah: Animals and the Liberation of Theology* (New York: Cassell, 1997), 23.

69. Isaiah 66:3.

70. Aviva Cantor, *Jewish Women, Jewish Men: The Legacy of Patriarchy in Jewish Life* (San Francisco: Harper and Row, 1995), 84.

71. Quoted in Richard Schwartz, "Tsa'ar Ba'alei Chayim—Judaism and Compassion for Animals" in Roberta Kalechofsky, ed. *Judaism and Animal Rights: Classical and Contemporary Responses* (Marblehead, MA: Micah Publications, 1992), 61. See also Richard Schwartz, *Judaism and Vegetarianism*, revised edition (New York: Lantern, 2001).

72. Genesis 1:29.

73. Quoted in Cartmill, *View*, 255 #38.

74. Quoted in Wise, *Rattling the Cage*, 13.

75. Thomas, *Man and the Natural World,* 17; Wise, *Rattling the Cage,* 14–5. Today this deeply entrenched view of western culture is being increasingly challenged. "The animals of the world exist for their own reasons," writes Alice Walker. "They were not made for humans any more than black people were made for whites or women for men." Foreword in Spiegel, *Dreaded Comparison,* 14.

76. Quoted in Cartmill, *View*, 40–1.

77. Aristotle, *Politics.* Quoted in Mason, *Unnatural Order,* 228.

78. Anthony Pagden, *The Fall of Natural Man: The American Indian and the Origins of Comparative Ethnology* (Cambridge: Cambridge University Press, 1982), 43.

79. Quoted in Wise, *Rattling the Cage*, 15.

80. Quoted in Ibid, 16.

81. Quoted in Mason, *Unnatural Order*, 34.

82. Wise, *Rattling the Cage,* 32.

83. Cartmill, *View*, 41. See also Serpell, *In the Company*, 219–20. J. M. C. Toynbee writes about the pleasure the Roman mind took "in the often hideous sufferings and agonizing deaths of quantities of magnificent and noble creatures." J. M. C. Toynbee, *Animals in Roman Life and Art* (Ithaca, NY: Cornell University Press, 1973), 21.

84. Dio Cassius, 39.38.2. Quoted in Cartmill, *View*, 41.

85. Cicero, *Ad familiares* 7.1.3. Quoted in Ibid, 42.

86. Quoted in Ascione and Arkow, *Child Abuse,* 45. Joyce Salisbury writes that during the Middle Ages the use of animals as models for human behavior in fables and bestiary literature, as well as folk beliefs in half-human creatures, was blurring the line that separated people from animals even as Aquinas and other Christian thinkers were asserting the absolute difference between the species. See Salisbury, *Beast Within,* especially Chapters 4 and 5.

87. Quoted in Salisbury, *Beast Within,* 16–17.

88. Ascione and Arkow, *Child Abuse,* 45–6.

89. Other Christian writers addressing the issue of respect and justice for animals include John Baker, Stephen Webb, Gary Kowalski, J. R. Hyland, and Jay McDaniel. For a good overview of the attempt of contemporary Christianity to transcend its human-centered tradition, see Roger S. Gottlieb, ed., *This Sacred Earth: Religion, Nature, Environment* (New York: Routledge, 1996).

90. *Satya* (January 2000), 3–4.

91. Plato, *Timaeus*, 40–1; Arthur O. Lovejoy, *The Great Chain of Being* (Cambridge, MA: Harvard University Press, 1936), 46ff.

92. Mason, *Unnatural Order*, 211.

93. Thomas, *Man and the Natural World,* 18.

94. E. M. W. Tillyard, *The Elizabethan World Picture* (New York: Random House, 1959), 27.

95. John Weiss, *Ideology of Death: Why the Holocaust Happened in Germany* (Chicago: Ivan R. Dee, 1996), 45.

96. Lovejoy, *Great Chain*, 80.

97. Pagden, *Fall of Natural Man*, 22.

98. Hayden White, "The Forms of Wildness: Archaeology of an Idea," in Edward Dudley and Maximillian E. Novak, ed., *The Wild Man Within: An Image of Western Thought from the Renaissance to Romanticism* (Pittsburgh: University of Pittsburgh Press, 1972), 14. Quoted in David Stannard, *American Holocaust: The Conquest of the New World* (New York: Oxford University Press, 1992), 173.

99. Thomas, *Man and the Natural World*, 134.

100. The Jesuit Joseph Francois Lafitan's highly regarded "Customs of the American Indians Compared with the Customs of Primitive Times" included an illustration of a headless native American whose face was embedded in his chest. Stannard, *American Holocaust*, 227.

101. Thomas, *Man and the Natural World*, 18.

102. Ibid, 19.

103. Ibid, 33.

104. Ibid, 34.

105. Ibid.

106. Serpell, *In the Company of Animals*, 170.

107. Thomas, *Man and the Natural World*, 34–6.

108. Ibid, 40–1.

109. Sagan and Druyan, *Shadows*, 365. Albert Schweitzer criticized western philosophy for not taking "the decisive step of making kindness to animals an ethical demand, on exactly the same footing as kindness to human beings." He wrote: "Ethics in our western world has hitherto been largely limited to the relation of man to man. But that is a limited ethics. We need a boundless ethic which will include the animals also." Albert Schweitzer, *The Animal World of Albert Schweitzer: Jungle Insights into Reverence for Life* (Boston: Beacon Press, 1950), 30, 183.

110. Thomas, *Man and the Natural World*, 41, 46–7.

111. Robert Jay Lifton, *The Nazi Doctors: Medical Killing and the Psychology of Genocide* (New York: Basic Books, 1986), 441–2 (emphasis added by Lifton). German anthropologists trained in the Haeckelian tradition became enthusiastic advocates of Nazi "race hygiene" in the 1930s.

112. Cartmill, *View*, 135. According to Nick Fiddes, author of *Meat: A Natural Symbol*, meat eating is the quintessential symbol of human supremacy, in that it "represents human control of the natural world. Consuming the muscle flesh of other highly evolved animals is a potent statement of our supreme power." Quoted in Salisbury, *Beast Within*, 55.

113. Cartmill, *View*, 135–6. See also Part III ("Animals and Empire") of Harriet Ritvo, *The Animal Estate: The English and Other Creatures in the Victorian Age* (Cambridge, MA: Harvard University Press, 1987), 205–88.

114. Leo Kuper, *Genocide: Its Political Use in the Twentieth Century* (New Haven: Yale University Press, 1981), 88.

2 WOLVES, APES, PIGS, RATS, VERMIN

1. Sigmund Freud, "A Difficulty in the Path of Psycho-Analysis" (1917) in *The Standard Edition of the Complete Psychological Works of Sigmund Freud,* James Strachey, trans. (London: Hogarth Press, 1955), Vol. XVII, 140. Donald C. Peattie made a similar point in 1942 while writing about the appeal of the Walt Disney movie *Bambi* to children: "To a child, in his simplicity, the life of an innocent, harmless, and beautiful animal is just as precious as that of a human being, so many of whom do not appear altogether innocent and harmless and beautiful." Donald C. Peattie, "The Nature of Things" in *Audubon Magazine,* 44: 266–71 (July 1942). Quoted in Matt Cartmill, *A View to a Death in the Morning: Hunting and Nature Through History* (Cambridge, MA: Harvard University Press, 1993), 180.

2. David Stannard, *American Holocaust: The Conquest of the New World* (New York: Oxford University Press, 1992), 242.

3. Ervin Staub, *The Roots of Evil: The Origins of Genocide and Other Group Violence* (Cambridge: Cambridge University Press, 1989), 175. The precedent was reassuring to Adolf Hitler, who asked, "Who remembers now the massacres of the Armenians?" Ibid, 187.

4. Neil J. Kressel, *Mass Hate: The Global Rise of Genocide and Terror* (New York: Perseus Books, 1996), 250.

5. Margaret T. Hodgen, *Early Anthropology in the Sixteenth and Seventeenth Centuries* (Philadelphia: University of Pennsylvania Press, 1964), 410–11.

6. Ibid, 411–12, 417.

7. Ibid, 422.

8. Keith Thomas, *Man and the Natural World: A History of the Modern Sensibility* (New York: Pantheon Books, 1983), 42.

9. Ibid, 136.

10. Quoted in Stephen Jay Gould, *The Mismeasure of Man,* revised edition (New York: Norton, 1981), 69.

11. Quoted in Ibid.

12. Quoted in Ibid, 118.

13. Henry Friedlander, *The Origins of Nazi Genocide: From Euthanasia to the Final Solution* (Chapel Hill: University of North Carolina Press, 1995), 1.

14. Quoted in Gould, *Mismeasure,* 133.

15. Ibid, 135.

16. Friedlander, *Origins,* 2.

17. Gould, *Mismeasure,* 88.

18. Gould, *Mismeasure,* 85–6.

19. Jim Mason, *An Unnatural Order: Why We Are Destroying the Planet and Each Other* (New York: Continuum, 1997), 241.

20. Philip P. Hallie, *The Paradox of Cruelty* (Middletown, CT: Wesleyan University Press, 1969), 110.

21. *Southwestern Christian Advocate* (April 27, 1893). Quoted in Charles Patterson, "Social Perspectives of Protestant Journals During the Depression of 1893–97" (Doctoral dissertation, Columbia University, 1970), 209.

22. Quoted in Gould, *Mismeasure*, 111.

23. Quoted in Ibid, 112.

24. Stannard, *American Holocaust*, 246.

25. Ibid, 248.

26. The first book about America published in the English language in 1511 described the Indians as "lyke bestes without any reasonablenes." Ibid, 225–6.

27. Ibid, 67.

28. Bartolomé de Las Casas, *The Devastation of the Indies: A Brief Account* (New York: Seabury Press, 1974), 43.

29. Tzvetan Todorov, *The Conquest of America: The Question of the Other* (New York: Harper and Row, 1984), 141.

30. Las Casas, *Devastation of the Indies*, 52, 70.

31. Quoted in Stannard, *American Holocaust*, 220.

32. Quoted in Mason, *Unnatural Order*, 231.

33. Thomas, *Man and the Natural World*, 42.

34. Robert F. Berkhofer, Jr., *The White Man's Indian: Images of the American Indian from Columbus to the Present* (New York: Vintage Books, 1979), 21.

35. Francis Jennings, *The Invasion of America: Indians, Colonialism, and the Cant of Conquest* (Chapel Hill: University of North Carolina, 1975), 78.

36. Hodgen, *Early Anthropology*, 22.

37. Thomas, *Man and the Natural World*, 42.

38. Richard Drinnon, *Facing West: The Metaphysics of Indian-Hating and Empire-Building* (Norman: University of Oklahoma Press, 1997), 53.

39. Thomas F. Gossett, *Race: The History of an Idea in America*, second edition (New York: Oxford University Press, 1997), 229–30.

40. Jennings, *Invasion of America*, 60.

41. Ibid, 12.

42. Ibid, 244; Gossett, *Race*, 243–4.

43. Stannard, *American Holocaust*, 145.

44. Ibid, 243.

45. Ibid.

46. Ibid, 245.

47. Quoted in Ibid, 126.

48. Ibid, 127. General William Colby took possession of an infant who survived the massacre to display her for profit as a "war curio." When he first put Lost Bird, as she came to be called, on display, his hometown newspaper reported, "not less than 500 persons called at his house to see it [sic]." Lost Bird, who was later put on display in Buffalo Bill's Wild West Show, died in Los Angeles at the age of 29.

49. Ibid.

50. Mason, *Unnatural Order*, 241.

51. *California Christian Advocate* (July 31, 1895). Quoted in Charles Patterson, "Social Perspectives of Protestant Journals During the Depression of 1893–97" (Doctoral dissertation, Columbia University, 1970), 228. For the story of Ishi, the last "wild Indian," see Theodora Kroeber, *Ishi in Two Worlds: A Biography of the Last Wild Indian in North America* (Berkeley: University of California Press, 1961).

52. John Toland, *Adolf Hitler* (Garden City, NY: Doubleday, 1976), 702. The camps the British built for the captured Boers in South Africa during the Boer War (1899–1902) convinced Hitler of the usefulness of concentration camps. Ibid.

53. John W. Dower, *War Without Mercy: Race and Power in the Pacific War* (New York: Pantheon, 1986), 89. For most people in America, a nation full of hunters to begin with, writes Dower, killing animals was much easier than killing people since hunters are accustomed to closing their minds to the fact that the animals they kill "are sentient beings that know fear and feel pain." Ibid.

54. Drinnon, *Facing West*, 287.

55. Ibid, 287, 315.

56. Ibid, 321.

57. Ibid, 325.

58. Dower, *War Without Mercy*, 152.

59. Stuart Creighton Miller, *"Benevolent Assimilation": The American Conquest of the Philippines, 1899–1903* (New Haven: Yale University Press, 1982), 188.

60. Quoted in Ibid, 188–9. In Austria during World War II, after some prisoners escaped from the Mauthausen concentration camp, the police commander noted that the local people who gathered with their guns, knives, and pitchforks to hunt down the prey "were arrayed as if for a chase." After they tracked down and brutally killed the prisoners, the local people referred to the bloodletting as the "rabbit hunt." Gordon J. Horwitz, *In the Shadow of Death: Living Outside the Gates of Mauthausen* (New York: Free Press, 1990), 134.

61. Quoted in Miller, *"Benevolent Assimilation"*, 189. The fact that fifteen Filipinos were killed for every one wounded suggested that the massacre of civilians was standard operating procedure. When a U.S. Senate committee asked General Arthur MacArthur why there was such a high ratio of killed to wounded, his answer was that "inferior races succumbed to wounds more readily than Anglo-Saxons." Dower, *War Without Mercy*, 152.

62. Drinnon, *Facing West*, 325–6. Drinnon writes that the apathy of these "little brown rats" resembled that of the walking corpses (*Muselmänner*) of the kind Bruno Bettelheim encountered in Dachau and Buchenwald. Ibid, 326 (footnote).

63. Ibid, 314.

64. Dower, *War Without Mercy*, 81.

65. Ibid, 78.

66. Ibid, 82. A Russian visitor to a Spanish mission in California in 1818 wrote that the Indians there lived in "specially constructed cattle-pens" in what he said can only be described as a "barnyard for domestic cattle and fowl." Stannard, *American Holocaust*, 138. At Auschwitz-Birkenau Anne Frank lived with more than 1,000 women in a barrack

which had originally be designed as a barn for fifty-two horses. Melissa Müller, *Anne Frank: The Biography* (New York: Henry Holt, 1998), 250.

67. Dower, *War Without Mercy*, 82–4.
68. Ibid, 84–6.
69. Ibid, 90–2.
70. Iris Chang, *The Rape of Nanking: The Forgotten Holocaust of World War II*. (New York: Basic Books, 1997), 44.
71. Ibid, 94.
72. Ibid, 56.
73. Ibid, 30.
74. Ibid, 218. The Japanese were not alone in calling the Chinese "pigs." In the nineteenth and early twentieth centuries European labor merchants, who recruited and seized thousands of Chinese "coolies" in port cities and shipped them off as "indentured laborers" to distant places like Malaya, Peru, and the West Indies, called their business the "pig trade." V. G. Kiernan, *The Lords of Human Kind: Black Man, Yellow Man, and White Man in an Age of Empire* (Boston: Little, Brown, 1969), 163.
75. Karl A. Menninger, "Totemic Aspects of Contemporary Attitudes Toward Animals," in George B. Wilbur and Warner Muensterberger, eds., *Psychoanalysis and Culture: Essays in Honor of Géza Róheim* (New York: International Universities Press, 1951), 50.
76. Ibid.
77. Drinnon, *Facing West*, 449.
78. Quoted in Stannard, *American Holocaust*, 252–3, and Drinnon, *Facing West*, 448–9.
79. Stannard, *American Holocaust*, 254.
80. Staub, *Roots of Evil*, 101.
81. John Weiss, *Ideology of Death: Why the Holocaust Happened in Germany* (Chicago: Ivan R. Dee, 1996), 22–4.
82. Gossett, *Race*, 12.
83. Weiss, *Ideology of Death*, 67.
84. Ibid, 118.
85. Ibid, 138.
86. Ibid, 125
87. Ibid, 140–1
88. Ian Kershaw, *Hitler: 1889–1936 Hubris* (New York: Norton, 1998), 152.
89. Charles Patterson, *Anti-Semitism: The Road to the Holocaust and Beyond* (New York: Walker, 1982), 65.
90. Eugen Kogon, Hermann Langbein, and Adalbert Ruckerl, eds., *Nazi Mass Murder: A Documentary History of the Use of Poison Gas* (New Haven: Yale University Press, 1993), 213.
91. Kershaw, *Hitler: 1889–1936*, 244.
92. Fritz Redlich, *Hitler: Diagnosis of a Destructive Prophet* (New York: Oxford University Press, 1999), 172. On another occasion Hitler said, "there is nothing else open to modern

peoples than to terminate the Jews." Ian Kershaw, *Hitler: 1936–1945 Nemesis* (New York: Norton, 2000), 589.

93. John K. Roth and Michael Berenbaum, eds., *Holocaust: Religious and Philosophical Implications* (St. Paul, MN: Paragon House, 1989), xvii.

94. Weiss, *Ideology of Death*, 301.

95. Boria Sax, *Animals in the Third Reich: Pets, Scapegoats, and the Holocaust* (New York: Continuum, 2000), 159. *Der Ewige Jude* was the German title of Henry Ford's *The International Jew*, which had been circulating widely in Germany for years (see next chapter). I saw "The Eternal Jew" at the Yad Vashem Summer Institute for Holocaust Education in Jerusalem, which I attended in 1983.

96. Weiss, *Ideology of Death*, 343.

97. Kershaw, *Hitler: 1936–1945*, 249. Goebbels did not like what he saw of the Poles, either: "More animals than human beings....The filth of the Poles is unimaginable." Ibid, 245. Goebbels recorded in his diary that the Russians "are not a people, but a conglomeration of animals." Louis P. Lochner, ed., *The Goebbels Diaries*, 1942–1943 (Garden City, NY: Doubleday, 1948), 52.

98. Ernst Klee, Willi Dressen, and Volker Riess, eds., *"The Good Old Days": The Holocaust as Seen by Its Perpetrators and Bystanders* (New York: Free Press, 1991), 159. Some prisoners at labor camps near Auschwitz were harnassed to ploughshares to replace horses requisitioned by the army, while in the men's camp in Birkenau boys were harnassed to heavy wagons, called *Rolwagen*, as a replacement for horses. The first prisoners of war marched to Auschwitz in its early days were not fed along the way, but instead were led into nearby fields and told to "graze" like cattle on everything that was edible. Yisrael Gutman and Michael Berenbaum, eds., *Anatomy of the Auschwitz Death Camp* (Bloomington: Indiana University Press, 1994), 207, 221–2, 119.

99. Konnilyn G. Feig, *Hitler's Death Camps* (New York: Holmes and Meier, 1981), 11.

100. Richard Breitman, *The Architect of Genocide: Himmler and the Final Solution* (New York, Knopf, 1991), 177.

101. In the trenches in World War I, Hitler liked to stay up at night and shoot rats. Redlich, *Hitler*, 39, 266.

102. Marion Kaplan, *Between Dignity and Despair: Jewish Life in Nazi Germany* (New York: Oxford University Press, 1998), 53, 108, 160; Eric A. Johnson, *Nazi Terror: The Gestapo, Jews, and Ordinary Germans* (New York: Basic Books, 1999), 102, 103, 159, 168, 387; Edwin Black, *IBM and the Holocaust: The Strategic Alliance Between Nazi Germany and America's Most Powerful Corporation* (New York: Crown, 2001), 139, 363; Wolfgang W. E. Samuel, *German Boy: A Refugee's Story* (Jackson: University Press of Mississippi, 2000), 75. Nazis also insulted each other with porcine epithets. Ernst Röhm told Hitler's onetime friend Hermann Rauschning, "Adolf is a swine." Johnson, *Nazi Terror*, 170. In his diary (October 26, 1925) Joseph Goebbels wrote, "Streicher spoke. Like a pig." Lochner, ed., *Goebbels Diaries*, 6.

103. Klee, *"Good Old Days,"* 204. "We are treated worse than pigs," wrote one ghetto diarist. Lawrence L. Langer, *Admitting the Holocaust: Collected Essays* (New York: Oxford University Press, 1995), 43.

104. Horwitz, *In the Shadow of Death*, 159.

105. Indictment of Gustav Laabs, Alois Haefele, and others at a court in Bonn, July 25, 1962. Raul Hilberg, *Perpetrators, Victims, Bystanders: The Jewish Catastrophe, 1933–1945* (New York: HarperCollins, 1992), 34.

106. James Serpell, *In the Company of Animals: A Study of Human-Animal Relationships* (London: Basil Blackwell, 1986), 229–30.

107. Robert Jay Lifton, *The Nazi Doctors: Medical Killing and the Psychology of Genocide* (New York: Basic Books, 1986), 378. The official German report on the destruction of the Warsaw Ghetto described the last ghetto residents as *Kreaturen* (creatures), *Untermenschen* (subhumans), *Banden* (gangs), *Banditen* (bandits), *Gesindel* (rabble), and *niedrigste Elemente* (lowest elements). Sybil Milton, trans., *The Stroop Report: The Jewish Quarter of Warsaw Is No More!* (New York: Pantheon, 1979). Introduction by Andrzej Wirth, 4.

108. Lifton, *Nazi Doctors*, 373.

109. Kressel, *Mass Hate*, 200.

110. Terrence Des Pres, "Excremental Assault" in Roth and Berenbaum, *Holocaust*, 210.

111. Daniel Jonah Goldhagen, *Hitler's Willing Executioners: Ordinary Germans and the Holocaust* (New York: Knopf, 1996), 387. For examples of the Germans' mockery and degradation of their victims, see Ibid, 256–61.

112. Gitta Sereny, *Into That Darkness: An Examination of Conscience* (New York: Vintage, 1983), 101. The denigration of animals serves the same function—to make killing them easier. "Taunting the victim before sacrifice is a widespread ritual observance in many societies. It probably helps to distance the killers both emotionally and symbolically from the animal." Serpell, *In the Company*, 184–5. "Just as we slander people we have wronged by attaching to them such labels as "congenitally lazy," "stupid," "dirty," or "barbarous" to justify our oppression and/or exploitation of them, in the same way we denigrate animals we want to slaughter in order to eat them with an untroubled conscience." Philip Kapleau, *To Cherish All Life: A Buddhist Case for Becoming Vegetarian*, second edition (Rochester, NY: The Zen Center, 1986), 39.

113. Quoted in letter from Simon Wiesenthal Center, June 1999.

114. Quoted in the National Christian Leadership Conference for Israel Background Paper, January 1998. Dr. Hanan Ashrawi, a member of the Palestinian Legislative Council, claims that Israelis also use animal epithets to reduce the humanity of the Palestinians. "The historical and familiar slurs used by Israeli officials and public figures (including cockroaches, two-legged vermin, dogs) have been expanded to include 'snakes' and 'crocodiles.' " *Satya* (November/December 2000), 16.

115. *Response* (Simon Wiesenthal Center World Report), Summer/Fall 1999, 11. At a rally in Montenegro during his final days in power, Yugoslav strongman Slobodan Milosovic called his opponents "rats and hyenas." Dusan Strojanovic, "Milosevic's Emotional Final Days" (Associated Press, October 7, 2000).

116. Judy Chicago, *Holocaust Project: From Darkness into Light* (New York: Viking Penguin, 1993), 8.

117. Ibid, 58.

118. The contribution of the industrialized slaughter of animals to the development of modern assembly-line production is discussed in the next chapter.

119. Ibid, 58–9.

120. Ibid, 59.

121. Ibid, 59–60.

3   THE INDUSTRIALIZATION OF SLAUGHTER

1. David Stannard, *American Holocaust: The Conquest of the New World* (New York: Oxford University Press, 1992), 184.

2. Ibid, 246.

3. Translation of "Auschwitz beginnt da, wo jemand auf Schlachthof steht und denkt: Es sind ja nur Tiere." Quoted in Christa Blanke, *Da krähte der Hahn: Kirche für Tier? Eine Streitschrift* (Eschbach, Germany: Verlag am Eschbach, 1995), 48.

4. Jeremy Rifkin, *Beyond Beef: The Rise and Fall of the Cattle Culture* (New York: Penguin, 1992), 45–6.

5. Keith Thomas, *Man and the Natural World: A History of the Modern Sensibility* (New York: Pantheon Books, 1983), 25–6.

6. Ibid, 26.

7. Jimmy M. Skaggs, *Prime Cut: Livestock Raising and Meatpacking in the United States, 1607–1983* (College Station: Texas A & M University Press, 1986), 34.

8. Ibid, 34–8.

9. Robert P. Swierenga, *Faith and Family: Dutch Immigration and Settlement in the United States, 1820–1920* (New York: Holmes and Meier, 2000), 286 #19.

10. Skaggs, *Prime Cut*, 38–9.

11. Ibid, 39.

12. Ibid.

13. Ibid, 39–41. In the South, where pork was the mainstay on plantations, most planters raised their own pigs and grew the corn they needed to feed both their pigs and slaves. They gave the job of killing the animals to the slaves. Kenneth M. Stampp, *The Peculiar Institution: Slavery in the Ante-Bellum South* (New York: Vintage, 1956), 45, 50–1.

14. Rifkin, *Beyond Beef*, 119.

15. James R. Barrett, *Work and Community in the Jungle: Chicago's Packinghouse Workers, 1894–1922* (Urbana: University of Illinois Press, 1987), 15, 19.

16. Quoted in Rifkin, *Beyond Beef*, 245.

17. Ibid, 246.

18. Ibid, 245.

19. Quoted in Ibid, 246.

20. Philip Kapleau, *To Cherish All Life. A Buddhist Case for Becoming Vegetarian*, second edition (Rochester, NY: The Zen Center, 1986), 46.

21. Skaggs, *Prime Cut*, 119.

22. Barrett, *Work*, 57.

23. Quotations are from Chapter 3 of Upton Sinclair, *The Jungle* (New York: Signet, 1990), 35–45.

24. Ibid, 311.

25. Ibid, 312.

26. Ibid, 136.

27. Afterword by Emory Elliott in Ibid, 344.

28. Upton Sinclair, *The Autobiography of Upton Sinclair* (New York: Harcourt, Brace and World, 1962), 126.

29. personal communication to author from David Cantor.

30. Donald D. Stull and Michael J. Broadway, "Killing Them Softly: Work in Meatpacking Plants and What It Does to Workers" in Donald D. Stull, Michael J. Broadway, and David Griffith, eds., *Any Way You Cut It: Meat-Processing and Small-Town America* (Lawrence: University Press of Kansas, 1995), 62.

31. Gail Eisnitz, *Slaughterhouse: The Shocking Story of Greed, Neglect, and Inhumane Treatment Inside the U.S. Meat Industry* (Amherst, NY: Prometheus, 1997), 182.

32. Ibid, 183–4.

33. Sue Coe, *Dead Meat* (New York: Four Walls Eight Windows, 1996), 111.

34. Ibid, 111–2.

35. Ibid, 112.

36. Ibid, 112–3.

37. For the story of how IBM's Hollerith punch card technology expedited Nazi Germany's industrialized killing of Jews and others, see Chapter 13 ("Extermination") of Edwin Black, *IBM and the Holocaust: The Strategic Alliance Between Nazi Germany and America's Most Powerful Corporation* (New York: Crown, 2001), 351–74.

38. Coe, *Dead Meat*, 118.

39. Ibid, 119.

40. Gitta Sereny, *Into That Darkness: An Examination of Conscience* (New York: Vantage, 1983), 157. When Karen Davis read the description of the scene, she said it reminded her of the atmosphere at the annual Hegins pigeon shoot in Pennsylvania where people used to eat, drink, and enjoy themselves while shooters spent the day killing and wounding pigeons released from boxes. personal communication to author.

41. Coe, *Dead Meat*, 120. For a description of how chickens are slaughtered, see Karen Davis, *Prisoned Chickens, Poisoned Eggs: An Inside Look at the Modern Poultry Industry* (Summertown, TN: Book Publishing Company, 1996), 105–24.

42. Coe, *Dead Meat*, 72.

43. Betsy Swart, "Interview with Gail Eisnitz" in Friends of Animals, *ActionLine* (Fall 1998), 29.

44. Ibid.

45. Farm Animal Reform Movement (FARM), *FARM Report* (Winter 1999), 7.

46. See David J. Wolfson, *Beyond the Law: Agribusiness and the Systemic Abuse of Animals Raised for Food or Food Production* (New York: Archimedian Press, 1996).

47. Gene Bauston, "Farm Sanctuary Government Affairs and Legislative Campaigns" letter to Farm Sanctuary members, July 17, 2000.

48. Henry Ford, *My Life and Work*, in collaboration with Samuel Crowther (Garden City, NY: Doubleday, Page & Company, 1922), 81. The slaughterhouse Ford visited was most likely located in the Union Stock Yards, although he did not specify which slaughterhouse it was.

49. Carol Adams, *The Sexual Politics of Meat* (New York: Continuum, 1991), 52.

50. Rifkin, *Beyond Beef*, 120.

51. J. M. Coetzee, *The Lives of Animals* (Princeton, NJ: Princeton University Press, 1999), 53.

52. Rifkin, *Beyond Beef*, 119–20.

53. Ibid, 120–1.

54. Barrett, *Work*, 20.

55. From 1923 to 1927 the magazine's circulation exceeded 500,000. David L. Lewis, *The Public Image of Henry Ford: An American Folk Hero and His Company* (Detroit: Wayne State University Press, 1976), 135.

56. Dealers who filled their subscription quotas received Ford cars as prizes, while dealers reluctant to sell subscriptions received threatening legalistic letters insisting they sell the newspaper. Reprints of the newspaper were bound into booklets and distributed to libraries and YMCAs throughout the country. Edwin Black, *The Transfer Agreement: The Untold Story of the Secret Agreement Between the Third Reich and Jewish Palestine* (New York: Macmillan, 1984), 27.

57. Norman Cohn, *Warrant for Genocide: The Myth of the Jewish World Conspiracy and the "Protocols of the Elders of Zion"* (London: Serif, 1996), 176–7.

58. Keith Sward, *The Legend of Henry Ford* (New York: Rinehart, 1948), 149.

59. Lewis, *Public Image*, 142–3.

60. Robert Waite writes that some three million copies were sold or given away as a public service to high school, municipal, and college libraries. Robert G. L. Waite, *The Psychopathic God Adolf Hitler* (New York: Basic Books, 1977), 138.

61. Albert Lee, *Henry Ford and the Jews* (New York: Stein and Day, 1980), 51.

62. Robert Wistrich, *Who's Who in Nazi Germany* (London: Weidenfeld and Nicolson, 1982), 271.

63. Lewis, *Public Image*, 143.

64. Lee, *Ford and the Jews*, 45. After discussing the question of Ford's alleged financial support of Hitler, Lee concludes that while the issue may never be resolved completely, "enough credible sources express belief and cite plausible reasons to indicate that such contributions were highly likely." Ibid, 52–7.

65. Cohn, *Warrant*, 178.

66. Adolf Hitler, *Mein Kampf* (Boston: Houghton Mifflin, 1971), 639.

67. Lee, *Ford and the Jews*, 46.

68. Nathan C. Belth, *A Promise to Keep: A Narrative of the American Encounter with Anti-Semitism* (New York: Times Books, 1979), 76.

69. Lewis, *Public Image*, 140.

70. Charles Patterson, *Anti-Semitism: The Road to the Holocaust and Beyond* (New York: Walker, 1989), 52.

71. Lewis, *Public Image*, 148–9.

72. Ibid, 148.

73. A photo showing Ford in his office in 1938, receiving the medal from the German counsuls can be found in Belth, *Promise*, 86 (World Wide Photos) and Lewis, *Public Image*, 171 (Detroit Free Press photo). The previous year in Wannsee, just outside Berlin, American businessman, Thomas Watson, president of International Business Machines, received the Merit Cross of the German Eagle with Star, specially created by Hitler. Edwin Black, *IBM and the Holocaust: The Strategic Alliance Between Nazi Germany and America's Most Powerful Corporation* (New York: Crown, 2001), 131–4, 217.

74. Lewis, *Public Image*, 149.

75. Cohn, *Warrant*, 86.

76. Yisrael Gutman and Michael Berenbaum, eds., *Anatomy of the Auschwitz Death Camp* (Bloomington: Indiana University Press, 1994), 6.

77. For a full account of the close ties between another large American company and Nazi Germany, see Black, *IBM and the Holocaust*.

78. Ken Silverstein, "Ford and the Führer: New Documents Reveal the Close Ties Between Dearborn and the Nazis" in *The Nation* (January 24, 2000), 11–16. My thanks to Allen Bergson for bringing this article to my attention. It should be noted that subsequent efforts by Henry Ford II, the Ford family, and company to improve relations with the Jewish community have included substantial donations to Yeshiva University and the Albert Einstein Medical Center, a gift of $1,000,000 to the National Conference of Christians and Jews for a national headquarters building in New York, and contributions to various national Jewish organizations and causes, such as the United Jewish Appeal, the Israel Emergency Fund, the Jewish Welfare Federation, and the Anti-Defamation League of B'nai B'rith. Henry Ford II also built a Ford assembly plant in Israel, even though it meant a boycott of all Ford products in Egypt, Syria, Lebanon, Iraq, and Saudi Arabia. Lewis, *Public Image*, 154–9; Albert Lee, *Henry Ford and the Jews*, iii.

4   IMPROVING THE HERD

1. Keith Thomas writes that in the early modern period in England animal breeding was "ruthlessly eugenic." A seventeeth-century handbook declared, "As soon as the bitch hath littered, it is requisite to choose them you intend to preserve, and throw away the rest." Keith Thomas, *Man and the Natural World: A History of the Modern Sensibility* (New York: Pantheon Books, 1983), 60.

2. Henry Friedlander, *The Origins of Nazi Genocide: From Euthanasia to the Final Solution* (Chapel Hill: University of North Carolina Press, 1995), 4.

3. Ibid, 2–3.

4. Robert N. Proctor, "Nazi Biomedical Policies" in Arthur L. Caplan, ed., *When Medicine Went Mad: Bioethics and the Holocaust* (Totowa, NJ: Humana Press, 1992), 27.

5. Barbara A. Kimmelman, "The American Breeders' Association: Genetics and Eugenics in an Agricultural Context, 1903–13" in *Social Studies of Science* 13 (1983), 164.

6. Quoted in Garland E. Allen, *Life Science in the Twentieth Century* (Cambridge: Cambridge University Press, 1978), 52.

7. Alexandra Oleson and John Voss, eds., *The Organization of Knowledge in Modern America, 1860–1920* (Baltimore: John Hopkins University Press, 1979), 226–7.

8. Richard Weiss, "Racism and Industrialization" in Gary B. Nash and Richard Weiss, eds., *The Great Fear: Race in the Mind of America* (New York: Holt, Rinehart and Winston, 1970), 136–7.

9. Friedlander, *Origins*, 4.

10. Daniel J. Kevles, *In the Name of Eugenics: Genetics and the Uses of Human Heredity* (Berkeley: University of California Press, 1985), 47.

11. Friedlander, *Origins*, 7.

12. Kevles, *In the Name*, 48.

13. Weiss, "Racism and Industrialization," 137.

14. Aviva Cantor, *Jewish Women, Jewish Men: The Legacy of Patriarchy in Jewish Life* (San Francisco: Harper and Row, 1995), 316.

15. Stephen Jay Gould, *The Mismeasure of Man*, revised edition (New York: Norton, 1981), 263. Assuming that immigration could have continued at its pre-1924 rate, the U.S. quotas kept out an estimated six million southern, central, and eastern Europeans between 1924 and the outbreak of World War II. Ibid.

16. Kevles, *In the Name*, 102–3, 108.

17. Nicole Hahn Rafter, ed., *White Trash: The Eugenic Family Studies, 1877–1919* (Boston, Northeastern University Press, 1988), 3–11.

18. Ibid, 27.

19. Ibid, 26.

20. Carl N. Degler, *In Search of Human Nature: The Decline and Revival of Darwinism in American Social Thought* (New York: Oxford University Press, 1991), 44.

21. Ibid, 45.

22. Ibid.

23. Ibid.

24. Ibid, 46.

25. Ibid, 47.

26. Quoted in Friedlander, *Origins*, 8–9.

27. Stefan Kühl, *The Nazi Connection: Eugenics, American Racism, and German National Socialism* (New York: Oxford University Press, 1994), 13.

28. Friedlander, *Origins*, 14–16.

29. Eugen Kogon, Hermann Langbein, and Adalbert Ruckerl, eds., *Nazi Mass Murder: A Documentary History of the Use of Poison Gas* (New Haven: Yale University Press, 1993), 13.

30. Kühl, *Nazi Connection*, 19. For more about the eugenics movement in America after World War I, see Barry Mehler, "A History of the American Eugenics Movement, 1921–1940," Doctoral dissertation, University of Illinois, 1988.

31. Kühl, *Nazi Connection*, 20.

32. Ibid, 22.

33. Edwin Black, *IBM and the Holocaust: The Strategic Alliance Between Nazi Germany and America's Most Powerful Corporation* (New York: Crown, 2001), 49.

34. Proctor, "Nazi Biomedical Policies," 27.

35. Friedlander, *Origins*, 25–6.

36. Marion Kaplan, *Between Dignity and Despair: Jewish Life in Nazi Germany* (New York: Oxford University Press, 1998), 82. In 1940 the Nazi public prosecutor in Graz recommended the univeral sterilization of all Gypsies as "the only effective way I can see of relieving the population of the Burgenland from this nuisance....These wandering work-shy beings of an alien race will never become faithful to the Reich and will always endanger the moral level of the German population." Donald Kenrick and Grattan Puxon, *The Destiny of Europe's Gypsies* (New York: Basic Books, 1972), 97.

37. Proctor, "Nazi Biomedical Policies," 29–30.

38. Kühl, *Nazi Connection*, 37.

39. Ibid, 85.

40. In 1937, in accordance with secret orders from Hitler, about 500 *Rheinlandbastarde* children, the offspring of black French occupation troops and German women, were sterilized. The action was carried out by the Gestapo working in conjunction with the genetic health courts. Guenter Lewy, *The Nazi Persecution of the Gypsies* (New York: Oxford University Press, 2000), 40.

41. Kühl, *Nazi Connection*, 38–9.

42. Ibid, 42–3.

43. Ibid, 43–5.

44. Reliable estimates put the total number of sterilizations performed before the onset of the war in 1939 at 290,000–300,000. Lewy, *Nazi Persecution of Gypsies*, 40.

45. Proctor, "Nazi Biomedical Policies," 30.

46. Kühl, *Nazi Connection*, 39–42.

47. Ibid, 38–9.

48. Proctor, "Nazi Biomedical Policies," 33–4.

49. Kühl, *Nazi Connection*, 46.

50. Kevles, *In the Name*, 116. On February 2, 2001, Virginia's House of Delegates, the state's lower house, passed a resolution by an 85–10 vote that expressed "profound regret over the Commonwealth's role in the eugenics movement in this country." It is estimated that Virginia forcibly sterilized about 8,000 people after state lawmakers passed a law that targeted people they considered "feebleminded" in 1924. Although eugenics was eventually discredited, the last eugenics language was not removed from the Virginia law until 1979. The bill's sponsor, Mitchell Van Yahres, said it was important to face up to the past now because of recent advances in genetic engineering. "We don't want to go down that road

again," he said, "when we were compared with the Nazis and the Holocaust." Chris Kahn, "Virginia Lower House OKs Bill on Eugenics" Associated Press, Feb. 2, 2001.

51. Kühl, *Nazi Connection*, 37.

52. Ibid, 53.

53. Ian Kershaw, *Hitler 1936–45: Nemesis* (New York: Norton, 2000), 257.

54. Michael Burleigh, *Death and Deliverance: "Euthanasia" in Germany c.1900–1945* (Cambridge: Cambridge University Press, 1994), 194. Nazi propaganda films praised thoroughbred animals but disapproved of the affection single women showed toward their pets. "What You Have Inherited" (*Was du ererbt*) accused female dog owners of misdirecting their affection and maternal instincts. "An exaggerated love for an animal is degenerate," it declares. "It doesn't raise the animal, but rather degrades the human being!"

55. Kühl, *Nazi Connection*, 48.

56. Ibid, 48–9.

57. Ibid, 86.

58. Ibid.

59. Laughlin expressed his appreciation in his letter of acceptance to Schneider: "I stand ready to accept this very high honor. Its bestowal will give me gratification, coming as it will from a university deeply rooted in the life history of the German people, and a university which has been both a reservoir and a fountain of learning for more than a half a millennium. To me this honor will be doubly valued because it will come from a nation which for many centuries nurtured the human seed-stock which later founded my own country and thus gave basic character to our present lives and institutions." Ibid, 87.

60. Friedlander, *Origins*, 66.

61. Kühl, *Nazi Connection*, 59–60.

62. Ibid, 61.

63. Stanley Cohen, "The Failure of the Melting Pot" in Gary B. Nash and Richard Weiss, *The Great Fear: Race in the Mind of America* (New York: Holt, Rinehart and Winston, 1970), 154.

64. Kühl, *Nazi Connection*, 61–3. For American eugenic developments in the later part of the 20th century, see Barry Mehler, "Foundation for Fascism: The New Eugenics Movement in the United States" in *Patterns of Prejudice*, Vol. 23, No. 4 (1989), 17–25.

65. Hitler also saw the Nazi eugenic goal as one of breeding a better race. On September 7, 1937, he told the faithful gathered for the opening of the Reichparteitag that the goal of National Socialism was the preservation of Germans by keeping their blood pure and uncontaminated. He invited them to see for themselves how the German human being was faring under National Socialist leadership. "Measure not only the increased numbers of births, but most of all the appearance of our youth....How beautiful are our boys and our girls, bright their eyes, how healthy and vigorous their posture, how wonderful the bodies of hundreds of thousands and millions that have been trained and cared for by our organizations....Where are better men than you see here? It is really the rebirth of a nation as the result of conscious breeding of a new man." Fritz Redlich, *Hitler: Diagnosis of a Destructive Prophet* (New York: Oxford University Press, 1999), 125.

66. Ibid, 107.

67. John K. Roth and Michael Berenbaum, eds., *Holocaust: Religious and Philosophical Implications* (St. Paul, MN: Paragon House, 1989), 197.

68. Jochen von Lang, *The Secretary: Martin Bormann—The Man Who Manipulated Hitler* (New York: Random House, 1979), 200.

69. Bradley F. Smith, *Heinrich Himmler: A Nazi in the Making, 1900–1926* (Stanford, CA: Hoover Institution Press, 1971), 67–165.

70. von Lang, *Secretary*, 84. The *Lebensborn* program, responsible for the Germanization of children from the East, placed children with foster families and special institutions, arranged adoptions, issued testimonials and false birth certificates, changed first and family names, and ran its own registration office. Yisrael Gutman and Michael Berenbaum, eds., *Anatomy of the Auschwitz Death Camp* (Bloomington: Indiana University Press, 1994), 421, 426 #25. About slave breeding farms in the antebellum American South, see Richard Sutch, "The Breeding of Slaves for Sale and the Westward Expansion of Slavery, 1850–1860" in Stanley L. Engerman and Eugene D. Genovese, eds., *Race and Slavery in the Western Hemisphere: Quantitative Studies* (Princeton: Princeton University Press, 1975), 173–210.

71. Quoted in Ervin Staub, *The Roots of Evil: The Origins of Genocide and Other Group Violence* (Cambridge: Cambridge University Press, 1989), 97.

72. Richard Breitman, *The Architect of Genocide: Himmler and the Final Solution* (New York, Knopf, 1991), 249–50.

73. Zygmunt Bauman, *Modernity and the Holocaust* (Ithaca, NY: Cornell University Press, 1989), 114.

74. Breitman, *Architect of Genocide*, 34.

75. John Weiss, *Ideology of Death: Why the Holocaust Happened in Germany* (Chicago: Ivan R. Dee, 1996), 272. Darré's successor, Herbert Backe, was a tenant farmer who, after he joined the Nazi Party, became head of the farmers' political organization in his district in 1931. He served as Reich Minister for Food and Agriculture during the last year of the Nazi regime. On April 6, 1947, he committed suicide in his cell at Nuremberg. Robert Wistrich, *Who's Who in Nazi Germany* (London: Weidenfeld and Nicolson, 1982), 10.

76. Breitman, *Architect of Genocide*, 188.

77. Rudolf Höss, *Commandant of Auschwitz: The Autobiography of Rudolf Höss* (Cleveland: World Publishing Company, 1959), 230. According to Irena Strzelecka, more than 1,000 women prisoners were placed in agricultural and cattle-breeding satellite camps created near Auschwitz, and over 2,000 more were put in similar camps in Silesia and Czechoslovakia. Gutman and Berenbaum, *Anatomy*, 407.

78. Gutman and Berenbaum, *Anatomy*, 269.

79. Hugh Gregory Gallagher, *By Trust Betrayed: Patients, Physicians, and the License to Kill in the Third Reich* (New York: Henry Holt, 1990), 52.

80. Friedlander, *Origins*, 39.

81. Burleigh, *Death and Deliverance*, 98.

82. Friedlander, *Origins*, 62.

83. Ibid, 49–59.

84. Ibid, 62. When T4 asked Dr. Albert Widmann, acting head of the chemistry department of the Reich Criminal Police Office, if he could manufacture large amounts of poison, he asked "For what? To kill people?" "No." "To kill animals?" "No" "What for, then?" "To kill animals in human form." Burleigh, *Death and Deliverance*, 119.

85. Friedlander, *Origins*, 68.

86. Ibid, 209. The gas chamber at the Mauthausen concentration camp in Austria underwent a trial run in April 1942, first on rats, then on more than 200 Soviet prisoners of war. Gordon J. Horwitz, *In the Shadow of Death: Living Outside the Gates of Mauthausen* (New York: Free Press, 1990), 18.

87. Kershaw, *Hitler 1936–1945*, 261, 430. See also Burleigh, *Death and Deliverance*, 144; Proctor, "Nazi Biomedical Policies," 34; and Friedlander, *Origins*, 109.

88. Proctor, "Nazi Biomedical Policies," 34.

89. Friedlander, *Origins*, 300. Omer Bartov, who believes the Great War (1914–18) was the birthplace of the industrial killing that culminated in the Holocaust, writes about the discontinuity between T4 and the extermination camps in Poland in Omer Bartov, *Murder in Our Midst: The Holocaust, Industrial Killing, and Representation* (New York: Oxford University Press, 1996).

90. John K. Roth, "On Losing Trust in the World" in Roth and Berenbaum, *Holocaust*, 244.

91. Friedlander, *Origins*, 22. Gordon Horwitz makes a similar point: "The operations demonstrated the effectiveness of assembly-line procedures for mass murder, and established the technical feasibility of the gas chamber as an instrument of mass killing. The integrated killing unit containing gas chamber, corpse-storage area, and crematorium first was used in the euthanasia centers. By 1942 the experience of the euthanasia killing centers had been applied on a monumental scale in the extermination centers: Treblinka, Sobibor, Belzec, Lublin-Maidanek, Auschwitz. In that year, too, Mauthausen established its own gas chamber." Horwitz, *In the Shadow*, 200 #5.

92. Friedlander, *Origins*, 68, 41; Robert Jay Lifton, *The Nazi Doctors: Medical Killing and the Psychology of Genocide* (New York: Basic Books, 1986), 52.

93. Friedlander, *Origins*, 71, 206–8.

94. Horwitz, *In the Shadow*, 79, 204 #96.

95. Friedlander, *Origins*, 243, 241, 238, 232.

96. Ibid, 239, 241. Hitler's personal body guard, Ulrich Graf, was also a former butcher. John Toland, *Adolf Hitler* (Garden City, NY: Doubleday, 1976), 107. The head of the Krefeld Gestapo, Ludwig Jung, was the son of a master butcher. Eric A. Johnson, *Nazi Terror: The Gestapo, Jews, and Ordinary Germans* (New York: Basic Books, 1999), 52. An Austrian woman recalled that after two escaped prisoners were captured in her town seven miles from the Mauthausen concentration camp, the butcher's daughter shouted, "Drive them right inside onto the meat bench, we'll cut them right up like calves." Horwitz, *In the Shadow*, 133.

97. Gitta Sereny, *Into That Darkness: An Examination of Conscience* (New York: Vintage, 1983), 236.

5   WITHOUT THE HOMAGE OF A TEAR

1. Boria Sax, *Animals in the Third Reich: Pets, Scapegoats, and the Holocaust* (New York: Continuum, 2000), 150.

2. Judy Chicago thinks there is something very modern about the Holocaust. "The medical mind, scientific method, technology, the Industrial Revolution, the assembly line, the concept of conquest—the conquest of space, of foreign lands, of cancer—these realities have shaped the world we live in, and this is the world that produced the Holocaust." She sees the industrialized slaughter which Nazi Germany implemented against the Jews as an outgrowth of modern industrial society. "The Nazis had cunningly applied the assembly-line techniques of the Industrial Revolution to the Final Solution; everything was engineered with maximum, but entirely dehumanized, efficiency." Judy Chicago, *Holocaust Project: From Darkness into Light* (New York: Viking Penguin, 1993), 58 and 60. See also Zygmunt Bauman, *Modernity and the Holocaust* (Ithaca, NY: Cornell University Press, 1989) and Omer Bartov, *Murder in Our Midst: The Holocaust, Industrial Killing, and Representation* (New York: Oxford University Press, 1996).

3. Eugen Kogon, Hermann Langbein, and Adalbert Ruckerl, eds., *Nazi Mass Murder: A Documentary History of the Use of Poison Gas* (New Haven: Yale University Press, 1993), 110.

4. Henry Friedlander, *The Origins of Nazi Genocide: From Euthanasia to the Final Solution* (Chapel Hill: University of North Carolina Press, 1995), 93.

5. Neil J. Kressel, *Mass Hate: The Global Rise of Genocide and Terror* (New York: Perseus Books, 1996), 199.

6. Upton Sinclair, *The Jungle* (New York: Signet, 1990), 40.

7. Kogon, *Nazi Mass Murder*, 170.

8. Gail Eisnitz, *Slaughterhouse: The Shocking Story of Greed, Neglect, and Inhumane Treatment Inside the U.S. Meat Industry* (Amherst, NY: Prometheus, 1997), 181.

9. Ibid, 44.

10. Ibid, 82.

11. Ibid.

12. Ibid, 119.

13. Jimmy M. Skaggs, *Prime Cut: Livestock Raising and Meatpacking in the United States, 1607–1983* (College Station: Texas A&M University Press, 1986), 191.

14. Donald D. Stull, "Knock 'em Dead: Work on the Killfloor of a Modern Beefpacking Plant" in Louise Lamphere, Alex Stepick, and Guillermo Grenier, eds., *Newcomers in the Workplace: Immigrants and the Restructuring of the U.S. Economy* (Philadelphia: Temple University Press, 1994), 57. Richard Rhodes found that watching pigs being driven down a pen which "narrows like a funnel" to a moving ramp was "a frightening experience; seeing their fear, seeing so many of them go by, it had to remind me of things no one wants to be reminded of anymore, all mobs, all death marches, all mass murders and extinctions." Richard Rhodes, "Watching the Animals," *Harper's*, March 1970. Quoted in Philip Kapleau, *To Cherish All Life: A Buddhist Case for Becoming Vegetarian*, second edition (Rochester, NY: The Zen Center, 1986), 12.

15. Kogon, *Nazi Mass Murder*, 113.

16. Ernst Klee, Willi Dressen, and Volker Riess, eds., *"The Good Old Days": The Holocaust as Seen by Its Perpetrators and Bystanders* (New York: Free Press, 1991), 240.

17. Alexander Donat, ed., *The Death Camp Treblinka: A Documentary* (New York: Holocaust Library, 1979), 310–1.

18. Gitta Sereny, *Into That Darkness: From Mercy-Killing to Mass Murder* (New York: McGraw-Hill, 1974), 115, 148, 165.

19. Kogon, *Nazi Mass Murder*, 132.

20. *New York Times*, August 5, 1997, C1, C6.

21. Donat, *Treblinka*, 309.

22. *New York Times*, June 24, 1865. Quoted in Lawrence and Susan Finsen, *The Animal Rights Movement in America* (New York: Twayne, 1994), 1.

23. Ibid.

24. Eisnitz, *Slaughterhouse*, 130.

25. Ibid, 199.

26. Ibid, 219.

27. When former Secretary of Agriculture Edward Madigan was shown a videotape of the way downed animals were treated, he was "disgusted and repelled." Gene Bauston, *Battered Birds, Crated Herds: How We Treat the Animals We Eat* (Watkins Glen, NY: Farm Sanctuary, 1996), 47.

28. Sue Coe, *Dead Meat* (New York: Four Walls Eight Windows, 1996), 116.

29. Karen Davis, "UPC's Realtor Files Lawsuit to Stop Perdue" in *Poultry Press*, (Fall/Winter 1998), 5.

30. From *Familiar Studies of Men and Books*. Quoted in Jon Wynne-Tyson, ed., *The Extended Circle: A Commonplace Book of Animal Rights* (New York: Paragon House, 1989), 355.

31. Andrew Tyler, "Getting Away With Murder" in Laura A. Moretti, ed., *All Heaven in a Rage: Essays on the Eating of Animals* (Chico, CA: MBK Publishing, 1999), 49.

32. Eisnitz, *Slaughterhouse*, 43.

33. Rynn Berry, *The New Vegetarians* (New York: Pythagorean Publishers, 1993), 116.

34. Ibid.

35. Ibid.

36. Quoted in Moretti, *All Heaven*, 43.

37. Rapp was found guilty of murder and given ten life sentences. Guenter Lewy, *The Nazi Persecution of the Gypsies* (New York: Oxford University Press, 2000), 122.

38. Klee, *"Good Old Days,"* 197; Daniel Jonah Goldhagen, *Hitler's Willing Executioners: Ordinary Germans and the Holocaust* (New York: Knopf, 1996), 401.

39. Klee, *"Good Old Days,"* 204.

40. Raul Hilberg, *The Destruction of the European Jews* (New York: Holmes and Meier, 1985), 276–7.

41. Raul Hilberg, *Perpetrators, Victims, Bystanders: The Jewish Catastrophe, 1933–1945* (New York: HarperCollins, 1992), 58–61.

42. Dan Bar-On, *Legacy of Silence: Encounters with Children of the Third Reich* (Cambridge, MA: Harvard University Press, 1989), 196.

43. James M. Glass, *"Life Unworthy of Life": Racial Phobia and Mass Murder in Hitler's Germany* (New York: Basic Books, 1997), 123–4.

44. Kogon, *Nazi Mass Murder*, 163.

45. Hilberg, *Perpetrators*, 148. Later for *Shoah*, Claude Lanzmann's documentary film about the Holocaust, Srebnik sang some of the songs he had sung at Chelmno with a voice that was "still beautiful." Inga Clendinnen, *Reading the Holocaust* (Cambridge: Cambridge University Press, 1999), 77–8.

46. Kogon, *Nazi Mass Murder*, 216.

47. Richard Breitman, *The Architect of Genocide: Himmler and the Final Solution* (New York, Knopf, 1991), 174.

48. Rudolf Höss, *Commandant of Auschwitz: The Autobiography of Rudolf Höss* (Cleveland: World Publishing Company, 1959), 237; Robert Jay Lifton, *The Nazi Doctors: Medical Killing and the Psychology of Genocide* (New York: Basic Books, 1986), 316.

49. Kogon, *Nazi Mass Murder*, 113, 236, 240.

50. Ibid, 133.

51. Sereny, *Into That Darkness*, 166.

52. Klee, *"Good Old Days,"* 227.

53. Clendinnen, *Reading the Holocaust*, 151.

54. Melissa Müller, *Anne Frank: The Biography* (New York: Henry Holt, 1998), 246.

55. Kogon, *Nazi Mass Murder*, 126.

56. Donat, *Treblinka*, 312–3. See also Sereny, *Into That Darkness*, 202.

57. Yisrael Gutman and Michael Berenbaum, eds., *Anatomy of the Auschwitz Death Camp* (Bloomington: Indiana University Press, 1994), 55. For the German concern about the health of their police dogs, see Goldhagen, *Hitler's Willing Executioners*, 268.

58. Charles G. Roland, *Courage Under Seige: Starvation, Disease, and Death in the Warsaw Ghetto* (New York: Oxford University Press, 1992), 174. Emmanuel Levinas befriended the dog "Bobby" at a Nazi slave labor camp and called him "the last Kantian in Nazi Germany." Emmanuel Levinas, "The Name of a Dog, or Natural Rights" in *Difficult Freedom: Essays on Judaism* (Baltimore: John Hopkins Press, 1990), 151–3. See also David Clark, "On Being 'The Last Kantian in Nazi Germany': Dwelling with Animals after Levinas" in Jennifer Ham and Matthew Senior, eds., *Animal Acts: Configuring the Human in Western History* (New York: Routledge, 1997), 165–98.

59. Sax, *Animals in the Third Reich*, 22. Bella Fromm reported that in 1936 when a group of farmers in a small community pooled their money to buy a bull for their cows, local officials decided the bull was "Jewish" and therefore would not be allowed to reproduce. Ibid, 22–3.

60. Jeffrey Moussaieff Masson, *Dogs Never Lie About Love: Reflections on the Emotional World of Dogs* (New York: Crown, 1997), 166. In the Warsaw Ghetto, when Marian Filar went to an apartment of a family he knew, he found that they had already been deported. The apartment was empty except for the family dog waiting for their return. When Filar tried

to take the dog home, she snarled and refused to leave. He thinks she probably starved to death in the apartment. Marian Filar and Charles Patterson, *From Buchenwald to Carnegie Hall* (Jackson: University Press of Mississippi, 2002), 64–5. Isaiah Spiegel's short story, "A Ghetto Dog," is about an old widow in the Warsaw Ghetto who refuses to part with her dog, so the Germans shoot them both. In Saul Bellow, ed., *Great Jewish Short Stories* (New York: Dell, 1963).

61. Sax, *Animals in the Third Reich*, 87.

62. Ibid, 182.

63. Victor Klemperer, *I Will Bear Witness: A Diary of the Nazi Years, 1942–1945* (New York: Random House, 2000), 52.

64. Ibid, 55.

65. Klee, *"Good Old Days,"* 100.

66. Goldhagen, *Hitler's Willing Executioners*, 266.

67. Hamburg Institute for Social Research, ed., *The German Army and Genocide: Crimes Against War Prisoners, Jews, and Other Civilians, 1939–1944* (New York: New Press, 1999), 104.

68. Jochen von Lang, *The Secretary: Martin Bormann—The Man Who Manipulated Hitler* (New York: Random House, 1979), 150.

69. Lifton, *Nazi Doctors*, 403.

70. Klee, *"Good Old Days,"* 120.

71. After the details of the 1944 bomb plot began to emerge, Hitler said, "Now I finally have the swine who have been sabotaging my work for years." Ian Kershaw, *Hitler: 1936–1945 Nemesis* (New York: Norton, 2000), 687; see also 208.

72. Fritz Redlich, *Hitler: Diagnosis of a Destructive Prophet* (New York: Oxford University Press, 1999), 149.

73. Kershaw, *Hitler: 1936–1945*, 447, 470, 401.

74. Robert G. L. Waite, *The Psychopathic God Adolf Hitler* (New York: Basic Books, 1977), 90.

75. Redlich, *Hitler*, 142.

76. Waite, *Psychopathic God*, 469.

77. Ibid, 86.

78. Redlich, *Hitler*, 10.

79. Ibid, 113. Hitler insisted that only people with talent should be educated, believing it was "criminal lunacy to keep on drilling a half-born ape until people think they have made a lawyer out of him." Ibid, 119, 310.

80. Waite, *Psychopathic God*, 97. Here Hitler was echoing the view of his idol Richard Wagner, who wrote that the "lower races" traced their origin from "from the apes," while the Aryans traced theirs "from the gods." Sax, *Animals in the Third Reich*, 54.

81. Redlich, *Hitler*, 302.

82. Waite, *Psychopathic God*, 155. In 1926 Hitler beat his dog ferociously in the presence of Mimi Reiter, a 16-year-old girl who caught his fancy and whom he was apparently trying to impress: "He whipped his dog like a madman [*Irrsinniger*] with his riding whip as he held him tight on the leash. He became tremendously excited....I could not have believed

that this man would beat an animal so ruthlessly—an animal about which he had said a moment previously that he could not live without. But now he whipped his most faithful companion!" Ibid, 192. In front of another girl on a different occasion, when Hitler's Alsatian didn't obey him, "he gave a demonstration of his idea of masculinity, mastery, and power by brutally whipping the animal." Ibid, 259.

83. Louis P. Lochner, ed., *The Goebbels Diaries, 1942–1943* (Garden City, NY: Doubleday, 1948), 138, 442; Albert Speer, *Inside the Third Reich: Memoirs* (New York: Macmillan, 1970), 358, 360; Kershaw, *Hitler: 1936–1945*, 564. On April 29, 1945, the day before Hitler committed suicide, he poisoned Blondi to make sure the cyanide capsules Himmler gave him worked. Kershaw, *Hitler: 1936–1945*, 825; Waite, *Psychopathic God*, 489; Redlich, *Hitler*, 216.

84. Ian Kershaw, *Hitler: 1889–1936 Hubris* (New York: Norton, 1998), 93.

85. Redlich, *Hitler*, 66, 77.

86. Kressel, *Mass Hate*, 133. For Kressel's discussion of Hitler's mental health, see pages 132–4. One day during the 1932 electoral campaign, according to an intimate, Hitler, feeling sorry for himself as he ate his vegetable soup, "asked plaintively for assurance that the vegetable diet would cure his stomach cramps, excessive sweating, and melancholy." Waite, *Psychopathic God*, 47.

87. Colin Spencer, *The Heretic's Feast: A History of Vegetarianism* (London: Fourth Estate, 1990), 306.

88. Waite, *Psychopathic God*, 27.

89. Kapleau, *To Cherish All Life*, 103 #71. According to Otto Wagener, Hitler became a strict vegetarian after viewing the autopsy of his young niece Angela (Geli) Raubal in 1931, but Wagener is not a reliable source since no autopsy was performed. Redlich, *Hitler*, 77, 285.

90. Redlich writes that Hitler loved to eat the Austrian meat dish *Leberknodl* (liver dumpling). Redlich, *Hitler*, 78.

91. Dione Lucas, *The Gourmet Cooking School Cookbook: Classic Recipes, Menus, and Methods as Taught in the Classes of the Gourmet Cooking School*, (New York: Bernard Geis Associates, 1964), 89. Cited in Rynn Berry, "Humankind's True Moral Test" in *Satya* (June 1994), 3.

92. Robert Payne, *The Life and Death of Adolf Hitler* (New York: Praeger, 1973), 346. Late in the war Hitler's personal physician, Dr. Theodor Morell, put him on a restricted diet that included small quantities of bacon, as well as butter, lard, egg whites, buttermilk, and heavy cream. Redlich, *Hitler*, 249.

93. Spencer, *Heretic's Feast*, 308–9.

94. Payne, *Life and Death*, 346. Ralph Meyer writes that this portrayal of Hitler as a peaceful vegetarian by Goebbels fooled even leading statesmen and biographers. "This hoax is still repeated *ad nauseum* to discredit vegetarians and animal rights advocates. How many people have been discouraged from even considering these issues because they abhor anything that might be associated with Hitler?" Ralph Meyer, "The 'Hitler Diet' for Disease and War," 1. Mr. Meyer, a vegetarian since the age of nine, left Nazi Germany in 1935. "Is it possible," he asks, "that just maybe, if humans had an inhibition about mistreating ani-

mals, they might also have an inhibition about mistreating each other?" personal communication to author.

95. Hitler also "collected rare paintings and engravings, gave expensive presents to his mistress, and surrounded himself with servants, whose trustworthiness was ensured because they were under the supervision of the SS. He had a fleet of automobiles, and airplanes were always at his disposal. Nearly every evening there were private showings of films. His table service was of the best Meissen china, each plate, saucer, and teacup engraved in gold with 'A.H.' and a swastika." Payne, *Life and Death*, 346–7.

96. In his memoir Albert Speer wrote that once Hitler discovered the taste of caviar, he ate it "by the spoonful with gusto" until he found out from Kannenberg how expensive it was. Although the expense was insignificant compared to that of the entire Chancellor's household, Hitler rejected caviar as an extravagance since "the idea of a caviar-eating Leader was incompatible with Hitler's conception of himself." Albert Speer, *Inside the Third Reich: Memoirs* (New York: Macmillan, 1970), 154.

97. Payne, *Life and Death*, 346. In the final stages of the war, Hitler lived for his favorite meal of the day—chocolate and cakes. Robert Waite writes, "Whereas in earlier days he ate at most three pieces, he now had his plate heaped high three times. He said that he didn't eat much for supper, so that he could eat more cakes." Waite, *Psychopathic God*, 479.

98. Kershaw, *Hitler: 1936–1945*, 403, 405.

99. Meyer, "Hitler Diet," 1.

100. Kershaw, *Hitler: 1936–1945*, 588. "The strongest asserts its will," Hitler declared, "it is the law of nature." Hugh Gregory Gallagher, *By Trust Betrayed: Patients, Physicians, and the License to Kill in the Third Reich* (New York: Henry Holt, 1990), 53.

101. Peter Sichrovsky, *Born Guilty: Children of Nazi Families* (New York: Basic Books, 1988), 169. To stamp out anything weak and gentle, some members of the SS were required to rear a German shepherd for twelve weeks, then strangle the puppy under the supervision of an officer." Sax, *Animals in the Third Reich*, 169.

102. Kershaw, *Hitler: 1936–1945*, 178.

103. According to James Serpell, Nazi dog lovers included Göring, Goebbels, Hess, and Admiral Donitz. James Serpell, *In the Company of Animals: A Study of Human-Animal Relationships* (London: Basil Blackwell, 1986), 33.

104. Max Horkheimer and Theodor W. Adorno, *Dialectic of Enlightenment* (New York: Herder and Herder, 1972), 253. I am indebted to Dr. Roberta Kalechofsky of Jews for Animal Rights for bringing this reference to my attention.

105. Sax, *Animals in the Third Reich*, 146–7.

106. Klee, "*Good Old Days*," 164–5.

107. Ibid, 167.

108. Ibid, 168.

109. Ibid, 257–9.

110. Ibid, 261. The "feast" of eating slaughtered animals continues. When Isabel Fonesca visited Auschwitz to do research for her book about the Gypsies, she reported that inside the camp is "a tourist hotel and a cafeteria, racked with ham-and-cheese sandwiches." Isabel

Fonseca, *Bury Me Standing: The Gypsies and Their Journey* (New York: Vintage, 1996), 254.

111. Klee, *"Good Old Days,"* 263–4.

112. Ibid, 267.

113. Lifton, *Nazi Doctors*, 403.

114. Sereny, *Into That Darkness*, 170, 168.

115. Goldhagen, *Hitler's Willing Executioners*, 304.

116. Gallagher, *By Trust Betrayed*, 52.

117. Friedlander, *Origins*, 86. Hitler's interest in humane killing extended even to lobsters. A Nazi regulation, dated January 14, 1936, and approved by Hitler, decreed that lobsters should be thrown "in rapidly boiling water" rather than in cold water that was then slowly brought to a boil since abrupt immersion in boiling water would be a "more humane" way of killing the lobster. Waite, *Psychopathic God*, 45. However, according to Albert Speer, Hitler did not see lobsters as attractive creatures. "Once, when Helgoland fishermen presented him with a gigantic lobster, this delicacy was served at table, much to the satisfaction of the guests, but Hitler made disapproving remarks about the human error of consuming such ugly monstrosities." Speer, *Inside the Third Reich*, 143.

118. Redlich, *Hitler*, 170.

119. Hilberg, *Destruction*, 136–7.

120. Ervin Staub, *The Roots of Evil: The Origins of Genocide and Other Group Violence* (Cambridge: Cambridge University Press, 1989), 138.

121. Kogon, *Nazi Mass Murder*, 184.

122. Ibid, 120.

123. For an overview of animal protection legislation during the Nazi era, see Sax, *Animals in the Third Reich*, Chapter 11 ("Animals, Nature, and the Law") and Appendix 2 ("Brief Chronology of Legislation on Animals and Nature in the Third Reich"). See also Arnold Arluke and Boria Sax, "Understanding Nazi Animal Protection and the Holocaust," *Anthrozoos* 5 (1992): 6–31, and Lynda Birke, Paul Bookbinder, et al, "Comment on Arluke and Sax: 'Understanding Nazi Animal Protection and the Holocaust'" *Anthrozoos* 6 (1993): 72–114. In this legislation, writes Boria Sax, "there is something ominous in the Nazi preoccupation with methods of killing animals" in that it conditioned people to think of killing in a positive light. "By desensitizing people, the killing of animals helped open the way for the mass murder of human beings." Sax, *Animals in the Third Reich*, 169.

124. Gary Francione, *Rain Without Thunder: The Ideology of the Animal Rights Movement* (Philadelphia: Temple University Press, 1996), 95.

125. Ibid, 96.

126. Brian Klug, "Ritual Murmur: The Undercurrent of Protest Against Religious Slaughter of Animals in Britain in the 1980s" in Roberta Kalechofsky, ed., *Judaism and Animal Rights: Classical and Contemporary Reponses* (Marblehead MA: Micah Publications, 1992), 149.

127. Winthrop Jordan writes that laws which curbed some of the cruelest excesses of slavery in the American South, such as laws which prohibited the gross maltreatment of slaves, left slavery more firmly entrenched than ever. By trying to eliminate cruel treatment, "the

humanitarian impulse helped make slavery more benevolent and paternal and hence more tolerable for the slaveowner and even for the abolitionist. To the extent that cruelty was inherent in slavery, humanitarian amelioration helped perpetuate cruelty." Winthrop D. Jordan, *The White Man's Burden: Historical Origins of Racism in the United States* (New York: Oxford University Press, 1974), 142–3.

128. Francione, *Rain Without Thunder*, 96–8.

129. Hilberg, *Destruction*, 276.

6 WE WERE LIKE THAT TOO

1. Leo Eitinger, "Auschwitz—A Psychological Perspective" in Yisrael Gutman and Michael Berenbaum, eds., *Anatomy of the Auschwitz Death Camp* (Bloomington: Indiana University Press, 1994), 480. "The Holocaust sensitizes us to the hatred of strangers, of the weak, and the persecuted," said Zevulan Hammer, former Israeli Minister of Education and Culture. "These are the universal messages of the Holocaust." Quoted in Michal Morris Kamil, "Learn to Remember: A New Year Message from The Minister of Education and Culture Zevulan Hammer," *Yad Vashem Magazine*, Vol. 3, Tishrei 5757, September 1996, 3.

2. Alan L. Berger, *Children of Job: American Second-Generation Witnesses to the Holocaust* (Albany: State University of New York Press, 1997), 16; Alan L. Berger and Naomi Berger, eds., *Second Generation Voices: Reflections by Children of Holocaust Survivors and Perpetrators* (Syracuse, NY: Syracuse University Press, 2001), 3.

3. Wildlife Watch and Committee to Abolish Sport Hunting, P.O. Box 562, New Paltz, NY 12561; 845-255-4227; wildwatch@earthlink.net; www.wildwatch.org

4. personal communication to author. Anne's husband, Peter, spent his early childhood in Nazi Germany (see Chapter 8).

5. personal communication to author from Anne Muller.

6. Ingrid Newkirk, *Free the Animals!: The Untold Story of the U.S. Animal Liberation Front and Its Founder, "Valerie"* (Chicago: Noble Press, 1992), 180.

7. personal communication to author.

8. personal communication to author.

9. "Holocaust Survivor Heads State Animal Rights Group" by Loren Goloski, *Montgomery County Sentinel*, November 21, 1996.

10. FARM, P.O. Box 30654, Bethesda MD 20824; 1-888-ASK-FARM; farm@farmusa.org; www.farmusa.org Each spring, in conjunction with its Great American Meatout, FARM sponsors a vegan lunch for Congressional employees on Capitol Hill. The speaker at the 1999 lunch was Representative Tom Lantos, Democrat of California. Lantos, who with his wife Annette survived the Holocaust in Hungary, was interviewed for Stephen Spielberg's Holocaust documentary—"The Last Days." Representative Lantos is co-chair of the Congressional Friends of Animals Caucus and the only member of Congress who is a Holocaust survivor. Tom and Annette Lantos have explained their opposition to vivisection (animal research) by saying they cannot just stand by and do nothing while animals suffer the same fate Jews did during the Third Reich. Christa Blanke, *Da krähte der*

Hahn: Kirche für Tier? Eine Streitschrift (Eschbach, Germany: Verlag am Eschbach, 1995), 167 #32.

11. Andrew Silow Carroll, "The Oppressive Mindset is the Issue," *Jewish World,* June 15–21, 1990, 9.

12. "Warning: This Book May Change Your Life," *FARM Report* (Summer 1998), 3.

13. personal communication to author.

14. "Freedom Tour in Context: Evil Roots of Vivisection Demand Long-Term Commitment," *Committee to End Primate Experiments (CEPE) News* (Spring 1999), 7.

15. personal communication to author.

16. personal communication to author.

17. "There Is Something I Can Do—I Can Teach People," *The AV* (January/February 1996), 2.

18. Ibid.

19. Center for Compassionate Living, P.O. Box 260, Surry, ME 04684; 207-667-1025; ccl@arcadia.net; www.compassionateliving.org

20. Humane Farming Association, P.O. Box 3577, San Rafael, CA 94912; 415-771-CALF; hfa@hfa.org; www.hfa.org

21. personal communication to author.

22. *Voice for the Voiceless,* North Carolina Network for Animals, Raleigh, NC (April-June 1994), 1.

23. personal communication to author.

24. *Voice for the Voiceless,* 1.

25. Rocky Mountain Animal Defense, 2525 Arapahoe—#E4–335, Boulder, CO 80302; 303-449-4422; info@rmad.org; www.rmad.org

26. personal communication to author.

27. Pamela D. Frasch, Sonia S. Waisman, Bruce A. Wagman, Scott Beckstead, eds., *Animal Law* (Durham, NC: Carolina Academic Press, 2000).

28. personal communication to author.

29. personal communication to author.

30. Project Equus, P.O. Box 18030, Boulder, CO 80308-1030; 720-565-2889; equus@projectequus.org; www.projectequus.org

31. personal communication to author.

32. personal communication to author.

33. Erik Marcus, *Vegan: The New Ethics of Eating,* second edition (Ithaca, NY: McBooks Press, 2000), 186.

34. personal communication to author.

35. "Princeton's New Philosopher Draws a Stir," *New York Times,* April 10, 1999, A1, B11. Young Albert Schweitzer had an aversion to fishing. "Twice, in the company of other boys, I went fishing with a rod," he wrote. "But then my horror at the mistreatment of the impaled worms—and at the tearing of the mouths of the fishes when they were caught— made it impossible for me to continue. Indeed, I even found the courage to dissuade others from fishing." Albert Schweitzer, *The Animal World of Albert Schweitzer: Jungle Insights into Reverence for Life,* (Boston: Beacon Press, 1950), 46.

36. Peter Singer, *Ethics Into Action: Henry Spira and the Animal Rights Movement* (Lanham, MD: Rowman and Littlefield, 1998), 47.

37. Ibid, 49.

38. "Living and Dying with Peter Singer," *Psychology Today* (January/February 1999), 58. "Since the Exodus, freedom has always spoken with a Hebrew accent" is a quotation that has been attributed to the German Jewish poet Heinrich Heine (1797–1856).

39. Singer, *Ethics Into Action*, 50.

40. Ibid, 1–3.

41. personal communication from Peter Singer (January 10, 2001).

42. Quoted in Singer, *Ethics Into Action*, 50.

43. From Spira's obituary in *Animals' Agenda* (November/December 1998).

44. Talk in church basement on West 40th Street in New York City on April 28, 1996.

45. *Ms.* (August 1983), 27.

46. personal communication to author.

47. Aviva Cantor, *Jewish Women, Jewish Men: The Legacy of Patriarchy in Jewish Life* (San Francisco: Harper and Row, 1995), 84.

48. Ibid.

49. Ibid, 406.

50. After reading an article in the international edition of the *Jerusalem Post* (May 5, 2001) about the resignation of the chairman of the Israeli Council on Animal Experimentation after he received death threats, Kaplan wrote: "I am all in favor of vivisecting vivisectors. I propose a vivisection laboratory for vivisectors. The vivisectors will be kept in cages, of course, in circumstances and conditions with which they are quite familiar. And they will be experimented on, laboratory models that they are. All kinds of experiments whose purpose is the betterment of non-human animals." personal communication to author.

51. personal communication to author.

7   THIS BOUNDLESS SLAUGHTERHOUSE

1. Singer was the first winner of the Nobel Prize for Literature who wrote in a language for which there was no country (Yiddish), and he was the second vegetarian to win the award (the first was George Bernard Shaw, who won the prize in 1925). According to Rynn Berry, Singer also had the distinction of being "the first American male to win the Nobel Prize for Literature who was not an alcoholic (Steinbeck, Hemingway, Sinclair Lewis, Faulkner, and Eugene O'Neill were among world literature's most bibulous scribes)." Rynn Berry, "Humankind's True Moral Test" in *Satya* (June 1994), 3.

2. Paul Kresh, *Isaac Bashevis Singer: The Story of a Storyteller* (New York: Dutton, 1984), 5. Another Nobel Laureate, Albert Schweitzer (winner of the Nobel Peace Prize in 1952), wrote that the suffering of animals was painful to see. "The sight of an old, limping horse being dragged along by one man while another man struck him with a stick—he was being driven to the Colmar slaughterhouse—tortured me for weeks." Albert Schweitzer, *The Animal World of Albert Schweitzer: Jungle Insights into Reverence for Life* (Boston: Beacon Press, 1950), 44.

3. "The Beginning" in Isaac Bashevis Singer, *Love and Exile: A Memoir* (Garden City, NY: Doubleday, 1984), xxi–xxii.

4. *Shosha* was serialized in the *Forward* in 1974 and published in English in 1978.

5. *Shosha* (New York: Farrar, Straus and Giroux, 1978), 239.

6. "The Beginning" in *Love and Exile*, xxii.

7. *The Family Moskat* (New York: Noonday Press, 1950), 158.

8. *Shosha*, 73–4.

9. "The Beginning" in *Love and Exile*, xxiii.

10. *The Certificate* was serialized in the *Forward* in 1967, but it was not published in English until 1992.

11. *The Certificate* (New York: Farrar, Straus and Giroux, 1992), 227.

12. Ibid.

13. *Meshugah* was serialized in the *Forward* in 1981–83 and published in English in 1994.

14. *Meshugah*, (New York: Farrar, Straus and Giroux, 1994), 45.

15. Dr. Richard Schwartz points out that in Jewish tradition "Thou shalt not kill" is generally translated "Thou shalt not murder" since Jewish tradition permits killing in certain circumstances, such as for self-defense and in wartime. However, he says, some later translations use "kill" rather than "murder".

16. "A Young Man in Search of Love" in Singer, *Love and Exile*, 129. Albert Schweitzer also found the religion passed on to him as a child too limited. "It was wholly unreasonable to me—this was even before I had gone to school—that in my evening devotions I should pray only for men. So when my mother had prayed with me and kissed me goodnight, I used secretly to add another prayer which I had composed for all living creatures. It ran like this: 'Dear God, guard and bless everything that breathes; keep it from all evil and give it a quiet sleep.'" Schweitzer, *Animal World*, 44.

17. "Lost in America" in *Love and Exile*, 234–7.

18. Ibid, 246–7.

19. Ibid, 345.

20. Ibid, 299.

21. *The Estate* (New York: Farrar, Straus and Giroux, 1968), 233–4.

22. *The Slave* (New York: Farrar, Straus and Giroux, 1962), 193.

23. *Shadows on the Hudson*, 548.

24. Foreword to Dudley Giehl, *Vegetarianism: A Way of Life* (New York: Harper and Row, 1979), viii.

25. "Lost in America" in *Love and Exile*, 350–1. Judaism condemns hunting for "sport" as wanton destruction, and the Talmud prohibits association with hunters (*Yorah Deah*, Second Series, 10). When a man asked Rabbi Ezekiel Landau (1713–93) if he could hunt in the forests and fields on his large estate, the rabbi answered: "In the Torah the sport of hunting is imputed only to fierce characters like Nimrod and Esau, never to any of the patriarchs and their descendents....I cannot comprehend how a Jew could ever dream of killing animals merely for the pleasure of hunting." Richard Schwartz, *Judaism and Vegetarianism*, revised edition (New York: Lantern Books, 2001), 25.

26. The Warsaw literary monthly *Globus* serialized *Satan in Goray* between January and September 1933, and the Yiddish section of the PEN Club in Warsaw published it as a novel in Yiddish in 1935. Because Singer left Poland in April of 1935, before the book's publication, he did not see it until after he arrived in America. In the United States, *Satan in Goray*, together with several of Singer's stories, was published in Yiddish in 1943. The Noonday Press published an English edition in 1955. Quotations are from the Noonday paperback edition (1996).

27. *Satan in Goray*, 55–6.

28. Clive Sinclair, *The Brothers Singer* (London: Allison and Busby, 1983), 8.

29. "Blood" is in *Short Friday and Other Stories* (New York: Farrar, Straus and Giroux, 1964).

30. "The Slaughterer" is in *The Seance and Other Stories* (New York: Farrar, Straus and Giroux, 1968) and *The Collected Stories* (New York: Farrar, Straus and Giroux, 1982).

31. "The Letter Writer" is in *The Seance and Other Stories* (New York: Farrar, Straus and Giroux, 1968) and *The Collected Stories* (New York: Farrar, Straus and Giroux, 1982).

32. Kresh, *Story*, 112.

33. *The Penitent* was serialized in the *Forward* in 1973 and published in English in 1983.

34. In Singer's short story "Tanhum," a young yeshiva student is similarly troubled by "questions and doubts [that] wouldn't let him rest." While he believes there's mercy in Heaven, he wants to know "why did little children or even dumb animals have to suffer? Why did man have to end up dying, and a steer under the slaughterer's knife?" Like Joseph Shapiro, Tanhum feels "an aversion to meat." At the table of his prospective father-in-law when he is asked which he prefers—beef or chicken, the words stick in his throat. "No doubt everything here was strictly kosher, but it seemed to him that the meat smelled of blood and that he could hear the bellowing of the cow writhing beneath the slaughterer's knife." "Tanhum" is in the short story collection *Old Love* (New York: Farrar, Straus and Giroux, 1979).

35. "Author's Note" at end of *The Penitent* (New York: Farrar, Straus and Giroux, 1983), 168–9. Singer told Richard Burgin in an interview that since he was born in a home where his parents thought like Joseph Shapiro, he knows exactly how he thinks. Although Joseph Shapiro expresses a number of opinions that are Singer's own, Singer denies a close identification. "He represents the extreme Orthodox Jew for whom the Torah is everything, and everything besides the Torah is nothing." Singer said that if he believed that, he would not have become a writer. Isaac Bashevis Singer and Richard Burgin, *Conversations with Isaac Bashevis Singer* (Garden City, NY: Doubleday, 1985), 151.

36. *Enemies, A Love Story* (New York: Farrar, Straus and Giroux, 1972). Quotations are from the paperback edition (1998).

37. Tiny creatures fascinated Singer. In *Shadows on the Hudson*, when Boris Makaver finds a ladybug on his sleeve, he thinks, "It was needed for some purpose—of that there can be no doubt." *Shadows on the Hudson* (New York: Farrar, Straus and Giroux, 1997), 394. At the end of *Shosha*, a Holocaust survivor living in Israel explains the change in her attitude about insects: "We battle here constantly with flies, beetles, even mice. Years ago I didn't

consider that insects or mice were God's creatures too; but since I've been treated as if I were a beetle myself, I've come to accept things one doesn't want to accept." *Shosha*, 275.

38. Singer wrote in his memoir: "On my long walks through New York I passed fish stores and butcher shops. The huge fish that yesterday was swimming in the Atlantic now lay stretched out on the ice with a bloody mouth and blank eyes, fare for millions of microbes and for a glutton to stuff his potbelly with." Singer, *Love and Exile*, 348.

39. The custom, not mentioned in the Torah or Talmud, is first discussed by Jewish scholars in the Middle Ages. Richard H. Schwartz, "The Custom of Kapparot in the Jewish Tradition"; see also Rabbi Chaim Dovid Halevy (late Sephardic Chief Rabbi of Tel Aviv), "The Custom of Kapparot Customarily Practiced Between Rosh Hashanah and Yom Kippur."

40. *Enemies*, 145. A similar situation occurs in *Shosha* when Shosha's mother buys two hens for Yom Kippur, one for herself and the other for Shosha. "She wanted to buy a rooster for me," says the narrator, "but I refused to let a rooster die for my sins." Still, "from all the apartments on Krochmalna Street one could hear the clucking of hens and the crowing of roosters." *Shosha*, 141.

41. *Shadows on the Hudson* (New York: Farrar, Straus and Giroux, 1997). Quotations are from the paperback edition (1999).

42. For more about the massacre of Jews in a Romanian slaughterhouse, see note #31 in Chapter 8.

43. Kresh, *Story*, 80.

44. *Family Moskat*, 260.

45. "The Yearning Heifer" is in *Passions and Other Stories* (New York: Farrar, Straus and Giroux, 1976) and *The Collected Stories* (New York: Farrar, Straus and Giroux, 1982).

46. "Brother Beetle" is in *Old Love* (New York: Farrar, Straus and Giroux, 1979) and *The Collected Stories* (New York: Farrar, Straus and Giroux, 1982).

47. "Cockadoodledoo" is in *The Seance and Other Stories* (New York: Farrar, Straus and Giroux, 1968).

48. *The Certificate*, 172–3.

49. "The Parrot" is in *The Seance and Other Stories* (1968).

50. *Shosha*, 14.

51. Dorthea Straus, *Under the Canopy: The Story of a Friendship with Isaac Bashevis Singer That Chronicles a Reawakening of Jewish Identity* (New York: George Braziller, 1982), 20.

52. Kresh, *Story*, 111.

53. Quotations from *Enemies: A Love Story* are from the paperback edition (1998).

54. Marshall Breger and Bob Barnhart, "A Conversation with Isaac Bashevis Singer" in Irving Malin, ed., *Critical Views of Isaac Bashevis Singer* (New York: New York University Press, 1969), 27–43.

55. Paul Kresh, *Isaac Bashevis Singer: The Magician of West 86th Street* (New York: Dial Press, 1979), 243–4.

56. Straus, *Under the Canopy*, 19.

57. Kresh, *Magician*, 271.

58. Straus, *Under the Canopy*, 141.
59. Dvorah Telushkin, *Master of Dreams: A Memoir of Isaac Bashevis Singer* (New York: Morrow, 1997), 40. I have kept Singer's conversation consistent with the rest of the chapter rather than using Telushkin's practice of rendering the sound of Singer's Yiddish accent with phonetic spellings ("vone" for "one," "vhich" for "which," etc.).
60. Ibid, 40–1.
61. Ibid, 179.
62. *Enemies*, 205. Singer's affection for animals is also evident in his children's stories, which he did not start writing until he was sixty-two and already a world-famous author. His first—"Zlateh the Goat"—is about a boy named Aaron and how he saves the family goat, Zlateh, from being sold for slaughter. Other Singer animal stories for children include "Naftali the Storyteller and His Horse, Sus," "A Parakeet Named Dreidel," "The Cat Who Thought She Was a Dog and the Dog Who Thought He Was a Cat," "Hershele and Hanukkah," and "Topiel and Tekla."
63. "Pigeons" is in *A Friend of Kafka and Other Stories* (New York: Farrar, Straus and Giroux, 1970).
64. Breger and Barnhart, "Conversation," 27–43.
65. *Newsweek*, October 16, 1978. Quoted in *CHAI Lights* (Spring 1992), 5.
66. Singer and Burgin, *Conversations*, 116, 151–2, 161, 175–8.
67. Foreword to Dudley Giehl, *Vegetarianism: A Way of Life* (New York: Harper and Row, 1979), vii–ix.
68. "The Man Who Talked Back to God: Isaac Bashevis Singer, 1904–91," *New York Times Book Review* (August 11, 1991). CHAI (Concern for Helping Animals in Israel), an organization which American activist Nina Natelson established in 1984, built an "Isaac Bashevis Singer Humane Education Center" at the SPCA in Tel Aviv. The center contains an extensive library of books and videos about animals and animal issues and conducts educational programs, including CHAI's "Living Together" program that brings together Jewish and Arab children to learn about and help animals. In 1986 the Jewish Vegetarians of North America presented Singer with its first "Jewish Vegetarian of the Year Award."

8 THE OTHER SIDE OF THE HOLOCAUST

1. personal communication to author.
2. Tom Regan, *The Case for Animal Rights* (Berkeley: University of California Press, 1983).
3. personal communication to author. Peter is married to Anne Muller (see Chapter 6).
4. "I Was Born as a Gift to Hitler: Liesel Appel's Unlikely Journey to Judaism," *Palm Beach Jewish Times*, June 30, 1995.
5. Alan L. Berger and Naomi Berger, eds., *Second Generation Voices: Reflections by Children of Holocaust Survivors and Perpetrators.* (Syracuse, NY: Syracuse University Press, 2001), 306.
6. Robert Wistrich, *Who's Who in Nazi Germany* (London: Weidenfeld and Nicolson, 1982), 175–6. Due to an article in the Polish penal code which prevented the execution of bedridden persons, Koch's sentence was later commuted to life imprisonment.
7. personal communication to author.

8. Dan Bar-On, *Legacy of Silence: Encounters with Children of the Third Reich* (Cambridge, MA: Harvard University Press, 1989). See also Gerald L. Posner, *Hitler's Children: Sons and Daughters of Leaders of the Third Reich Talk About Their Fathers and Themselves* (New York: Random House, 1991); Peter Sichrovsky, *Born Guilty: Children of Nazi Families* (New York: Basic Books, 1988); and Martin S. Bergmann and Milton E. Jucovy, eds., *Generations of the Holocaust* (New York: Basic Books, 1982), 159–244.

9. Bar-On, *Legacy*, 25.

10. Gitta Sereny, *Into That Darkness: An Examination of Conscience* (New York: Vintage, 1983).

11. Ibid, 201.

12. Ibid, 344.

13. Bar-On, *Legacy*, 25.

14. Robert Jay Lifton, *The Nazi Doctors: Medical Killing and the Psychology of Genocide* (New York: Basic Books, 1986), 197.

15. Bar-On, *Legacy*, 31.

16. Ibid, 40.

17. Ibid, 331.

18. Ibid, 244.

19. Thanks to Peter Muller and Dietrich von Haugwitz for providing information about Edgar Kupfer-Koberwitz before and after his Dachau years.

20. Edgar Kupfer-Koberwitz, *Animal Brothers: Reflections on an Ethical Way of Life* (*Die Tierbrüder*), fourth edition (Mannheim, Germany: Warland-Verlagsgenossenschaft eG Mannheim, no date). Translated by Ruth Mossner for Vegetarian Press, Denver, CO. A carbon copy of this 38-page essay is preserved with the original Dachau Diaries—*Die Mächtigen und die Hilflosen: als Häftling in Dachau* (*The Mighty and the Helpless as Prisoners in Dachau*)—in the Special Collection of the Library of the University of Chicago. Excerpts from the essay were reprinted in the Postscript of Mark Mathew Braunstein's *Radical Vegetarianism* (Los Angeles: Panjandrum Books, 1981).

21. Gandhi had a similar thought: "I hold that, the more helpless a creature, the more entitled it is to protection by man from the cruelty of man." Mohandas K. Gandhi, *An Autobiography: The Story of My Experiments with Truth* (Boston: Beacon Press, 1957), 235.

22. Albert Schweitzer also cared about the safety of worms. Once in England when he was on his way to catch a train with a friend, each carrying one end of a stick on which Schweitzer's knapsack was slung, Schweitzer suddenly stopped and, putting down his end of the stick, "tenderly picked up from a rut in the road a poor, half-frozen worm, which he carefully placed in the hedge-row." When he came back and picked up his end of the stick, he explained with a gentle smile that if it had remained there a few minutes longer it would certainly have been crushed by some auto traveling along the road. They hurried on to the station, where Schweitzer barely caught his train. Albert Schweitzer, *The Animal World of Albert Schweitzer: Jungle Insights into Reverence for Life* (Boston: Beacon Press, 1950), 26.

23. After the war Kupfer-Koberwitz lived in Ascona in the Italian-speaking part of Switzerland, the United States (Chicago), San Teodoro on the island of Sardinia, and Germany, where he died in 1991 at the age of 85. According to the author E. Garbani Nerini, Kupfer-Koberwitz never wore or used leather; even the leashes he used to take care of stray dogs on Sardinia were made of fabric.

24. personal communication to author.

25. Helmut Kaplan, *Tierrechte: Die Philosophie einer Befreiungsbewegung* (Göttingen: Echo Verlag, 2000).

26. personal communication to author.

27. In July 2000, Blanke told an Israeli journalist her church had demonstrated total indifference toward the concept of animal rights which she is committed to advancing. "They consider animals inferior beings that exist for the use of humans. They are not even willing to discuss the ideas I support. I consider animals my brothers and sisters in the world from a spiritual and religious aspect." Zafrir Rinat, "Sheep and cows have their guardian angels too," *Ha'aretz* (August 2, 2000).

28. Animals' Angels, Bismarckallee 22, D-79098 Freiburg, Germany; AnimalsAngels@ t-online.de; www.animals-angels.de

29. Animals' Angels Newsletter, May 2000.

30. Rinat, "Sheep and cows."

31. During the fascist rebellion in Bucharest in January 1941, Romanian Iron Guard militants brought Jews to the slaughterhouse in the Bucharestii Noi District, not to transport them to their deaths elsewhere, but to kill them there. After they dismembered and disemboweled the bodies of their victims, they hung their intestines "like neckties on other corpses, which were displayed on meat hooks and labeled 'Kosher meat.'" Ioanid Radu, *The Holocaust in Romania: The Destruction of Jews and Gypsies Under the Antonescu Regime, 1940–1944* (Chicago: Ivan R. Dee, 2000), 57–8.

32. Marion Kaplan, *Between Dignity and Despair: Jewish Life in Nazi Germany* (New York: Oxford University Press, 1998), 187. In Dortmund, a *Mischling* daughter who went into a large hall to say a last good-bye to her mother wrote: "They were in the 'Exchange,' which was at the cattle market by the slaughterhouse, they were brought to the slaughterhouse(!)....There lay the Schacher family....He was half dead." Ibid.

33. Eric A. Johnson, *Nazi Terror: The Gestapo, Jews, and Ordinary Germans* (New York: Basic Books, 1999), 402. The Nazis also treated the Germans accused of being behind the July 20, 1944 bomb plot to assassinate Hitler like animals slaughtered for food. Hitler ordered that each of the accused be hung on a meathook and strangled to death slowly with piano wire. Hitler had photographs and color film made of the scene, which he is reported to have looked at repeatedly. The film became "one of his favorite entertainments." Robert G. L. Waite, *The Psychopathic God Adolf Hitler* (New York: Basic Books, 1977), 23; Ian Kershaw, *Hitler: 1936–45 Nemesis* (New York: Norton, 2000), 693.

34. On Sunday, August 30, 1991, a Commemorative Walk retraced the last journey of Wiesbaden's murdered Jews. Starting in front of city hall, the walk ended at the site of the former slaughterhouse where some of the cattle grids are still visible. "Selbstmord war für

viele der letzte Ausweg" by Christoph Zehler, a serialization of the *TAGBLATT* (last segment) in the "Wiesbaden" section of the *Rhein-Main-Presse*, June 1, 1992.

35.   The Soviet secret police (NKVD) used a slaughterhouse in the city of Smolensk as one of the sites where they murdered Polish officers and then transported the corpses in trucks to the Katyn forest for burial in mass graves. "The pre-existence of an animal slaughterhouse made the job easy for the NKVD." I am indebted to Waclaw Godziemba-Maliszewski for this information.

36.   After numerous church publications, including the progressive Catholic newspaper *Publik-Forum*, declined to publish Blanke's article, it was finally published by the animal rights/environmental magazine *Gaia*. Most of the material in the article is included in her book, *Da krähte der Hahn: Kirche für Tiere? Eine Streitschrift* (*Then the Rooster Crowed: Church for Animals? A Critical Plea*) (Eschbach, Germany: Verlag am Eschbach, 1995).

BIBLIOGRAPHY

Adams, Carol. *The Sexual Politics of Meat: A Feminist-Vegetarian Critical Theory.* New York: Continuum, 1991.

Adams, Carol and Josephine Donovan, eds. *Animals and Women: Feminist Theoretical Explorations.* Durham, NC: Duke University Press, 1995.

Adorno, Theodor W., Else Frenkel-Brunswik, Daniel J. Levinson, and R. Nevitt Sanford. *The Authoritarian Personality.* New York: Harper and Row, 1950.

Allen, Garland E. *Life Science in the Twentieth Century.* Cambridge: Cambridge University Press, 1978.

Allison, Alida. *Isaac Bashevis Singer: Children's Stories and Childhood Memoirs.* New York: Twayne, 1996.

Aly, Gotz, Peter Chroust, and Christian Pross. *Cleansing the Fatherland: Nazi Medicine and Racial Hygiene.* Baltimore: John Hopkins University Press, 1994.

Aptheker, Herbert. *Abolitionism: A Revolutionary Movement.* Boston: Twayne, 1989.

Arendt, Hannah. *Eichmann in Jerusalem: A Report on the Banality of Evil.* New York: Viking, 1965.

Ascione, Frank R. and Phil Arkow, eds. *Child Abuse, Domestic Violence, and Animal Abuse: Linking the Circles of Compassion for Prevention and Intervention.* West Lafayette, IN: Purdue University Press, 1999.

Barnes, Jonathan, ed. *The Complete Works of Aristotle,* 2 vols. Princeton: Princeton University Press, 1984.

Bar-On, Dan. *Legacy of Silence: Encounters with Children of the Third Reich.* Cambridge, MA: Harvard University Press, 1989.

Barrett, James R. *Work and Community in the Jungle: Chicago's Packinghouse Workers, 1894–1922.* Urbana: University of Illinois Press, 1987.

Bartov, Omer, ed. *The Holocaust: Origins, Implementation and Aftermath.* New York: Routledge, 2000.

Bartov, Omer. *Murder in Our Midst: The Holocaust, Industrial Killing, and Representation.* New York: Oxford University Press, 1996.

Bauman, Zygmunt. *Modernity and the Holocaust.* Ithaca, NY: Cornell University Press, 1989.

Bauston, Gene. *Battered Birds, Crated Herds: How We Treat the Animals We Eat.* Watkins Glen, NY: Farm Sanctuary, 1996.

Bellow, Saul, ed. *Great Jewish Short Stories.* New York: Dell, 1963.

Belth, Nathan. *A Promise to Keep: A Narrative of the American Encounter with Anti-Semitism.* New York: Schocken, 1981.

Berger, Alan L. *Children of Job: American Second-Generation Witnesses to the Holocaust.* Albany: State University of New York Press, 1997.

Berger, Alan L. and Naomi Berger, eds. *Second Generation Voices: Reflections by Children of Holocaust Survivors and Perpetrators.* Syracuse, NY: Syracuse University Press, 2001.

Bergmann, Martin S. and Milton E. Jucovy, eds. *Generations of the Holocaust.* New York: Basic Books, 1982.

Berkhofer, Robert F., Jr. *The White Man's Indian: Images of the American Indian from Columbus to the Present.* New York: Knopf, 1978.

Berry, Rynn. *Famous Vegetarians and Their Favorite Recipes: Lives and Lore from Buddha to Beatles.* New York: Pythagorean Publishers, 1995.

Black, Edwin. *IBM and the Holocaust: The Strategic Alliance Between Nazi Germany and America's Most Powerful Corporation.* New York: Crown, 2001.

——. *The Transfer Agreement: The Untold Story of the Secret Agreement Between the Third Reich and Jewish Palestine.* New York: Macmillan, 1984.

Blanke, Christa. *Da krähte der Hahn: Kirche für Tier? Eine Streitschrift.* Eschbach, Germany: Verlag am Eschbach, 1995.

Braunstein, Mark Mathew. *Radical Vegetarianism.* Los Angeles: Panjandrum Books, 1981.

Breitman, Richard. *The Architect of Genocide: Himmler and the Final Solution.* New York: Knopf, 1991.

Buchen, Irving. *Isaac Bashevis Singer and the Eternal Past.* New York: New York University Press, 1968.

Burleigh, Michael. *Death and Deliverance: "Euthanasia" in Germany c.1900–1945.* Cambridge: Cambridge University Press, 1994.

Cantor, Aviva. *Jewish Women, Jewish Men: The Legacy of Patriarchy in Jewish Life.* San Francisco: Harper and Row, 1995.

Caplan, Arthur L., ed. *When Medicine Went Mad: Bioethics and the Holocaust.* Totowa, NJ: Humana Press, 1992.

Cartmill, Matt. *A View to a Death in the Morning: Hunting and Nature Through History.* Cambridge, MA: Harvard University Press, 1993.

Chang, Iris. *The Rape of Nanking: The Forgotten Holocaust of World War II.* New York: Basic Books, 1997.

Chicago, Judy. *Holocaust Project: From Darkness into Light.* New York: Viking Penguin, 1993.

Clendinnen, Inga. *Reading the Holocaust.* Cambridge: Cambridge University Press, 1999.

Clutton-Brock, Juliet. *Domesticated Animals from Early Times.* Austin: University of Texas Press, 1981.

Coe, Sue. *Dead Meat.* New York: Four Walls Eight Windows, 1995.

Coetzee, J. M. *The Lives of Animals.* Princeton, NJ: Princeton University Press, 1999.

Cohn, Norman. *Warrant for Genocide: The Myth of the Jewish World Conspiracy and the Protocols of the Elders of Zion.* London: Serif, 1996.

Davis, Karen. *Prisoned Chickens, Poisoned Eggs: An Inside Look at the Modern Poultry Industry.* Summertown, TN: Book Publishing Company, 1996.

Degler, Carl N. *In Search of Human Nature: The Decline and Revival of Darwinism in American Social Thought.* New York: Oxford University Press, 1991.

Des Pres, Terrence. *The Survivor: An Anatomy of Life in the Death Camps.* New York: Oxford University Press, 1976.

Diamond, Jared. *Guns, Germs, and Steel: The Fates of Human Societies.* New York: Norton, 1997.

——. *The Third Chimpanzee: The Evolution and Future of the Human Animal.* New York: HarperCollins, 1992.

Donat, Alexander, ed. *The Death Camp Treblinka: A Documentary.* New York: Holocaust Library, 1979.

Donovan, Josephine and Carol Adams, eds. *Animals and Women: Feminist Theoretical Explorations.* Durham, NC: Duke University Press, 1995.

——. eds. *Beyond Animal Rights: A Feminist Caring Ethic for the Treatment of Animals.* New York: Continuum, 1996.

Dower, John W. *War Without Mercy: Race and Power in the Pacific War.* New York: Pantheon, 1986.

Drinnon, Richard. *Facing West: The Metaphysics of Indian-Hating and Empire-Building.* Norman: University of Oklahoma Press, 1997.

Dudley, Edward and Maximillian E. Novak, eds. *The Wild Man Within: An Image in Western Thought from the Renaissance to Romanticism.* Pittsburgh: University of Pittsburgh Press, 1972.

Ehrenreich, Barbara. *Blood Rites: Origins and History of the Passions of War.* New York: Henry Holt, 1997.

Eisnitz, Gail. *Slaughterhouse: The Shocking Story of Greed, Neglect, and Inhumane Treatment Inside the U.S. Meat Industry.* Amherst, NY: Prometheus Books, 1997.

Engerman, Stanley L. and Eugene D. Genovese, eds. *Race and Slavery in the Western Hemisphere: Quantitative Studies.* Princeton: Princeton University Press, 1975.

Feig, Konnilyn G. *Hitler's Death Camps.* New York: Holmes and Meier, 1981.

Fein, Helen. *Accounting for Genocide: National Responses and Jewish Victimization During the Holocaust.* New York: Free Press, 1979.

Filar, Marian and Charles Patterson. *From Buchenwald to Carnegie Hall.* Jackson: University Press of Mississippi, 2002.

Finsen, Lawrence and Susan. *The Animal Rights Movement in America.* New York: Twayne, 1994.

Fisher, Elizabeth. *Woman's Creation: Sexual Evolution and the Shaping of Society.* New York: Doubleday, 1979.

Fonseca, Isabel. *Bury Me Standing. The Gypsies and Their Journey.* New York: Vintage, 1996.

Ford, Henry. *My Life and Work.* Garden City, NY: Doubleday, Page and Company, 1922.

Francione, Gary. *Rain Without Thunder: The Ideology of the Animal Rights Movement.* Philadelphia: Temple University Press, 1996.

Frasch, Pamela D., Sonia S. Waisman, Bruce A. Wagman, Scott Beckstead, eds. *Animal Law.* Durham, NC: Carolina Academic Press, 2000.

Freud, Sigmund. *The Standard Edition of the Complete Psychological Works of Sigmund Freud,* trans. by James Strachey. London: Hogarth Press, 1955.

Friedlander, Henry. *The Origins of Nazi Genocide: From Euthanasia to the Final Solution.* Chapel Hill: University of North Carolina Press, 1995.

Friedman, Lawrence S. *Understanding Isaac Bashevis Singer.* Columbia: University of South Carolina Press, 1988.

Gaard, Greta, ed. *Ecofeminism: Women, Animals, Nature.* Philadelphia: Temple University Press, 1993.

Gallagher, Hugh Gregory. *By Trust Betrayed: Patients, Physicians, and the License to Kill in the Third Reich.* New York: Henry Holt, 1990.

Gandhi, Mohandas K. *An Autobiography: The Story of My Experiments with Truth.* Boston: Beacon Press, 1957.

Giehl, Dudley. *Vegetarianism: A Way of Life.* New York: Harper and Row, 1979.

Glacken, Clarence J. *Traces on the Rhodian Shore: Nature and Culture in Western Thought from Ancient Times to the End of the Eighteenth Century.* Berkeley: University of California Press, 1967.

Glass, James M. *"Life Unworthy of Life": Racial Phobia and Mass Murder in Hitler's Germany.* New York: Basic Books, 1997.

Godlovitch, Stanley and Roslind, and John Harris, eds. *Animals, Men and Morals: An Enquiry into the Maltreatment of Non-humans.* New York: Taplinger, 1972.

Goldhagen, Daniel Jonah. *Hitler's Willing Executioners: Ordinary Germans and the Holocaust.* New York: Knopf, 1996.

Gossett, Thomas F. *Race: The History of an Idea in America,* second edition. New York: Oxford University Press, 1997.

Gottlieb, Roger S., ed. *This Sacred Earth: Religion, Nature, Environment.* New York: Routledge, 1996.

Gould, Stephen Jay. *The Mismeasure of Man.* New York: Norton, 1981.

Grandin, Temple. *Thinking in Pictures and Other Reports of My Life with Autism.* New York: Doubleday, 1995.

Gutman, Yisrael, and Michael Berenbaum, eds. *Anatomy of the Auschwitz Death Camp.* Bloomington: Indiana University Press, 1994.

Hallie, Philip P. *The Paradox of Cruelty.* Middletown, CT: Wesleyan University Press, 1969.

Ham, Jennifer and Matthew Senior. *Animal Acts: Configuring the Human in Western History.* New York: Routledge, 1997.

Hamburg Institute for Social Research, ed. *The German Army and Genocide: Crimes Against War Prisoners, Jews, and Other Civilians, 1939–1944.* New York: New Press, 1999.

Higham, John. *Strangers in the Land: Patterns of American Nativism, 1860–1925.* New York: Atheneum, 1969.

Hilberg, Raul. *The Destruction of the European Jews*, revised edition. New York: Holmes and Meier, 1985.

Hilberg, Raul. *Perpetrators, Victims, Bystanders: The Jewish Catastrophe, 1933–1945*. New York: HarperCollins, 1992.

Hitler, Adolf. *Mein Kampf.* Boston: Houghton Mifflin, 1971.

Hodgen, Margaret T. *Early Anthropology in the Sixteenth and Seventeenth Centuries*. Philadelphia: University of Pennsylvania Press, 1964.

Horkheimer, Max, and Theodor W. Adorno. *Dialectic of Enlightenment.* New York: Herder and Herder, 1972.

Horwitz, Gordon J. *In the Shadow of Death: Living Outside the Gates of Mauthausen*. New York: Free Press, 1990.

Höss, Rudolf. *Commandant of Auschwitz: The Autobiography of Rudolf Höss.* Cleveland: World Publishing Company, 1959.

Jacobs, Wilbur R. *Dispossessing the American Indian: Indians and Whites on the Colonial Frontier.* Norman: University of Oklahoma Press, 1984.

Jennings, Francis. *The Invasion of America: Indians, Colonialism, and the Cant of Conquest.* Chapel Hill: University of North Carolina, 1975.

Johnson, Allen W. and Timothy Earle. *The Evolution of Human Societies: From Foraging Group to Agrarian State.* Stanford, CA: Stanford University Press, 1987.

Johnson, Eric A. *Nazi Terror: The Gestapo, Jews, and Ordinary Germans.* New York: Basic Books, 1999.

Jordan, Winthrop D. *The White Man's Burden: Historical Origins of Racism in the United States.* New York: Oxford University Press, 1974.

Kalechofsky, Roberta, ed. *Judaism and Animal Rights: Classical and Contemporary Responses.* Marblehead, MA: Micah Publications, 1992.

Kaplan, Helmut F. *Tierrechte: Die Philosophie einer Befreiungsbewegung.* Göttingen, Germany: Echo Verlag, 2000.

Kaplan, Marion. *Between Dignity and Despair: Jewish Life in Nazi Germany.* New York: Oxford University Press, 1998.

Kapleau, Philip. *To Cherish All Life: A Buddhist Case for Becoming Vegetarian,* second edition. Rochester, NY: The Zen Center, 1986.

Kenrick, Donald, and Grattan Puxon. *The Destiny of Europe's Gypsies.* New York: Basic Books, 1972.

Kershaw, Ian. *Hitler: 1889–1936 Hubris.* New York: Norton, 1998.

——. *Hitler: 1936–45 Nemesis.* New York: Norton, 2000.

Kevles, Daniel J. *In the Name of Eugenics: Genetics and the Uses of Human Heredity.* Berkeley: University of California Press, 1985.

Kiernan, V. G. *The Lords of Human Kind: Black Man, Yellow Man, and White Man in an Age of Empire.* Boston: Little, Brown, 1969.

Klee, Ernst, Willi Dressen, and Volker Riess, eds. *"The Good Old Days": The Holocaust as Seen by Its Perpetrators and Bystanders.* New York: Free Press, 1991.

Klemperer, Victor. *I Will Bear Witness: A Diary of the Nazi Years, 1933–45*, 2 vols. New York: Random House, 1998, 2000.

Kogan, Eugen, Hermann Langbein, and Adalbert Ruckerl, eds. *Nazi Mass Murder: A Documentary History of the Use of Poison Gas*. New Haven, CT: Yale University Press, 1993.

Krausnick, Helmut and Martin Broszat. *Anatomy of the SS State*. New York: Walker, 1968.

Kresh, Paul. *Isaac Bashevis Singer: The Magician of West 86th Street*. New York: Dial Press, 1979.

——. *Isaac Bashevis Singer: The Story of a Storyteller*. New York: Dutton, 1984.

Kressel, Neil J. *Mass Hate: The Global Rise of Genocide and Terror*. New York: Perseus Books, 1996.

Kroeber, Theodora. *Ishi in Two Worlds: A Biography of the Last Wild Indian in North America*. Berkeley: University of California Press, 1961.

Kühl, Stefan. *The Nazi Connection: Eugenics, American Racism, and German National Socialism*. New York: Oxford University Press, 1994.

Kundera, Milan. *The Unbearable Lightness of Being*. New York: Harper and Row, 1984.

Kuper, Leo. *Genocide: Its Political Use in the Twentieth Century*. New Haven: Yale University Press, 1981.

Kupfer-Koberwitz, Edgar. *Animal Brothers* (*Die Tierbrüder*), fourth edition, translated by Ruth Mossner. Mannheim, Germany: Warland-Verlagsgenossenschaft eG Mannheim, 1988.

Lamphere, Louise, Alex Stepick, and Guillermo Grenier, eds. *Newcomers in the Workplace: Immigrants and the Restructuring of the U.S. Economy*. Philadelphia: Temple University Press, 1994.

Lang, Jochen von. *The Secretary: Martin Bormann—The Man Who Manipulated Hitler*. New York: Random House, 1979.

Langer, Lawrence L. *Admitting the Holocaust: Collected Essays*. New York: Oxford University Press, 1995.

Las Casas, Bartolomé de. *The Devastation of the Indies: A Brief Account*. New York: Seabury Press, 1974.

Leakey, Richard E. and Roger Lewin. *Origins: What Discoveries Reveal About the Emergence of Our Species and Its Possible Future*. London: Futura, MacDonald and Company, 1982.

Lee, Albert. *Henry Ford and the Jews*. New York: Stein and Day, 1980.

Lee, Richard B. and Irven DeVore, eds. *Man the Hunter*. Chicago: Aldine Publishing Company, 1968.

Lerner, Gerda. *The Creation of Patriarchy*. New York: Oxford University Press, 1986.

Lerner, Richard M. *Final Solutions: Biology, Prejudice, and Genocide*. University Park: Pennsylvania State University Press, 1992.

Levinas, Emmanuel. *Difficult Freedom: Essays on Judaism*. Baltimore: John Hopkins Press, 1990.

Lewis, David L. *The Public Image of Henry Ford: An American Folk Hero and His Company*. Detroit: Wayne State University Press, 1976.

Lewy, Guenter. *The Nazi Persecution of the Gypsies*. New York: Oxford University Press, 2000.

Lifton, Robert Jay. *The Nazi Doctors: Medical Killing and the Psychology of Genocide.* New York: Basic Books, 1986.

Lifton, Robert Jay and Eric Markusen. *The Genocidal Mentality: Nazi Holocaust and Nuclear Threat.* New York: Basic Books, 1990.

Linzey, Andrew and Dan Cohn-Sherbok. *After Noah: Animals and the Liberation of Theology.* New York: Cassell, 1997.

Lochner, Louis P., ed. *The Goebbels Diaries, 1942–1943.* Garden City, NY: Doubleday, 1948.

Lovejoy, Arthur O. *The Great Chain of Being.* Cambridge, MA: Harvard University Press, 1936.

Lucas, Dione. *The Gourmet Cooking School Cookbook: Classic Recipes, Menus, and Methods as Taught in the Classes of the Gourmet Cooking School.* New York: Bernard Geis Associates, 1964.

Malin, Irving, ed. *Critical Views of Isaac Bashevis Singer.* New York: New York University Press, 1969.

Marcus, Erik. *Vegan: The New Ethics of Eating,* second edition. Ithaca, NY: McBooks Press, 2000.

Marrus, Michael R. *The Holocaust in History.* Hanover, NH: University Press of New England, 1989.

Mason, Jim. *An Unnatural Order: Why We Are Destroying the Planet and Each Other.* New York: Continuum, 1997.

Mason, Jim and Peter Singer, *Animal Factories: What Agribusiness Is Doing to the Family Farm, the Environment and Your Health,* revised edition. New York: Crown, 1990.

Masson, Jeffrey Moussaieff. *Dogs Never Lie About Love: Reflections on the Emotional World of Dogs.* New York: Crown Publishers, 1997.

Miller, Stuart Creighton. *"Benevolent Assimilation": The American Conquest of the Philippines, 1899–1903.* New Haven: Yale University Press, 1982.

Milton, Sybil, trans. *The Stroop Report: The Jewish Quarter of Warsaw is No More!* New York: Pantheon, 1979.

Moretti, Laura A. *All Heaven in a Rage: Essays on the Eating of Animals.* Chico, CA: MBK Publishing, 1999.

Müller, Melissa. *Anne Frank: The Biography.* New York: Henry Holt, 1998.

Muller-Hill, Benno. *Murderous Science: Elimination by Scientific Selection of Jews, Gypsies, and Others, Germany 1933–1945.* New York: Oxford University Press, 1988.

Nash, Gary B. and Richard Weiss. *The Great Fear: Race in the Mind of America.* New York: Holt, Rinehart and Winston, 1970.

Noske, Barbara. *Beyond Boundaries: Human and Animals.* Montreal: Black Rose Books, 1997.

Oleson, Alexandra and John Voss, eds. *The Organization of Knowledge in Modern America, 1860–1920.* Baltimore: Johns Hopkins University Press, 1979.

Pagden, Anthony. *The Fall of Natural Man: The American Indian and the Origins of Comparative Ethnology.* Cambridge: Cambridge University Press, 1982.

Patterson, Charles. *Anti-Semitism: The Road to the Holocaust and Beyond.* New York: Walker, 1982.

Patterson, Orlando. *Slavery and Social Death: A Comparative Study.* Cambridge, MA: Harvard University Press, 1982.

Payne, Robert. *The Life and Death of Adolf Hitler*. New York: Praeger, 1973.

Pearce, Roy Harvey. *The Savages of America: A Study of the Indian and the Idea of Civilization*, revised edition. Baltimore: Johns Hopkins University Press, 1965.

Posner, Gerald L. *Hitler's Children: Sons and Daughters of Leaders of the Third Reich Talk About Their Fathers and Themselves*. New York: Random House, 1991.

Radu, Ioanid. *The Holocaust in Romania: The Destruction of Jews and Gypsies Under the Antonescu Regime, 1940–1944*. Chicago: Ian R. Dee, 2000.

Rafter, Nicole Hahn, ed. *White Trash: The Eugenic Family Studies 1877–1919*. Boston: Northeastern University Press, 1988.

Redlich, Fritz, *Hitler: Diagnosis of a Destructive Prophet*. New York: Oxford University Press, 1999.

Regan, Tom. *The Case for Animal Rights*. Berkeley: University of California Press, 1983.

Rifkin, Jeremy. *Beyond Beef: The Rise and Fall of the Cattle Culture*. New York: Dutton, 1992.

Ritvo, Harriet. *The Animal Estate: The English and Other Creatures in the Victorian Age*. Cambridge, MA: Harvard University Press, 1987.

Roland, Charles G. *Courage Under Seige: Starvation, Disease, and Death in the Warsaw Ghetto*. New York: Oxford University Press, 1992.

Roth, John K. and Michael Berenbaum, eds. *Holocaust: Religious and Philosophical Implications*. St. Paul, MN: Paragon House, 1989.

Ryder, Richard. *Animal Revolution: Changing Attitudes Towards Speciesism*. Oxford: Basil Blackwell, 1989.

Sagan, Carl. *The Dragons of Eden: Speculations on the Evolution of Human Intelligence*. New York: Random House, 1977.

Sagan, Carl and Ann Druyan. *Shadows of Forgotten Ancestors: A Search for Who We Are*. New York: Ballantine, 1992.

Salisbury, Joyce E. *The Beast Within: Animals in the Middle Ages*. New York: Routledge, 1994.

Samuel, W. E. Wolfgang. *German Boy: A Refugee's Story*. Jackson: University Press of Mississippi, 2000.

Sax, Boria. *Animals in the Third Reich: Pets, Scapegoats, and the Holocaust*. New York: Continuum, 2000.

Schwartz, Richard. *Judaism and Vegetarianism*, revised editon. New York: Lantern Books, 2001.

Schweitzer, Albert, *The Animal World of Albert Schweitzer: Jungle Insights into Reverence for Life*, edited by Charles R. Joy. Boston: Beacon Press, 1950.

Sereny, Gitta. *Into That Darkness: An Examination of Conscience*. New York: Vintage, 1983.

Serpell, James. *In the Company of Animals: A Study of Human-Animal Relationships*. London: Basil Blackwell, 1986.

Sichrovsky, Peter. *Born Guilty: Children of Nazi Families* New York: Basic Books, 1988.

Sinclair, Clive. *The Brothers Singer*. London: Allison and Busby, 1983.

Sinclair, Upton. *The Autobiography of Upton Sinclair*. New York: Harcourt, Brace and World, 1962.

——. *The Jungle*. New York: Signet, 1990.

Singer, Isaac Bashevis. *The Certificate*. New York: Farrar, Straus and Giroux, 1992.

——. *The Collected Stories*. New York: Farrar, Straus and Giroux, 1982.

——. *The Death of Methuselah and Other Stories*. New York: Farrar, Straus and Giroux, 1972.

——. *Enemies, A Love Story*. New York: Farrar, Straus and Giroux, 1972.

——. *The Estate*. New York: Farrar, Straus and Giroux, 1968.

——. *The Family Moskat*. New York: Noonday Press, 1950.

——. *A Friend of Kafka and Other Stories*. New York: Farrar, Straus and Giroux, 1970.

——. *In My Father's Court*. New York: Farrar, Straus and Giroux, 1966.

——. *Love and Exile: A Memoir*. Garden City, NY: Doubleday, 1984.

——. *Meshugah*. New York: Farrar, Straus and Giroux, 1994.

——. *Old Love*. New York: Farrar, Straus and Giroux, 1979.

——. *Passions and Other Stories*. New York: Farrar, Straus and Giroux, 1976.

——. *The Penitent*. New York: Farrar, Straus and Giroux, 1983.

——. *Satan in Goray*. New York: Noonday Press, 1955.

——. *The Seance and Other Stories*. New York: Farrar, Straus and and Giroux, 1968.

——. *Shadows on the Hudson*. New York: Farrar, Straus and Giroux, 1997.

——. *Short Friday and Other Stories*. New York: Farrar, Straus and Giroux, 1964.

——. *Shosha*. New York: Farrar, Straus and Giroux, 1978.

——. *The Slave*. New York: Farrar, Straus and Giroux, 1962.

——. *The Spinoza of Market Street*. New York: Farrar, Straus and Giroux, 1961.

Singer, Isaac Bashevis and Richard Burgin. *Conversations with Isaac Bashevis Singer*. Garden City, NY: Doubleday, 1985.

Singer, Peter. *Animal Liberation*, second edition. New York: Avon Books, 1990.

Skaggs, Jimmy M. *Prime Cut: Livestock Raising and Meatpacking in the United States, 1607–1983*. College Station: Texas A&M University Press, 1986.

Smith, Bradley F. *Heinrich Himmler: A Nazi in the Making, 1900–1926*. Stanford, CA: Hoover Institution Press, 1971.

Speer, Albert. *Inside the Third Reich: Memoirs*. New York: Macmillan, 1970.

Spencer, Colin. *The Heretic's Feast: A History of Vegetarianism*. London: Fourth Estate, 1990.

Spiegel, Marjorie. *The Dreaded Comparison: Human and Animal Slavery*, revised edition. New York: Mirror Books, 1996.

Stampp, Kenneth M. *The Peculiar Institution: Slavery in the Ante-Bellum South*. New York: Knopf, 1956.

Stannard, David E. *American Holocaust: Columbus and the Conquest of the New World*. New York: Oxford University Press, 1992.

Staub, Ervin. *The Roots of Evil: The Origins of Genocide and Other Group Violence*. Cambridge: Cambridge University Press, 1989.

Stoltfus, Nathan. *Resistance of the Heart: Intermarriage and the Rosenstrasse Protest in Nazi Germany*. New York: Norton, 1996.

Straus, Dorthea. *Under the Canopy: The Story of a Friendship with Isaac Bashevis Singer That Chronicles a Reawakening of Jewish Identity*. New York: George Braziller, 1982.

Stull, Donald D., Michael J. Broadway, and David Griffith, eds. *Any Way You Cut It: Meat-processing and Small-town America.* Lawrence: University Press of Kansas, 1995.

Sward, Keith. *The Legend of Henry Ford.* New York: Rinehart, 1948.

Swierenga, Robert P. *Faith and Family: Dutch Immigration and Settlement in the United States, 1820–1920.* New York: Holmes and Meier, 2000.

Telushkin, Dvorah. *Master of Dreams: A Memoir of Isaac Bashevis Singer.* New York: Morrow, 1997.

Thomas, Keith. *Man and the Natural World: A History of the Modern Sensibility.* New York: Pantheon Books, 1983.

Tillyard, E. M. W. *The Elizabethan World Picture.* New York: Random House, 1959.

Todorov, Tzvetan. *The Conquest of America: The Question of the Other.* New York: Harper and Row, 1984.

Toland, John. *Adolf Hitler.* Garden City, NY: Doubleday, 1976.

Toynbee, J. M. C. *Animals in Roman Life and Art.* Ithaca, NY: Cornell University Press, 1973.

Ucko, Peter J. and G. W. Dimbleby, eds. *The Domestication and Exploitation of Plants and Animals.* Chicago: Aldine Publishing Company, 1969.

Waite, Robert G. L. *The Psychopathic God Adolf Hitler.* New York: Basic Books, 1977.

Weiss, John. *Ideology of Death: Why the Holocaust Happened in Germany.* Chicago: Ivan R. Dee, 1996.

Wilbur, George B. and Warner Muensterberger, eds. *Psychoanalysis and Culture: Essays in Honor of Géza Róheim.* New York: International Universities Press, 1951.

Wise, Steven M. *Rattling the Cage: Toward Legal Rights for Animals.* Cambridge, MA: Perseus Books, 2000.

Wistrich, Robert. *Who's Who in Nazi Germany.* London: Weidenfeld and Nicolson, 1982.

Wolfson, David J. *Beyond the Law: Agribusiness and the Systemic Abuse of Animals Rasied for Food or Food Production.* New York: Archimedian Press, 1996.

Wynne-Tyson, Jon, ed. *The Extended Circle: A Commonplace Book of Animal Rights.* New York: Paragon House, 1989.

Zeuner, Frederick E. *A History of Domesticated Animals.* London: Hutchinson, 1963.

ACKNOWLEDGMENTS

My special thanks to Lucy Rosen Kaplan for reading the manuscript and writing the Foreword and also to those who read early drafts of the manuscript and made valuable suggestions—Aviva Cantor, cofounder of the Jewish feminist magazine *Lilith*; David Cantor, a consultant to national animal rights organizations; Robert Cohen, executive director of the Dairy Education Board; Karen Davis, president of United Poultry Concerns; Albert Kaplan, consultant for Laidlow Global Securities; and Barbara Stagno and Eliott Katz of In Defense of Animals. I also want to express my gratitude to those who read individual chapters and made helpful comments—Ingrid Newkirk, president of PETA; Alex Press, copy chief of the New York weekly *Village Voice*; and Richard Schwartz, author of *Judaism and Vegetarianism*.

Those who shared their stories that appear in Part III also deserve a special word of thanks—Liesel Appel, Dan Berger, Marc Berkowitz, Christa Blanke, Aviva Cantor, David Cantor, Stewart David, Robin Duxbury, Gail Eisnitz, Dietrich von Haugwitz, Alex Hershaft, Susan Kalev, Albert Kaplan, Helmut Kaplan, Lucy Kaplan, Anne Kelemen, Eric Marcus, Jennifer Melton, Anne Muller, Peter Muller, Rhoda Ruttenburg, Peter Singer, Barbara Stagno, Sonia Waisman, Zoe Weil, and the late Henry Spira.

I also want to express my appreciation to Yoël Arbeitman, Peter Muller, Valerie Paradiz, and Dietrich von Haugwitz for helping me with the translation of German materials and to the staffs of the New York

Public Library and Columbia University library systems for helping me find the materials I needed for my research.

Those who offered me a helping hand, valuable advice, or an encouraging word along the way also deserve mention—Batya Bauman, Allen Bergson, Georgianna Bishop, Andrea daVinci Braun, Gert Bregman, Waclaw Godziemba-Maliszewski, Roberta Kalechofsky, Albert Kaplan, Marilyn Klein, Michael Larsen, Ralph Meyer, Elizabeth Pomada, and Debby Tanzer, among others. My very special thanks to Meredith Dunham for designing the book and to Dave Rietz for setting up and maintaining the book's website (www.powerfulbook.com).

I want to express my fond appreciation for Professor Marian Filar, a retired concert pianist and Holocaust survivor, whom I met during the final stages of writing this book and whose amazing life story—*From Buchenwald to Carnegie Hall*—it was my privilege to work on with him.

A well-deserved word of thanks and praise for Martin Rowe, publisher of Lantern Books, for recognizing the merits of *Eternal Treblinka* and for helping make it happen.

My grateful acknowledgment to Farrar, Straus and Giroux, for permission to use an excerpt from "The Letter Writer" from *The Seance and Other Stories* by Isaac Bashevis Singer, and to Four Walls Eight Windows for permission to quote from *Dead Meat* by Sue Coe.

For a complete listing of organizations around the world which have expressed support for the book on its way to publication, see the Support page on the book website.

INDEX